The
BÜRGERMEISTER'S
DAUGHTER

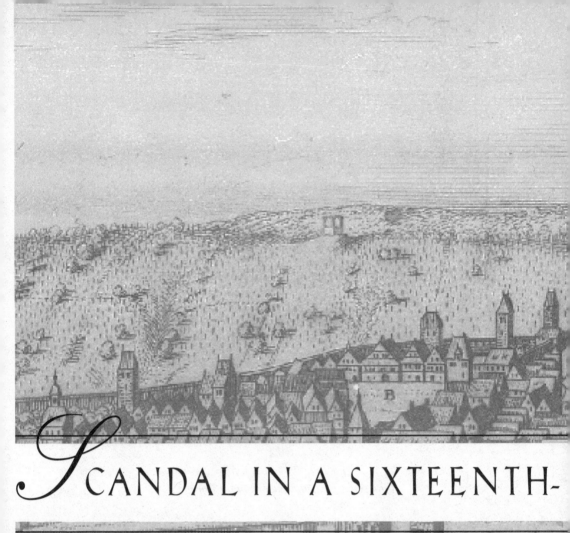

SCANDAL IN A SIXTEENTH-

The BÜRGERMEISTER'S DAUGHTER

CENTURY GERMAN TOWN

 STEVEN OZMENT

St. Martin's Press
NEW YORK

Front cover: Lucas Cranach's (1472–1553) "Justice as a Naked Woman with Sword and Scales," 1537. Amsterdam, Fridart Stichting. Cranach was the most productive and economically successful German painter of his time, perhaps of all time. His altars, woodcuts, nudes, and especially portraits, made him an influential political as well as powerful cultural figure, court-painter for the Saxon princes and lifelong friend and ally of Martin Luther and the Reformation. Only Albrecht Dürer (1471–1528), who admired and painted Cranach, was deemed by contemporaries to excel him, but not by much. For the most up-to-date account, see Claus Grimm, et al., *Lucas Cranach. Ein Maler-Unternehmer aus Franken* (Augsburg, 1994), pp. 19–27, 347–348.

Back cover: Castle Limpurg. Georg Widmann, Hallischer Chronick SA Hall (HV II/8, fol. 8r). Castle Limpurg commanded the heights bordering the southeastern wall of Hall. At its foot lay the market-village of Unterlimpurg, which embraced the Schauenburg (directly beneath), home of the Schenks' noble retinue and servants. The steepled Church of Mary, since 1283 the parish church of the Schenks, can be seen at the Schauenburg's center. The large house (center left) was once the Limpurg toll house, on the boundary between Limpurg and Hall. With the sale of Limpurg to the city in 1541, all of these properties were incorporated into Hall. The lords of the Schauenburg, however, continued to enjoy freedom from taxation.

Title-page spread (background): Mathias Merian, *Schwäbisch Hall*, Stadtarchiv Schwäbisch Hall BS 193.

DESIGN BY BARBARA M. BACHMAN

MAP ON P. 7 BY MARK STEIN STUDIOS

Library of Congress Cataloging-in-Publication Data

Ozment, Steven E.
  The bürgermeister's daughter : scandal in a sixteenth-century German town / Steven Ozment.
      p.   cm.
  Includes bibliographical references.
  ISBN 0-312-13939-X
  1. Büschler, Anna, ca. 1496–1552.   2. Women—Germany—Schwäbisch Hall—Biography.   3. Schwäbisch Hall (Germany)—Social conditions. 4. Fathers—Germany—Schwäbisch Hall—History.   5. Courts—Germany—Schwäbisch Hall—History.   6. Schwäbisch Hall (Germany)—Social life and customs.   7. Women—History—Middle Ages, 500–1500.   8. Social history—Medieval, 500–1500.   I. Title.
DD901.S3652096   1996
943'.471031'092—dc20   95-40408
[B]   CIP

10 9 8 7 6 5 4 3 2

TO MY DEAR MOTHER

SHIRLEY M. EDGAR

I WILL BE AS HARSH AS TRUTH AND AS

UNCOMPROMISING AS JUSTICE.

—*William Lloyd Garrison, 1831*

CONTENTS

LIST OF ILLUSTRATIONS

Nun gråß dich got du frewndtlichs kindt.
Got danck euch Junckher was habt ir im synn.
Liebe Junckfraw laßt mich zu ewr Rosen schmecken.
Lieber Junckher sie wachssen nit in allen hecken.
Liebe Junckfra wåd as ich het ein solchen garten.
Wolt ich sein so fleissig warten.
Lieber Junckher man leßt nit yederman dynnen geten.
Ir müßt gar fleissig darumb peten.
Darumb mögt ir euch woll weyter versehen.
Gûte wort soll man nit verschmehen.

1521

BUDDING ROMANCE

God greets you, dear, kind girl.

God thanks you, junker. What's on your mind?

Dear maiden, let me smell your roses.

Dear junker, they do not grow in every thicket.

Dear maiden, if I had a garden such as yours,

I would tend it oh so diligently.

Dear junker, not everyone may go in there;

To enter, you must first pray constantly.

So you continue to make yourself worthy.

Kind words shall not be spurned.

CHAPTER ONE

The Story

ON JANUARY 27, 1552, IN THE COURTHOUSE OF THE CENTURIES-old south German imperial city of Schwäbisch Hall, a notorious case of parental brutality and denial of family inheritance abruptly ended with the announcement of the death of the plaintiff, Anna Sporland, born Anna Büschler (1496/98–1552). Anna was, at her death, in her mid-fifties and had spent fully half her life, since 1525, battling her father, siblings, and city hall. She died impoverished and embittered between the testimonies of the penultimate and the last witness—the bürgermeister of distant Rothenberg, who was her first cousin, and the bürgermeister of Hall, who led the opposition to her.[1] To the end, she held the spotlight in the internal politics and life drama of Hall.[2]

In the early 1520s, Anna Büschler seemed destined to a prosperous and serene life, not one of interminable personal and legal conflict. Born into a highly respectable family, confident and exuberant in her youth, and a woman of acknowledged beauty, she had a reputation as the belle of her hometown, and as something of a free spirit. But the center of attention could also be a perilous place in the sixteenth century, and those who put themselves in it flirted with danger.

Both men and women were then expected to adhere to clearly defined standards of behavior specific to gender, social class, and contemporary community values. On such conformity were social order and civic peace seen to hang. Character and reputation accordingly carried great weight in legal proceedings, which judged present behavior in light of past, carefully examining a person's life from every angle.

Anna was peculiarly vulnerable to such scrutiny. Both in her late teens and in her twenties, she had behaved in a manner scandalous to the society in which she lived. Her story is one of multiple collapsing relationships: between a daughter and a father, a sister and her siblings, a servant and her mistress, a woman and her lovers, a citizen and her town. Twice, in original and unforgettable ways, she brought shame and embarrassment to her family and the city of Hall: the first time, when she deceived her father and incurred his undying wrath, the second, twenty years later, when she defied the city council and provoked its retaliation.

The whole disputed record of her "scandalous, undisciplined, and reprehensible life"[3] has survived largely intact, thanks to the undying animus of her father and her brother. It is because of their actions that we have the unusual testimony to the events in question of dozens of her fellow citizens and well-positioned outside observers, taken decades later by the imperial court. And her father and brother were the ones who discovered, confiscated, and preserved the extremely rare cache of her love letters—not with one, but with two men—by which her character was impeached before the same court.

What exactly had this woman done to cause her father, then bürgermeister, to denounce her as "an evil serpent" and the government of Hall to declare her a renegade, and in both instances to draw the intervention of the imperial supreme court, Germany's highest? Why did the behavior of one woman rivet the attention and disrupt the lives of so many important people for so long a time? The answers to those questions lie in the internal workings of a distant society and in the inner lives of people who were both like and unlike ourselves.

Our story is set in northern Europe in the first half of the sixteenth century, when the age of chivalry had passed and the creative period of the Italian Renaissance was nearing its climax. Rome would be tragically sacked and looted by imperial soldiers, many of them German mercenaries, in 1527. But already in the late fourteenth and fifteenth centuries, the comparatively ordered medieval world of knights, priests, and peasants had begun to give way to the more adventurous world of nouveau riche merchants, zealous religious reformers, and politically ambitious artisan guilds in the economically and culturally ascendant urban centers.

The Black Death, which peaked in 1349 and especially ravaged the cities and towns along the major overland trade routes, ironically helped tip the balance of power from the landed nobility in the countryside to the new bourgeoisie in the cities. In the wake of the plague's devastation, thousands of peasants bought, or simply declared, their freedom from their landlords and departed for the cities, where skilled hands were more in demand and better paid than on the waning manors.

In the recovering cities, the immigrants found good jobs in urban industries, and increasingly became part of a confident new lay world created by another revolution in these same centuries. Between 1300 and 1500, the number of universities more than tripled across Europe, and the opportunities for vernacular secular education multiplied as well to meet the need for educated personnel in urban businesses and governments. The printing press became a reality because of the new multitudes of literate laity. A scant fifty years after Johann Gutenberg, bankrolled by his father-in-law, had opened his print shop in Mainz (in the 1440s), two hundred presses were in operation across Europe, sixty of them in Germany alone. In the late fifteenth and early sixteenth centuries, these various forces had created a bourgeoisie more knowledgeable about and involved in their world than ever before, and ready to challenge both the old nobility and the old Church for control of their lives.[4]

Nowhere was such lay self-confidence bolder than in Germany, the site of our story. Emperor Maxmilian I (1493–1519) attested the new unruly spirit of the age when, in a famous comparison of his rule in the Holy Roman Empire with that of the kings of Spain and France in their lands, he described himself as a "king of kings." In Spain, subjects both obeyed and disobeyed their king, as one might expect them to do, while in (rival) France, contrary to expectations, they did the king's bidding without question, behaving more like animals than humans. But in the empire, where Germany was the crown jewel, people did just as they pleased, as if each were a king![5]

The 1520s were Germany's most revolutionary decade before modern times. In these years, the Protestant Reformation, led by Martin Luther, captured the imagination of people in scores of German cities and towns, including Hall. Charging the Church of Rome with spiritual deceit and tyranny, the Reformation divided families, universities, and city governments alike, as region after region was forced to choose between the old religion and the new. Amid resentments that would flame up in a near century of religious conflict, Protestants demolished shrines, emptied and secularized cloisters, forbade the Mass and other sacraments, permitted the clergy to marry and subjected them to taxation, and conceded lay magistrates—no longer the clergy—the last word in moral and domestic affairs.

The Church of Rome was not the only traditional institution at this time to incur the wrath of revolutionaries. The years 1524–25 saw tens of thousands of peasants revolt in the countrysides of southern and central Germany, as they challenged their masters' greed and exploitation. A number of peasant leaders invoked Luther's teaching to justify such action, as the new spiritual egalitarianism of the Reformation gave a spur to social revolution. But Luther soon condemned the peasants for mixing religion and politics, and powerful noble armies, both Catholic and Protestant, suppressed the rebellious peasants everywhere, killing tens of thousands.

Scholars today argue whether these two great events in German history—the Reformation and the Peasants' War—really liberated anyone. The near consensus is that the 1520s were truly a dark, not an enlightened decade, and these events created new forms of bondage for all save a privileged few. Removing the counterweight of the papacy, the Reformation seemed to concede absolute political authority to the German princes and ruling elites, while the Peasants' War gave these same rulers a pretext for crushing the common man as well.[6]

These same years are also viewed today as a low point in the history of women. Whereas the centuries between 1300 and 1500 had been something of a golden age for women—their educational and vocational opportunities increased, and with them their civic freedom—the sixteenth century turned back the clock. Women were again squeezed out of the guilds and public places and increasingly confined to the home—a reversal of fortunes for which some scholars have held the patriarchal ideals of Protestant reformers especially responsible.[7]

Like many other comparable towns in this age of religious reform and social revolution, Hall had both a successful Lutheran reformation and a failed peasants' revolt, in one or both of which, characters in our story played a role. And its "star," Anna Büschler, could certainly attest to the difficulties of being a woman in the sixteenth century. Her story is also one of revolt against deceit, tyranny, and exploitation, but on a smaller scale and in a different dimension. Set in a medium-sized but central imperial city, and revolving around a single prominent family, her story, too, measures an age as well as its protagonist. As one person's quest for justice and equity in an uncharitable age, Anna Büschler's "revolt" may have something in common with the revolutionary movements of the 1520s. Certainly the odds against her succeeding against the traditional authorities in her life were as great as those that faced the religious and social revolutionaries. And whether in the end she, like them, can be said really to have won anything is a question the reader must decide in light of the evidence.

Finally, as a provocative tale about the primordial forces of human nature, our story could not have a more appropriate setting than the ancient town of Hall. The city and its environs have been described as "the classic land of the history of the earth," a reference to its unique geography and geological history.[8] The Celts first settled the area in the fifth century B.C., building a village near the great salt spring around which the town of Hall would subsequently grow; in the 1940s, excavations uncovered the remains of the original village. Although older than the Celts, the name "Hall" derives from them and is closely connected etymologically with "salt," Hall being from the beginning the great "salt place." German tribes and the Romans were subsequent invaders and settlers, their remains still visible in surviving roads and construction.

Over the centuries, the city painstakingly layered itself into the Kocher valley, whose walls, 850 meters apart and 97 meters above the city's lowest point, tower above it on the east and west. Around and about the city, the Kocher River runs, its original bed 300,000 years old. Over these millennia, the river's twists and turns have made the valley a wonder to behold. Descending from the train station 50 meters above the city and glimpsing for the first time the quaint old town set against the dark green of the valley walls takes the visitor's breath away.[9]

At greater distance, but still within sight, are the Limpurg mountains to the southeast, with the highest point in the area (the Einkorn, 510 meters), and to the west, the Waldenberg mountains, both densely forested. The wide Haller plain, running east and north of the city, is intensely farmed. At still greater distance and completely out of sight, yet serving as four corners of a box in which Hall's place within greater Germany may be showcased, are the great modern German cities of Stuttgart, 45 kilometers to the southwest, Heidelberg, 80 kilometers to the northwest, Nürnberg, 100 kilometers to the northeast, and Augsburg, 120 kilometers to the southeast.

0   miles   50

0   kilometers   80

• Places mentioned in the text
□ Other important places

SCHWÄBISCH HALL AND ITS SURROUNDINGS

The Father

A MERCHANT INVESTOR AND POLITICIAN, HERMANN BÜSCHLER (1470–1543) was a proud and powerful councilman and five times the city's bürgermeister, holding that top post in 1508, 1514, 1517,

1520, and 1525. At this time, Hall's twenty-four councilmen were not freely elected by the citizenry at large, but co-opted by the council itself, which also elected the bürgermeister annually (on July 25) from its own ranks—a system of government that kept the circles of political power exceedingly small, although not necessarily from a contemporary point of view. As the city's principal magistrate, the bürgermeister was similar to a modern mayor, save for the fact that he served at the will of the council rather than at that of an electorate. A "career" politician, Hermann Büschler had held some government post in the city since 1492. His family had grown rich by selling wine and investing in real estate. By 1499, when Anna was a toddler, he had attained a taxable wealth of 7,600 gulden, a notable sum at the time. By 1520, he was the city's richest man and his the grandest house on market square. Between 1513 and 1525, no man in Hall wielded greater influence over city policy or commanded more respect from the citizenry. Hermann Büschler spoke with equal authority to the outside world, often representing the city at territorial diets where key political decisions affecting the entire region were made.[10]

During the later Middle Ages, the family progressively became the center of work and life, as the responsibility for the production of society's goods shifted from the large manorial households to the small urban family and the industries its labor fueled, a process that has been described as the "familiarization" of work and life.[11] It was customary at this time for all children to work, girls as well as boys. This they did by age thirteen or fourteen at the latest, and orphaned children might be placed in service as early as six or eight. Because being able to support oneself independently was a condition of a proper marriage, girls who could not bring wealth into a marriage by means of a dowry from their fathers or an inheritance from their mothers might spend eight, ten, or even more years at domestic service before they and their prospective husbands had the means to marry.[12]

While all girls worked, the daughters of royalty and the urban nobility did not do so outside the home. Destined for marriage at an early age, if not sent away to a cloister at an even earlier one, they spent their entire childhood at home, where they were educated and taught the homemaking skills they would need as wives. It was also rare for girls from rich, burgher families like Hermann Büschler's to work out-side the home.[13]

Anna, however, did work outside the home, but in a special place: the nearby castle of the Limpurg Schenks just beyond the city walls to the south. For Anna, it was a brisk twenty-minute walk from her Hall home, but exhausting, as entry to the castle lay at the end of a long, serpentine climb. Although very minor royals in the service of the Holy Roman Emperor, the Schenks were nonetheless local poten-tates in the class-conscious world of the sixteenth century; they had a significantly higher social standing than the Büschlers, who were non-noble merchants. But as the bürgermeister's daughter, Anna was a spe-cial person wherever she was, and she became an informal friend and associate of the royal family as well as their servant. She kept house and sewed for Schenkin Margarete, the former countess of Schlick and the wife of Schenk Gottfried II (1474–1530), lord of castle Limpurg and the lands south and southeast of Hall. Margarete was also the mother of eight children, among them the teenage future Schenk As-mus, or Erasmus (1502–1553), who was four to six years Anna's junior.

After her mother's death in December 1520, Anna came back to her father's mansion on market square (today incorporated into the Hotel Adelshof) to take her mother's place as his full-time housekeeper. Anna was by this time a mature woman in her early twenties, between twenty-two and twenty-four. She returned home at her father's com-mand and against her own wishes. She had liked her position in castle Limpurg, and having just passed the age when most Hall women mar-ried (between nineteen and twenty-two)[14] and moved outside the pa-rental home, she must have felt very self-conscious about returning to hers.

By all accounts, her father was an extraordinary man, and towns-people considered his relationship with his daughter to be out of the ordinary as well. "They led a strange life together," one witness ob-served, alluding to the high degree of freedom the bürgermeister gave his daughter and her very bold exercise of it.[15] In 1527, Hermann Büschler would retire quietly from the city council in no small part because of the scandal he and his daughter created in the city in the years immediately preceding.[16]

But a decade and a half earlier, Hermann Büschler had been the town hero, and seemingly destined to lifelong tenure on the council. Between 1510 and 1512, his leadership had secured forever the political rights of nonpatrician burghers (*Mittelbürger*, the upper middle classes) and artisans (*Handwerker*) in city government. Deep social divisions had plagued Hall and its governing council for centuries, and in these years, they were being exacerbated again by the old waning noble patrician families'[17] habit of constantly reminding the ever larger burgher and artisan classes of their inferior lineage—all in a vain and occasionally tragicomic attempt to dampen the latter's political ambitions and drown out their voice in the city council. But these groups were now too many and too strong to be denied. Almost half of the city's roughly eleven hundred households would be headed by master artisans by 1550, and some of them, like the bakers and the butchers, were already wealthy men in 1510. And the city also coped with a large, restless underclass, as 40 percent of its households paid no tax or less than one-tenth of the average tax.[18]

Hall, however, was too important a city for its overlord, the Holy Roman Emperor, to permit crippling social and political division to continue. Long the site of a major imperial saltworks, supplying the needs of people in Franconia and Württemberg, Hall was also the home of the imperial coinworks. In 1156, the city had received from the imperial government its market regulations, which allowed it to levy tolls, and the right to coin its own money, thereby making it officially a "city." Its new coat of arms portrayed a cross above a hand or glove (or above two hands or gloves), indicating one or both of these new privileges. Around the same time, the famous Hall penny, the "Haller" or "Heller," was struck.

Then, in 1276, King Rudolf of Habsburg recognized Hall as an imperial city, thereby freeing it from the long resented "rule" (reduced to mere consensual "protection" in 1260) of the Limpurg Schenks, who from their castle on a neighboring hill had long acted as the "lords of Hall" on behalf of the emperor. They had also hoped and plotted for generations to absorb Hall into their own lands. Imperial city status gave Hall both a new autonomy (henceforth, it was directly answerable only to the emperor) and new protection from the Schenks of Limpurg and other noble predators in the surrounding lands, whose ambitions and designs on the city did not cease because of its imperial status. A *Reichsschultheiss*, or imperial mayor, would now reside in the city,

bearing the staff of royal authority in the emperor's name, adminis-
tering justice in matters affecting the emperor, and overseeing the tolls
and other sources of imperial income in the city.[19]

Internal social and political conflict of the kind besieging Hall in
1510 was not unprecedented. Already in 1261, as it was becoming a
self-governing free city, the noble aristocrats who then dominated city
government and the burghers who desired a greater role in it squared
off in "class warfare" fashion. In that year, the burghers rebelled
against a magistrate's ordinance to reduce the length of cellar entries
to attached houses and taverns to under seventy-five centimeters, as
people were falling into them when they walked the narrow streets of
the city at night. The intended result of the protest, however, was less
to delay the implementation of the new ordinance than to make a
successful show of burgher strength (although noblemen in the city,
who also were not councilmen and resented it, also joined the protest).
On both scores, the burghers made their point. Not only was the ordinance temporarily withdrawn, but twenty to thirty noble families
moved out of the city, ostensibly in search of more tranquil residence
elsewhere.[20]

A more serious protest came in the fourteenth century, after the city
council's controlling patrician chamber (*obere Rat*) passed a 10 percent
tax on all burghers. This brought swift resistance from the council's
lower chamber (*untere Rat*), which represented the guilds and had long
sought the merger of the two bodies and a fairer sharing of power.
Other noblemen in the city also joined the protest. When the patricians
stuck to their decision against the popular majority, the city erupted
in rebellion.

Emperor Louis of Bavaria (1314–1347) moved to contain the class
warfare by broadening the franchise along the lines desired by the
majority of citizens. He did this by a famous ruling in 1340 that both
restructured the city's political representation and merged the two representative bodies. In the new constitution, the old patrician families'
exclusive right to the highest council position was rescinded, and prop-
erty-owning burghers and artisans in the city were given majority representation in the council, regardless of their lack of noble lineage.
Under the new formula, Hall was henceforth to be ruled by a twenty-
six-member council composed of twelve noble patricians (variously
described as *Geschlechter*, *Junker*, or *Edelleuten*), who held the deci-

sive rank of judges (*Richter*); six wealthy "middle burghers" (*ritter-bürtige Mittelbürger, ehrbare Bürger*); and eight artisans (*Hand-werker*). The middle burghers were a fast-rising group between the old patriciate and the traditional artisan classes and included prosperous merchants and guildmasters, who had acquired significant propertied wealth and income from rents and trade. Although none of them were patrician by birth, or necessarily even of local ancestry, many in this group had married into noble families and believed themselves to be of equal worth in every way. Once again, in 1340 as in 1261, the burghers had successfully demonstrated their power, and again, as in 1261, some noble families moved out of the city in protest.[21]

The constitution of 1340 kept the peace in Hall for over a century and a half, but it did not end the social divisions within the council, much less within Hall society. In the early sixteenth century, that peace was again shattered by what began as a petty dispute over the right of nonpatrician members of the council to enter a special taproom, which the patrician members snobbishly reserved to themselves. Hermann Büschler's erstwhile friend and frequent companion in the conduct of council business, Rudolf Nagel, led the opposition to the entry of low-born burghers and artisans.

The taproom in question was on market square in the house of a rich widow and local philanthropist named Sibylla Egen (d. 1538), who later gained local fame as a patron of the Protestant Reformation.[22] Entrance was restricted to those who were members of a local patrician family either by birth or by marriage, a bit of arrogance that created over the years a festering sore within the council, threatening the city's political unity as well as its social harmony. In 1505, one wealthy non-patrician councilman dramatically protested his ostracism by be-queathing his wealth to another town.[23]

By what seemed to Hermann Büschler pure sophistry, he too was deemed to fail the test of nobility and denied entry. Although his family had lived for generations in Hall, it was not patrician, and while he had married into an old patrician family, it was not local; his wife, Anna Hornberger, was a Rothenburger, not a Haller. On the other hand, he did have a patrician lineage by marriage, and his taxable wealth at this time of 6,800 gulden ranked him fifth among the twenty-six councilmen.[24] And he also had served the city as bürgermeister in 1508. How could so wealthy and prominent a citizen be denied entry to a taproom for councilmen? For his noble counterparts on the council, the answer was simple and centuries old: without a noble birth, the bürgermeister lacked the requisite "honor."

Other nonpatrician members of the council shared Hermann Büschler's pride and resentment, and with their support, he made an issue of the discriminatory policy. Bursting into the forbidden taproom, he was advised that he might drink wine there as a courtesy, but that he would be welcomed by the patricians only as their guest, not as their equal.[25] Moralizes the contemporary chronicler Johann Herolt, who records the episode: "From such pride, which has never brought about anything good, the dissension grew."[26]

The spurned bürgermeister formally addressed the council on the issue of the taproom in November 1509. Was it not ridiculous, he asked his nonpatrician colleagues, that they, a sizable majority of the council, holding fourteen of the twenty-six slots, should have to stand in rain or snow in the churchyard, or by the fish market outside the taproom, while their noble counterparts lounged and bargained in the warmth and comfort of their special room? By an initial vote of sixteen to ten, rising to nineteen to seven in a second vote, now including two Junkers, the council approved the obvious solution: the nonpatricians would create their own taproom, where "ordinary councilmen and honorable burghers,"[27] together with their noble sympathizers, might meet as equals. A room in a virtually new house next to St. James's Church, built in 1499 and used as a city hospice or infirmary (*Spital*) under the direction of the Franciscan monks, was designated, and the necessary renovations were begun.

This development brought the dispute out of the taproom and onto the streets of Hall. As Hall was now the regional center of imperial industry and finance, Emperor Maximilian I (1493–1519), like emperors past, had watched the deterioration of social order in his showcase imperial city with alarm. By April 1510, he had concluded that he must intervene, and an imperial commission of inquiry was in the city within a month. As if the conflict were none of their doing, the seven patrician councilmen who had fought to the end to keep their colleagues out of the taproom complained loud and long to the commissioners about the great harm being done to the hospice by Hermann Büschler's construction of a taproom there.[28] They also denounced the bürgermeister as a man who had mismanaged the city's finances, unfairly fined the

servants of the nobility, and packed the council with cronies and relatives—the latter a reference to his recent filling of three vacant patrician slots with "honorable burghers," one of whom was a cousin.[29]

To the shock and dismay of most Haller, the commission concluded
its investigation by ruling in favor of the patricians, and a few weeks
later the emperor made their recommendations law. The latter not only
ordered the new taproom under construction in the hospice to be
"eternally closed," but reformulated the constitution of 1340, which
had given the city 170 years of relative civil peace, to increase the
powers of the minority patrician faction within city government. The
key provisions guaranteed the patricians their traditional twelve slots,
while adding to them the bürgermeistership, seven of the city's twelve
judgeships, and appointment to one of the two positions in every council office. In addition, the patricians were now put in a position to
dominate the all-powerful privy council of five (*der geheime Funffer*).
That was arranged by requiring two patrician and two nonpatrician
members to serve on the latter with the bürgermeister. Because of the
closer social relations and greater common political interests of patricians and burghers (wealth at least here proving to be thicker than
blood), the bürgermeister, who was almost always elected from one or
the other group, could be counted on to side with the interests of the
patricians against those of the artisans.[30]

For many Haller, the "dark ages" seemed to be returning to their
city. The hearings before the commission had been intense and angry,
so much so that at one point, patrician threats caused Hermann Büschler to flee the city in fear for his life. With the implementation of the
new ruling, he and four of his allies were voted out of office and re-
placed with three Junkers and two artisans. The defeated five protested
both the revolution and the terror to the imperial supreme court in
Speyer, but their opponents had the more influential contacts there.

Hermann Büschler was not, however, one to take insult and defeat
lying down. He knew how to get even and soon demonstrated his
mettle in a way not even his closest friends could have anticipated. He
decided to protest the commission's decision in a private audience with
the emperor himself, and to that end he set out for Frankfurt am Main.
As the protests in Hall against the new constitution were growing
louder, he believed the emperor might be persuaded to rescind it. Hall's
patricians, however, with Nagel in the forefront, were again one step

ahead of Hermann Büschler, and their friends at court effectively closed the emperor's door to him.

Not to be denied, the bürgermeister decided to accost the emperor directly in public, and in a most dramatic fashion. Barefoot and dressed in coarse wool, with dirt and ashes strewn over his bare head, a small wheel tied to his chest, a rope hung around his neck, an unsheathed sword in one hand and a written plea in the other, he waited along the emperor's route in Cologne. When his associates realized what was happening, they thought him mad and tried to conceal him from the emperor's sight, but they acted too late.

Thus confronted by the bürgermeister of Hall, the emperor received his petition, which asked for a private hearing of his case and also explained the supplicant's strange attire. It was Hermann Büschler's resolve to die gladly by rack (wheel), rope, or sword (the three traditional means of execution) should the emperor find his cause unjust upon hearing it. This was the kind of gamble legends are made of, and soon thereafter the emperor ordered a new commission, this time composed of distinguished delegates from over a dozen south German imperial cities, to take a second look at the situation in Hall. Given the popular outcry against the new constitution in Hall, that reassessment would very likely have occurred anyway. But Hermann Büschler's theatrics had hastened that decision, and he would forever be remembered for it.

The new commission met in Hall in mid-October 1512, confronted by a citizenry the greater part of which demanded the immediate restoration of the constitution of 1340. The result was a complete victory for Hermann Büschler's side. In a dramatic public ceremony, the prior of the Comburg monastery, acting in the person of the emperor, cut the imperial seal from the first commission's ruling, thereby declaring it null and void.

While the event was no social revolution, it did enhance the power and influence of the city's affluent nonpatricians. As in the past, several old patrician councilmen resigned their citizenship and departed Hall to live among more deferential folk, leaving behind still more vacancies in the council for Hermann Büschler's "honorable burghers" to fill.[31] Many of these burghers, like the bürgermeister himself, already fancied themselves patricians anyway. Philip Büschler (d. 1568), Hermann's eldest son, who would twice become bürgermeister himself at midcentury (1549, 1551), proudly claimed the title "Junker" on the grounds of his mother's noble lineage. Not only did he marry into a local patrician family, he took as his wife Afra Senft, the daughter of Gilg Senft, one of the seven patricians who had opposed his father to the very end during the confrontation of 1510.[32] For a generation after the second commission's restoration of Hall's constitution, the city's bürgermeister would be a patrician either by birth or by marriage.

Still, Hermann Büschler's defiance and daring had helped put new leadership permanently in city hall, one less bound to the social order of the Middle Ages and, as we will see, to the Church of Rome as well. That change spared the city some lethal political conflict during the second decade of the sixteenth century, and it made the city more receptive to the Protestant Reformation in the third.[33] The successful resolution of the constitutional crisis also established Hermann Büschler's heroic reputation in Hall's history.

 The Daughter

BY MANY ACCOUNTS, HERMANN BÜSCHLER HAD INDULGED HIS daughter enormously in the years immediately following her mother's death, when Anna moved back home to become his housekeeper. One witness, remembering Anna's behavior as "undisciplined enough," believed her father had driven her to it.[34] According to Anna's lawyer, her father indulged her with expensive clothes and jewelry, raising her "as if she were a born countess."[35] Numerous witnesses agreed that she had a taste for finery and loved to call attention to herself by dressing "immodestly and beyond what was proper."[36]

One of Anna's more notorious acquisitions, at an alleged cost of forty gulden, was a custom-made beret adorned with a white feather on the side and layered with fine pearls, including some her detractors claimed had been torn from a dress belonging to her deceased mother.[37] Her siblings recalled another striking headdress (or perhaps it was a different recollection of the same one) that Anna had had made for herself without her father's knowledge. They describe it as a round felt hat in a style more often worn by men than by women, which Anna decorated with white "gems" or dove's feathers.[38] Anna wore the hat properly enough to a city festival, but then dared also to wear it to St. Michael's Church, where it gave offense to so many parishioners that the pastor made her ostentatious display the topic of his sermon the following Sunday. In the week preceding that sermon, at her father's request, the superior of the Franciscan cloister visited Anna at home to remonstrate with her about the immodesty of her dress.

According to her siblings, neither the friar's remonstrance nor her father's earnest scolding had any lasting effect on Anna's behavior. However, a priest who also recalled the episode[39] described Hermann Büschler as having rebuked Anna for "having her clothes cut in such a way that one could see her naked body." Thereafter, the priest claimed never again to have noticed the scandalous feathered hat or a plunging neckline on Anna.[40] As to why Anna had dressed in such a provocative fashion in the first place, a tawer from nearby Oehringen offered the opinion that her father must have liked and encouraged it, "for if the plaintiff's late father had taken no pleasure in the way his daughter dressed, he would not have clothed her so."[41]

How far out of line with respectable Hall fashion was Anna? It was indeed the custom of urban men to wear felt hats and to adorn them with plumes on holidays (a high black hat with a white band was favored). Women wore fur hats and could choose among square (with satin borders), pointed, and flat or slouchy models. Formal outerwear was predominantly black and white and did not have a plunging neckline. Standard items of clothing were veils partly banded in black, white chemises extending up the neck, white collars, linen or black barchent sleeves, and satin hairnets. Among the accessories were gold buckles, silver brooches, and black knapsacks with yellow buttons. Bolder was the choice in underwear, with bodices of camel's hair for women and of silver and taffeta for girls. Among popular items of jewelry were pierced coins, both old and new, including a godfather's christening gift (usually a gold piece), worn together in bunches on necklaces. The favorite embellishment appears to have been pearls: on strings, lilies of pearl, and gold-encased mother-of-pearl. There were rings of every description: plain gold, crown gold with turquoise, fused metals, enameled; silver signet, silver rings with a crystal setting (so-called "vertigo rings," believed to protect one against gout as well, hence, also called "gout rings"); also rings encasing elkhoof, bloodstone,

Carol-zinc (a ring of stones set in zinc), and green malachite (so-called "fright stones" because they were thought to ward off fear—newborns and infants wore small heart-shaped versions).[42]

The preponderance of recorded testimony indicates that Hermann Büschler tolerated Anna's suggestive dressing for a while, but then strictly forbade it. Most witnesses had no idea whether he took any pleasure in it.[43] They did, however, agree completely that a father was responsible for the behavior of a daughter; her shortcomings directly reflected on him.

If her accusers are to be believed, Anna stole regularly from her father, using the money "to pretty herself up."[44] One widely rumored purloined item was a convertible bond (*Zinsbrief*) worth twelve hundred gulden, which her father managed to recover only after the city constable threatened to clap her in jail.[45] Other bonds of much lesser value Anna apparently did manage to cash. She also stole grain from her father's granary, once virtually emptying it. When he was away, she would send for the miller and let him take what he wanted, paying her for it directly on the spot.[46] On one occasion, her father's servant, Lienhard Vahmann, rescued two barrels she had secretly shipped to Kirchberg, packed with all kinds of wares taken from her father's stocks, intending to sell them there. And he claimed to know about other barrels she had successfully sold.[47] According to her siblings, Anna once pawned a family ring with a Jew in Wertheim and a silver necklace and gold brooch in Nördlingen. They also accused her of selling filched household linens, dish towels, and hand towels at the fair in Beinbach.[48]

It was not immodest dress, thievery, or "poor housekeeping,"[49] however, that made Hermann Büschler send his daughter packing in 1525, eventually hounding her from Hall and starting a quarter century of bitter family strife and litigation. In the eyes of her family and most of her neighbors, Anna's troubles resulted from her unrestrained and indiscreet amours.

 The Sin

WHEN HER MOTHER DIED IN 1520 AND SHE BEGAN TO KEEP HOUSE for her father, Anna, in her early twenties, was at the outer limits of normal marriageable age for Hall women. Although witnesses recalled several suitors during the early 1520s, only two are cited by name in the trial records. The more serious of these was Daniel Treutwein, a decorated cavalryman from the lower nobility, whom witnesses remembered as having been as much pursued by Anna as she by him.[50] Her father's servants, Lienhard Vahmann and Barbara Dollen, also recalled Daniel's sneaking in and out of the Büschler home, and staying late into the night—at least on those occasions when Herr Büschler was fast asleep or away on business.[51] At such times, Anna would command the servants to fetch wine for them, an order Vahmann claimed successfully to have resisted, while Dollen maintained that Anna several times put a knife to her heart when she hesitated, once forcing her to flee in fear for her life.[52]

Vahmann tried vainly to tame Anna's "disorderly nature," sometimes scolding her harshly, at other times trying to reason with her calmly. "Think, Miss Anna," he remembered telling her, "it won't be good in the long run, if you keep doing this."[53] But in the end, Vahmann was no match for Anna and her boyfriends' high mischief. Her father was no more successful. Dollen reports that when he realized how much she had stolen, he took away all of her keys. But Anna set a ladder against his window and sent a young girl through it to fetch his keys. She then made wax impressions of them all and soon had a new set that gave her free and unlimited access to all her father's valuables.[54]

Many witnesses believed that the root of Anna's hostility toward her father lay in his failure to arrange a good marriage for her when it was most opportune and proper for him to do so. Frequently she complained to her relatives that her father was not helping her find a husband. Her Rothenberg cousin Hans Hornberger, who reports this, could not say whether the charge was true. In his opinion, all the trouble arose from Anna's having remained in her father's house, unmarried, for too long a time.[55] Other witnesses disapproved in principle of a woman being still in her father's house at "twenty-eight or thirty years of age" (in 1525, Anna would have been in her late twenties), regardless of who was to blame for it.

Why, if Anna had "many good, honorable suitors," as her lawyer also claimed,[56] did she not marry in her early to middle-twenties when it was more than fitting for her to do so, and when her desires and behavior were jeopardizing the family's reputation? According to Anna, the fault was entirely her father's and intentional. He had simply chosen to shirk his paternal duty to give her a proper marriage, because he wanted to keep her dowry portion for himself, "preferring money to his daughter."[57] Her accusation is confirmed by witnesses, who maintain that her father approved of none of her suitors and blocked her every opportunity for marriage.[58] At her advanced age she might, of course, have married without her father's consent, but that could have jeopardized her dowry and inheritance and made her a far less attractive mate in the marriage market of the sixteenth century.

Anna's brother Philip and sister Agatha, on the other hand, scoffed both at the idea that she had many suitors and at the allegation that their father's greed threatened to make their sister a spinster.[59] As far as Hermann Büschler was concerned, his daughter's single state was entirely of her own making. He claimed to have arranged several good marriages for her, only to have her refuse them all.[60]

Vahmann, who probably resented Anna and had nothing to gain by siding with her, contradicted his master's claim. He recalled hearing him say that he had spoken with suitors on Anna's behalf, but had been unable to accept any of them; and he several times heard Anna say that she would gladly have married any one of them, if only her father had let her.[61] He hastened to add, however, that he could not be sure whether Anna had been sincere when she made such statements.

Judging from his other testimony about her in the 1520s, Vahmann agreed with his master that Anna was a confused and opportunistic young lady. Though he backs up her interpretation of why she could not marry at this time, it is possible that Anna also created problems for herself, much as her father claimed. She may unrealistically have hoped for a husband of higher social rank, perhaps even for a royal mate, and discouraged worthy but lesser suitors. Vahmann may have caught her at moments of sober reflection, when she honestly confronted the overwhelming odds against that happening, and was wishing she had made the most of her realistic choices. Be that as it may, a number of witnesses felt that Hermann Büschler had done far less on his daughter's behalf than a father might reasonably have been expected to do.

Had Anna and her father been able to agree on a candidate, caval-

ryman Daniel Treutwein would seem to have been that man. That he
and Anna several times raided her father's wine cellar certainly infu-
riated Hermann Büschler; and the bürgermeister certainly disapproved
of the pair's cavorting in his home into the early morning hours. However, in the sixteenth century courting couples did that sort of thing,
and parents then, as now, coped with it, especially when they believed
an acceptable permanent relationship was developing. So while Hermann Büschler had much to be aggrieved about when he contemplated
Anna's behavior, her indiscretions with Daniel Treutwein were hardly
a just reason to expel her from his house on that fall day in 1525.

Anna's banishment and lifelong feud with her family resulted from
a more shocking revelation. Unknowingly, the fastidious Vahmann
had made his master's terrible discovery possible. He recalled the very
day of its occurrence and the specific event leading to it. It happened
one evening at harvesttime, just as Vahmann had returned from an
errand at the tailor's. In one of the two barrels of stolen wares that
Anna had sent to Kirchberg and Vahmann had intercepted and returned to Hall, Hermann Büschler discovered a cache of private letters
to and from his daughter, which Anna had sent along with her personal
belongings, as she intended to sell those wares there herself. Clearly,
the letters were important to her and she wanted them in her custody
at all times. According to Vahmann, his master avidly read them and
seized on one in particular, an undated letter that Anna had apparently
recently written to Schenkin Margarete, her previous employer in Limpurg. Coincidentally, Hermann Büschler also received around the
same time a personal letter from the Schenkin concerning Anna.

Despite Anna's close relations with the Schenkin's family in Limpurg, it was no everyday occurrence for her to write to the Schenkin,
and certainly not for the Schenkin to write to her father. Together with
the Hohenlohe princes, the Limpurg Schenks were the region's true
royalty and for centuries had been the city's commercial rivals and
political enemies. The Schenks commanded an empire measuring almost seven square miles south and southeast of Hall and including the
town of Gaildorf and the villages of Unterlimpurg, which lay at the
foot of the castle, and Obersontheim.[62] Although on the bottom tier
in the hierarchy of imperial royalty, the Schenks were people to reckon
with in the region around Hall. As councilman and bürgermeister,
Hermann Büschler gave his relations with them a high priority, and

he could only have taken pride in his daughter's employment at castle Limpurg.

As a royal dynasty dating back to the 1230s, the Schenks[63] were older than the imperial city of Hall. The title "Schenk" literally means "cupbearer," and originally described unfree servants of the emperor known as *ministeriales*, who dated back to the eighth century. These men lived their lives in the saddle, accompanying kings on ceremonial occasions and providing them shelter and lodging whenever they passed through their lands. From such contacts evolved special commissions, which over the years transformed the Schenks into key agents in the administration of imperial lands and possessions in several regions of Germany.[64] In the process, they also became locally powerful landed nobility. In exchange for the use of royal land, they built and maintained castles on the emperor's behalf, from which, as virtual imperial governors, they monitored the emperor's possessions throughout the empire, in some places displacing the special imperial envoys and mayors who had previously performed such services. By the thirteenth century, the lands the Schenks governed began to be treated as hereditary, and the Schenks became locally powerful dynasties in their own right, even though in the hierarchy of imperial royalty they remained very small fish.

The first Schenk of Limpurg appeared in Hall in 1230 with a mission to oversee the imperial saltworks and other imperial possessions in the region on behalf of the Hohenstaufen emperors. Castle Limpurg was built only 750 meters southeast of the city's front wall, and the new Schenk held exclusive hunting rights on three sides of the city. He also controlled the forests on whose wood the city depended to fuel the cauldrons that created the salt that kept the city's economy strong. Better conditions for bitter, protracted conflict between city and Schenk could not have been arranged, and during the thirty-four-year reign of Schenk Walter II (1249–1283), every effort was made to incorporate the city into the little kingdom of the Limpurg Schenks.[65] Yet before his reign had ended, in 1276, Hall had become a free imperial city answerable only to the emperor, and no longer under the custody and oversight of Limpurg. By this time, the city was also the more economically and politically powerful of the two.

But if the Schenks were losing parity on the banks of the Kocher, they were receiving new recognition in the larger world of the Holy Roman Empire. In 1356, the emperor acknowledged them to be hereditary Schenks before all others in the empire, an honor they owed to the patronage of the king of Bohemia, the very "Lord High Cupbearer of the Holy Roman Empire" and one of the recently appointed seven electors, who were henceforth to choose the emperor. As the king's new vassals, the Limpurg Schenks represented him at the crownings of the emperor and Roman (imperial) kings, and whenever the emperor held court. On these ceremonial occasions, the Schenk of Limpurg, in full array, would ride toward the emperor (or king), bearing in his hand a gold-and-silver cup of twelve mark silver weight (which still exists today), in which a mixture of wine and water was contained, and coming abreast of his majesty, would dismount and extend the cup to him to drink from—a ceremony that both celebrated the occasion and reconfirmed the Schenks' allegiance and humble service to their overlord.[66]

Although after 1276, Hall and Limpurg were independent political entities, both locally and imperially they remained as adjacent to and dependent upon one another as two lands could possibly be. For this reason, they were destined to clash repeatedly over boundaries, tolls, hunting rights, and ultimate sovereignty. The seriousness with which such matters were taken is conveyed by the building of Hall's protective "hedges." Early in the fourteenth century, the new imperial city began digging trenches twelve feet deep and wide along the entire stretch of the borders of its land, into which brush was poured, creating an impenetrable hedge, so that riders would be able to enter Hall land and approach the city only along designated roads. Frequently inspected, these trenches were "rehedged" every seven years to maintain their deterrence. By the mid-fourteenth century, the hedges extended all the way to Leofels, five kilometers to the north, and anyone caught damaging them was fined fifty gold marks.[67]

The most serious in the long series of conflicts between Hall and Limpurg occurred in the late fifteenth century, when the brothers Egidius and Daniel Senft, Hall citizens, hacked to death the Schenk's gamekeeper, after the latter had cut down a rabbit hedge the two had built very near to, if not directly on, Schenkish land. The gamekeeper's body was subsequently found on the spot that marked the toll and territorial boundary between Hall and Limpurg. Not until 1541, when the city succeeded in purchasing castle Limpurg, then over three hundred years old and partially dilapidated, would such feuding end and clear and definitive boundaries be established between the two sovereignties.[68]

The walls that separate lands and polities are different from those that divide individuals, so Anna was not conscious of being in enemy territory during the years she worked in castle Limpurg. Indeed, she may not at first have lodged in, but gone back and forth across the border every day, as the distance between her home and the castle was short, and the Büschler house offered far the more comfortable accommodations. When royalty, including the emperor, visited Hall, it was in burgher mansions like Hermann Büschler's, not the local castle, that they preferred to stay.[69]

Assuming that Anna began her service around the age when it was common for Hall girls to do so, that is, by fifteen, she must have been in the Schenks' employment for at least five years before returning home in 1520 to become her father's housekeeper. During her years in castle Limpurg, she had gotten to know the royal family well, and after her return to Hall, she continued to perform services for them and to be a frequent visitor to the castle.

In the cache of Anna's letters through which her father now rummaged, there were no fewer than forty-two between Anna and Erasmus (eleven by Anna and thirty-one by Erasmus), written back and forth between 1520 and 1525, several containing frank talk about love and sex.[70] In the same bundle were nineteen love letters from Daniel Treutwein, along with still other correspondence connected with the two affairs. Twenty-five years later, her brother Philip and sister Agatha would submit the entire collection to the imperial commissioners in an effort to discredit their sister's character and justify her disinheritance. At that time, the two described them as letters no honorable daughter or maiden would write,[71] which was also their father's view of them on his first reading.

In Anna's letter to the Schenkin, which Vahmann says Hermann Büschler singled out in the collection, Anna dwelt on the care she was then taking to hire a trustworthy maid. Her comments may not have come as a revelation to the Schenkin, but they certainly did to her father:

It is my sincere request [Anna writes] that your grace not pay attention to all the talk she now hears. There is a man named Hermann Büschler, and if he were not, I would put an end to many things. It is my sincere request that your grace not allow anyone to suffer any [harm] because of me. My hope is that your grace shall make everything right.[72]

According to Vahmann, Hermann Büschler seized immediately upon the second line,[73] which Vahmann recalled him paraphrasing thus: "If Hermann Büschler were not, she would gladly return to the Schenkin."[74] Plaintively, he asked his servant: "Dear friend, what shall I say? What have I done to my child that she may not call me father?"

At about the same time that Hermann Büschler was discovering his daughter's secret life in her private correspondence, he also received a letter from the Schenkin herself. In it, as Vahmann recalled, the Schenkin informed him in diplomatic language of her intention to keep Anna and Erasmus apart. "Henceforth," as Vahmann paraphrased the Schenkin, "Anna may not make shirts for her son, she would again clothe her son well enough herself." "Because of this," Vahmann comments, "her father was moved to drive [Anna] out of the house."[75]

Erasmus was the third of six surviving children and the Schenkin's second son,[76] and obviously someone Anna had gotten to know well during the years she worked in castle Limpurg. Sewing for the royal family, and particularly for Erasmus, had been one of the services she performed during her years there. As the Schenkin's letter makes clear, it was a service she continued to perform after her tenure there ended. Thus had Hermann Büschler stumbled upon his daughter's secret affair with Schenk Erasmus, which, as their full correspondence made clear to him, had been going on since at least 1520.

The "talk" Anna wanted the Schenkin now to ignore was the mounting gossip about her and her suitors in Hall. The person she was trying to protect was, of course, Erasmus. And the "matters" she would put an end to, evidently by marrying, if her father were not in the way, were her amours with her suitors.

When her father read her letter to the Schenkin, he immediately interpreted it to mean that she preferred her previous life in castle Limpurg, with its easy and immoral access to her royal lover, over a respectable life with him in Hall. When she wished him gone, he saw not escape from tormenting gossip, but from her duty to him whom she could no longer call father. He may now also have recognized, perhaps for the first time, the depth of her resentment of his failure to settle a proper marriage.

Erasmus's mother probably knew about the relationship between the two for a longer period of time, and was now taking steps to contain it because of Anna's increasingly notorious reputation. No longer was Anna simply another young maid in castle Limpurg. She was the very public daughter of the bürgermeister of Hall, and not just any bürgermeister, but a local hero on whose goodwill political relations between Limpurg and Hall depended. Had it not been for the new potential for scandal to rub off on the young Schenk, the Schenkin might never have written to Hermann Büschler, but rather taken a presumed still secret and passing affair between her son and Anna in stride, for such amours were not unusual in royal households. Now she had to consider the possible consequences for Limpurg if and when, in conjunction with Anna's scandalous behavior with other men, her involvement with Erasmus also came to light. As she wrote to Hermann Büschler, the Schenkin had no way of knowing that the discovery she feared was then occurring.

Hermann Büschler's failure to learn of his daughter's relationship with Erasmus sooner can only be due to his servants' family loyalty and fear of telling him. Barbara Dollen certainly knew that Anna had frequent rendezvous with Erasmus, although she claimed in later testimony to have had no idea what they did on such occasions. She recalled once when she had gone to Weinsberg and Herr Büschler was out of town on business how Anna, then home alone, disguised herself in her (Dollen's) clothes and secretly spent three days in Limpurg castle with Erasmus.[77]

If the letters to and from Erasmus and Daniel were not evidence enough of Anna's depravity for her father, their dates and contents further indicated to him that the affairs had gone on concurrently: Anna had been sexually active not with one man, but with two men simultaneously, one of whom, Erasmus, was a completely unrealistic marriage prospect, making that relationship an affair for its own sake. That was the bombshell that moved Hermann Büschler to describe his daughter as an "evil serpent," a phrase he hereafter often used in referring to her,[78] and to remove her from his house.

If, from a modern point of view, Hermann Büschler appears to have overreacted, it must be remembered that at this time casual premarital sex and unwed motherhood could indelibly stain a person and irreparably damage a family's reputation, in addition to which the partners also faced punishment. Despite greater openness to and less prudery about sex than in later centuries, the sixteenth century rigidly defined and enforced the laws regulating proper sexual behavior. Such vigilance came primarily in reaction to the rapid expansion of brothels in the fifteenth century and the closely related rampant spread of syphilis in the sixteenth, and was as strongly supported by the religious reformers as by health-conscious public officials.

Prior to the sixteenth century, marriage had not been the dominant lifestyle for adult men and women, and those who did marry often waited until their mid to late twenties before they were financially able to do so. Given the large numbers of unmarried freemen, clergy, and religious, single young adults made up a sizable segment of society. City governments established public brothels during the fifteenth century as an outlet for the sexual needs of single young men and as a measure of protection for the marriageable daughters of burghers, whose purity and good reputation were essential for the best possible marriage.[79] The combination of a deadly new venereal disease and the success of a religious reform that exalted marriage over celibacy revised thinking about previous sexual practice. Historians have perceived a new "moral politics" emerging in German cities during the sixteenth century, closely tied to the desires of both Protestant and Catholic reformers to restrict all sexuality to marriage, which Martin Luther proclaimed to be the only "true chastity." To this end, the leaders of the Reformation and Counter Reformation sanctioned new measures against premarital, extramarital, and deviant sexual behavior.[80]

Whereas in the villages in the countryside, premarital sex and pregnancy continued to remain a normal, moral, and licit route to a proper marriage, city governments increasingly criminalized such behavior during the sixteenth century, especially when it was undertaken without any intention or prospect of marriage. Youth were admonished to remain chaste until marriage. Women who openly engaged in premarital sex or lived in open concubinage with no plans to marry could find themselves paraded barefoot through town, clad in penitential tunics and with their heads shaved.[81] The birth of a child to an artisan couple who had been married less than nine months could occasion the parents' expulsion from the guild.[82] As for adultery and sodomy (homosexuality), imperial law punished the former by pillory, flogging, and banishment, while the latter was a capital crime.[83]

In the great majority of cases, as in Anna Büschler's, partners engaging in premarital sex made every effort to keep it secret, knowing that they might survive gossip, but not the scandal of public disclosure. It was very likely for this reason, and not out of any diminished desire or heroic sexual restraint on the part of premodern youth,[84] that so little sexual deviance appears to have existed in early modern Europe. Even when discovered, premarital sex, unlike adultery and sodomy, was rarely as severely punished as the law prescribed, particularly if there was a chance of steering the couple toward a proper marriage. Despite the age's professed ideals of chastity and self-denial, people then—and the clergy as perceptively as any others—understood the temptations facing the young and the likelihood that they would succumb. Perhaps one-half of urban populations were unmarried youth under twenty years of age,[85] and financial considerations or the lack of proper opportunities could easily delay marriage into one's mid to late twenties.

During the later Middle Ages, townspeople had had considerable experience with this problem in the form of clandestine marriages or the private exchange of vows by young people of canonical age (twelve for women and fourteen for men), a practice against which a largely losing campaign had been waged. Such unions became possible after the Church in the tenth century recognized consent between the partners to be the primary element in a valid marriage. Thereafter, it was possible for a young man and a young woman of canonical age to exchange valid promises of marriage ("future vows") or even actual marriage vows ("present vows") privately at their own initiative and without parental knowledge or consent.

Such permissiveness was not only a proper theological position for the Church to take at the time; it was also an enterprising pastoral extension of the Church's authority over the sexual life of the laity. In one great stroke, it brought under the Church's moral authority the enormous world of teenage and young adult fornication. As a consequence, however, parents found themselves confronted by children who, without any prior consultation with them, had exchanged marriage vows, possibly engaged in sexual relations, and might even be expecting a child, yet by these very acts were proclaimed by the Church truly to be man and wife in the eyes of God and under the laws of the Church.[86]

For the majority of youth in late medieval and Reformation Europe, premarital sex seems not to have been a great issue of conscience, despite the clergy's determination to make it such. Nonetheless, for youth who found themselves in a society that both forbade premarital sex and expected it to occur, secret vows became a way to engage in sexual relations with minimum risk and a good conscience.[87] Yet, despite the flexibility clandestine marriage seemed to introduce into sexual relations, the practice often resulted in personally devastating and socially disruptive litigation. This was because the partners did not always agree that marriage vows had been exchanged as a condition of sexual intercourse. In the majority of such cases, an allegedly seduced and sometimes pregnant woman, fearing disgrace and ostracization, swore she had had sexual relations with an accused lover (and, if pregnant, the presumed father of her child) only after the two of them had exchanged marriage vows. He, however, in response swore just as fervently that only casual, consensual sex had occurred between them, insisting that he be punished, if he must be, only for fornication, and not declared the lawful husband of a woman he did not wish to marry and the father of a child he could not confidently call his own.

When, in such disputes, the evidence was insufficient to determine whether vows had in fact been exchanged, official efforts were made to persuade the couple to marry anyway. If, in the end, the man agreed to marry the woman and repair the damage done her by their mutual indiscipline, the couple were punished only by being denied a public wedding and the bride the traditional festive bridal wreath (her head remained covered during the ceremony). If, on the other hand, the man refused to marry her for whatever reason—which he was free to do, since a binding marriage could not occur without the voluntary consent of both parties—he then had to pay damages commensurate with the loss of the woman's sexual integrity and social standing. Since at this time virginity was viewed as a "second dowry," the marriage prospects of a woman thus damaged were seriously diminished. In such cases, fair compensation could more than double the original dowry. In addition, the accused man could also spend time in jail, depending on the circumstances of the offense and the court's findings regarding his character.[88]

In cases of disputed clandestine marriage and/or fornication, the courts generally presumed that the accusing women were the ones who had been deceived and seduced, and thus, as the comparatively guiltless party, exempted them from such punishment. However, if it could be demonstrated that a woman had encouraged the illicit activity by her previous behavior and reputation, or had freely solicited it, then she could be denied compensation from the alleged seducer, lose her right to a dowry from her parents, and even be imprisoned.[89]

To counter private marriage vows and the seeming sexual license they masked, late medieval towns passed laws making publicity a condition of a "licit" marriage. By this means, a marriage deemed valid in the eyes of God by the Church thus became legal in human society only as the marriage vows were also exchanged in a public forum before documented witnesses. Another weapon against private vows was the parents' power to disinherit children who married defiantly without their knowledge and consent. This latter course of action, however, had dire consequences for a child and was one few families were inclined to follow.[90]

To win the cooperation of young people and avoid socially disruptive scandal and litigation, sixteenth-century towns like Hall also tried to make premarital chastity appealing and entrance into a mature marriage as easy as possible. In doing so, they were aided by the Protestant reformers, who urged early marriage as a remedy to fornication and recommended regular, vigorous sex within marriage as the surest way to prevent adultery. Martin Luther, who has been said to have been as fixed on sex as Freud, absolutely opposed any restraints on sexual activity within marriage. Marriage opened the forbidden door to sex by investing it with love and legality, thereby making it something Christians could indulge in fully with a good conscience. According to the Strasbourg reformer Martin Bucer, no true marriage existed where there was not a joyous sharing of physical affection.[91]

At the same time, the moralists of the age glorified sexual abstinence and purity before marriage as the "vocation" of youth, the special "labor" to which God called single teenagers and young adults. As it was the divine vocation of fathers to work in the world and of mothers to labor in childbirth, God had burdened youth with self-sacrificing virginity until marriage.[92]

In church, school, and home, pastors, teachers, and parents drummed chastity and self-control into the young, who were taught early the liabilities of unwed motherhood, venereal disease, and immature marriages.[93] In the growing literature for girls published in the sixteenth and seventeenth centuries, the overriding concern was to diminish sexual thoughts and delay sexual activity until marriage. That literature was heavily religious in content, a medley of catechisms, Bible excerpts, prayer books, and the lives of virtuous people—reading that has been described as "the sixteenth century's alternative to sex education."[94] Catechetical sermons conveyed the same message to boys and girls entering puberty, as they prepared for their first communion.

That ordinary parents fully shared the concerns of the moralists can be seen in the advice a dying mother left her two surviving daughters in a seventeenth-century testament.

> Don't eat and drink too much at parties. Eat and drink ahead of time and accept drinks only from other girls. If a boy peels a fruit for you, do not accept it. When boys come and sit beside you, don't answer their questions; say only, "yes," "no," and "I don't know." And do not smile at them. When boys happen to come into your bedroom, hide behind the bed and threaten to hit them in the face.[95]

Against this background, Anna's confirmed sexual intimacy not with one but with two men, and at the same time, could only strike her father as bordering on prostitution, a charge he later made privately to her brother, by describing her as a whore.[96] Gossip about her relationship with a legitimate suitor like Daniel Treutwein was one thing for him to have to live with; the sudden, sure knowledge of her promiscuity with two men was quite another. Not only did his discovery destroy his trust in and respect for his daughter, it also threatened to bring scandal into his home and stigmatize forever the Büschler name. So he drove the "evil serpent" from his house and out of Hall.

As for the filthy letters, he kept them to himself, bequeathing them upon his death in 1543 to his son Philip, who later exposed them to the public during his litigation with his sister at mid-century. Until then, they were in all likelihood preserved under lock and key in an iron-hinged, metal-rimmed oaken chest (roughly 16×12×8 inches in size), or in one of the great oaken cabinets that were commonly used in contemporary Hall households to store valuable papers and documents, examples of which are today on display in the city's Hällisch-Fränkisches Museum. By suppressing the letters, Hermann Büschler succeeded in confining the scandal during his lifetime. To the vast majority of Anna's contemporaries, stealing and cavorting with Daniel Treutwein behind her father's back had been the worst of her wrong-doing—not the scandalous love triangle, involving a prominent person Anna had no chance to marry, that her father had uncovered. Anna thus remained in the contemporary public eye, as later also in her brief appearances in the accounts of modern historians, a willful and disobedient daughter who disgraced her father, not a notoriously promiscuous woman, liable, and deserving of punishment at law.

A memorial to Erasmus's grandfather, Schenk Georg von Limpurg
(d. 1475), in the chapel of the Schenks in Comburg monastery near castle
Limpurg. He wears the new tailored armor, and stands on a threatening
lion, symbol of manliness and power. Around his neck is the insignia of
the Cyprian Order of the Sword, a badge of honor awarded by the kings
of Cyprus to nobility returning from Jerusalem via the island after being
knighted at the Holy Sepulcher.

At the base are the words: "Limpurg from the bloodlines of the dukes of
Swabia and Franconia," a defensive assertion of Georg's lineage, which
was only partly royal (his grandmother was Elizabeth of Hohenlohe) and
not from his father's side of his family, which was originally unfree
knights.

CHAPTER

TWO

The **A**ffairs

ERASMUS IS KNOWN IN HISTORY BOOKS AS A CHAMPION OF THE Protestant Reformation in Hall and through his son, the future Schenk of Limpurg-Sontheim, Friedrich VII (1536–1596), as the progenitor of modern dynasties, including that of Queen Victoria of England.[1] Within the context of the Büschler drama, however, Erasmus may more appropriately be remembered as one of Germany's great cads. That is not to say that he did not play a role in the Reformation, which, with the great Peasants' War of 1525, historically frames his affair with Anna Büschler. Erasmus assumed that role only reluctantly, however, and well after the Reformation had established itself in the region. On the other hand, his womanizing began early and, as we shall see, was always wholeheartedly pursued.

Beginning in 1523, the people of Hall progressively embraced the new Lutheran faith, but ever so cautiously, as the city remained politically beholden to the new and very devout Catholic emperor, Charles V (1519–1550). At the turn of the century, Hall's religious life was served by twelve churches and chapels with twenty-four benefices and active orders of Benedictine, Franciscan, and Johannite monks— fifty-three clergy in all, thirty-two priests and twenty-one religious, serving a city of perhaps five thousand. The churches and cloisters of Hall were not in good repair, though, and corruption and concubinage were rife among the clergy.

As in many other cities and towns on the eve of their reform, popular religious culture in Hall remained lively and active, as both the spiritually secure and the spiritually anxious attempted to stifle any doubts they might have about traditional belief and practice by embracing all the more fervently the piety of their parents. Hall's churches were well attended, and most burghers belonged to a religious confraternity. St. Michael's Church displayed seventy-three relics, while two Marian churches in the area welcomed pilgrims.[2]

The depth and vitality of popular piety in and around the city is conveyed by a famous episode that led, in 1440, to the creation of a remarkable shrine to the Virgin in the nearby village of Tüngenthal, northeast of Hall. According to legend, around 1434, a Limpurg Schenk was hunting near the village church when his dogs flushed a hare from its burrow. The hare bounded into the church and in its panic began to leap repeatedly upon a statue of the Virgin that stood on a console at the south wall of the choir. The dogs, which had raced into the church in pursuit of the hare, froze at the altar. Viewing the episode as a miracle, the hunter took the frightened hare to the church cemetery and released it with the words: "Go forth, dear hare; you have sought freedom in the church and you have found it there. As the dogs have spared you, so will I."[3]

As the story was retold throughout the region, pilgrims flocked to the church to behold "Our Lady of the Hare," and Tüngenthal became a popular area shine. Very soon a sculpted figure of a hare appeared upon the original statue, securely attached to the Madonna's left foot. Our Lady of the Hare remained an object of veneration until the church was destroyed by Allied bombs on April 19, 1945.[4]

The popular piety of Hall also had a dark side. During the sixteenth century and arguably ever since, the city's most famous work of prose was *The Story of Dr. Faust (Das Volksbuch von Doktor Faust)*, about the physician and philosopher who sold his soul to the devil in exchange for magical powers. Written in 1599 by Georg Rudolf Widmann, a local author and son of the city's syndic, the book became the basis for the later, world-renowned versions of Christopher Marlowe and Johann Wolfgang von Goethe. Widmann based his popular tale on oral traditions about a foreign-born physician and philosopher, believed to possess magical powers, who visited Hall in 1516. According to legend, the famous doctor caroused with the gregarious salt-makers, who made up the city's largest trade, boasting a third again as many members (sixty) as the next-largest trade (the shoemakers). These were the men who boiled the water from the salt spring in 111 cauldrons, each five meters long and over a meter wide, and on whose labors the city's prosperity depended.[5]

One of the stories told about Dr. Faust during his stay describes the day the salt-makers challenged him to "conjure [literally, shit] a devil." Accepting the challenge, the famous doctor dropped his trousers and sent a great fiery bolt into the Kocher River, while the salt-makers watched from a footbridge in disbelief. At the very spot where the flash entered the water, a coal-black man emerged and proceeded to attack the salt-makers, who in their panic jumped from the bridge into the river.[6]

So closely associated with Hall is the Faust legend that a local establishment in the modern city has turned it to advantage by claiming to be the famous doctor's first stop during his visit to Hall (as reported in Georg Widmann's sixteenth-century chronicle). On the side of Schubach's Restaurant near the town square are chiseled the words:

> When Dr. Faust came one day to Hall,
>   He went directly to Schubach's,
> Where, from dawn to dusk, he drank
>   Many a strong drink with the honest salt-makers.
> But no harm was done him there;
>   The wine was pure, the hand sure,
> As the Chronicle [of Widmann] reports.
>   It really is true and no fiction.
> So you people listen up,
>   And, like Faust, drop by Schubach's.

If Hall's popular piety was lively and profound, the local churches and cloisters stood in need of moral and political reforms that were long overdue and their leaders disinclined to make. In the closing decades of the fifteenth century, the city council attempted to force reform upon them by its ordinary powers of taxation and zoning. It restricted church expansion, limited the tax exemptions of the clergy, and carefully monitored the financial and sexual behavior of the clergy.

In 1522, it took a bolder step by inviting a twenty-three-year-old Lutheran preacher, Johannes Brenz, to occupy the pulpit of St. Michael's Church.[7] Recommended by a Haller who was a fellow student with Brenz in Heidelberg, Brenz arrived in Hall for his "interview" in September, preaching on the 22nd a sermon that greatly impressed the councilmen, an event that may be said to mark the start of the city's conversion to Protestantism.

Although a zealot, the young preacher proved also to be politically astute and methodical in his work. During his first year, he continued to read the traditional Mass, but he also told his congregation that he did not believe the Mass to be a miracle of transubstantiation, as Church dogma proclaimed. Also in his first year, he directly attacked the practice of venerating saints and relics, something that brought him the undying enmity of the Franciscans.

In 1524, several changes heralded the transformation of Hall into a Protestant city: the dilapidated Franciscan cloister was torn down, the whorehouse closed, and the practice of clerical concubinage forbidden. In 1525, the first Evangelical Mass (with both bread and wine) was publicly celebrated, effectively suppressing the traditional Mass, which would, however, not be officially abolished until two years later, and then not in every church. In 1526, Brenz published an ambitious new church order, destined in the 1530s to shape the spiritual life of Protestants throughout Württemberg. With the publication of new school and welfare ordinances in the following year, the new discipline of the Protestant Reformation had indeed come to Hall.

Brenz, however, was moving faster and farther than the Haller desired, and they called a halt when he proposed the creation of a clerical synodal court to discipline the laity. By that system, the moral failings of laity, after warnings from their pastors, would, upon the latter's recommendation, be punished by excommunication and humiliation enforced by the magistrate. To the clerical mind, that was an admirable use of force in the service of the Gospel, while to the laity, it smacked of the old papal institutions the city had invited Brenz to reform. An old Haller may have spoken for the majority when he accused Brenz of utopianism as well. "You, sir, are up to something that won't work," he reportedly shouted at Brenz, when the synodal ordinance was proposed in 1531: "You want to make the devil pious, but you can't do that." "One cannot prevent all sins or offenses in the community," Brenz agreed in response, "but everything [will be] fine as long as one [only] punishes them!"[8]

At the imperial Diet of Augsburg in 1530, convened by the emperor to address the Reformation's success in the empire and, if possible, to reconcile the differences between Protestants and Catholics, Hall's delegation took its place with the other decidedly Protestant cities. None of the changes in the city's spiritual life, however, had come about easily, nor were they all at this time inflexible, or even secure. Catholics remained in the city council and continued to oppose Brenz's reforms—men like Volk von Rossdorf and Michael Seiboth, who would later testify at Anna's hearings. In 1529, Hall's delegation to the Diet of Speyer, where the name "Protestant" was coined, cooperated so eagerly with the papal side that Martin Luther lamented (inaccurately, but with cause) Hall's "falling away from the Gospel" in that year; Hermann Büschler was one-half of that wavering delegation.[9] And despite the outlawing of the Mass in 1527, it continued to be celebrated with the emperor's blessing at St. John's Church until 1534, drawing a sizable congregation from the old patrician families in and around the city, whose traditional faith remained unshaken throughout the religious revolt.[10]

In Limpurg, the ascendance of the Reformation in Hall and the region was watched with ambivalence at best. For generations, the Schenks had been patrons of the old Church, and their personal and political interests remained closely tied to its institutions. Erasmus's cousin Schenk Wilhelm of nearby Gaildorf illustrates the dilemma posed for those in the region who still professed Catholicism and maintained alliances with the larger Catholic world. In 1544, Schenk Wilhelm joined area counts in embracing the Lutheran Augsburg Confession (1530), an authoritative statement of Lutheran religious beliefs that had been placed before Emperor Charles V at the Diet of Augsburg and subsequently provided the basis for the Schmalkaldic League, a Protestant defense alliance against the emperor. Yet the Schenk remained a man both blessed and burdened with eleven children, five of whom he had earlier placed in cloisters he personally patronized. When a new daughter arrived in 1545, the now publicly Lutheran Schenk Wilhelm discreetly consecrated her to a cloister in faraway Quedlinburg. In light of his recent embrace of the Augsburg Confession, this may seen a most duplicitous act, but given the Schenk's needs and habits, it was, for the times, both logical and appropriate.[11]

For as long as one could remember, the Limpurg Schenks had patronized the cathedral chapters of Würzburg and Bamberg. Erasmus's younger brother Philip was a canon in both places, as well as prior of the nearby Comburg monastery. His uncle Georg was Bamberg's bishop. After his death in 1553, Erasmus joined his predecessors in Comburg's "Chapel of the Schenks," a special burial room at the back of the church with striking statuary. By 1553, burial at the monastery had little confessional meaning, however, since this most Catholic of convents had by then also fallen to Protestantism. Indeed, at the time of Erasmus's death, its ruling canon was living openly, as he would continue to do lifelong, in uncontested concubinage with the daughter of an Evangelical pastor.[12]

Still, in the 1530s, the confessional issues remained difficult for the Schenks of Limpurg. Erasmus's marriage to the widowed countess Anna of Lodron in 1533 immersed him even more deeply in the larger contemporary Catholic world at the very time his immediate world was succumbing to Lutheranism. His wife came from a wealthy south Tirol family with connections at the highest levels of Catholic royalty. During his midteens, their only son, Friedrich, would spend five years at the Catholic court of King Ferdinand in Prague.

Given his family's history and alliances, it might seem unthinkable that Erasmus could end up in the Protestant camp, much less gain the reputation of a hero of the Reformation. There were, however, other forces at work in Limpurg moving him to embrace Protestantism when he could do so in utmost safety. Having only one son and two daughters, he did not have his cousin Wilhelm's pressing need to board numerous children in cloisters. Also, his father had already accommodated Luther's teaching, allowing Evangelical preachers to move freely in Limpurg lands in the mid-1520s, while at the same time firmly resisting any efforts on their part to institutionalize their major reforms. Because of the enmity between Hall and Limpurg and the more radical nature of Hall's reforms, the Limpurg Schenks could not allow the city to be its model for religious reform. Schenk Gottfried pursued church reform of a milder and more political nature, giving Protestants a hearing, but discouraging a revolution in traditional belief and practice on the scale of Hall's Reformation.[13]

Erasmus was drawn into the religious conflict early. In 1524, when only twenty-two, he represented his father at a conference in Kitzingen, where the conferees (Franconian princes) drew up a list of economic and religious grievances against the Roman Church. As Schenk, he shared his father's cautious approach to religious change, inching toward it always with a finger in the wind. Only after far stronger noblemen than he had joined the Reformation did Erasmus openly embrace it. There is evidence that he supported basic Evangelical preaching in Limpurg as early as 1537, when the preachers in his land were required to swear an oath "to preach the gospel and God's word pure and clear, following the letter of Scripture without any distractions."[14]

The oath itself cannot, however, be taken as an acid test of Protestant sentiment, since unlike definitive Protestant oaths elsewhere, it required no explicit rejection of traditional doctrine or practice. Nonetheless, several of Erasmus's actions at this time confirm his growing political association with the ascending Protestant powers in the region. In 1534, Duke Ulrich of recently Protestantized Württemberg appointed him counsel and sheriff (*Obervogt*) of little Laufen, south of Hall on the Kocher, for a second time. A decade earlier, when the town had been Catholic, Erasmus had also held that position. Now he found himself working on a new Protestant religious order for the region. Seven years later (1541), the devoutly Lutheran Count Palatine Ottheinrich made Erasmus administrator (*Pfleger*) of the Evangelical village of Hilpoltstein. And in 1544, a Brandenburg prince put him in charge of deeply Evangelical Crailsheim.[15]

By the early 1540s, then, Erasmus had come to accept Lutheranism as the dominant religion in the region. Yet even at this late date, he still had to tread lightly on the divisive confessional issues. When, in 1541, his personal finances forced him to sell castle Limpurg to the city of Hall, he still looked to the Catholic emperor to help him build a smaller castle for himself in nearby Obersontheim, which was now also in the same sea of Protestantism as Limpurg.[16]

Whatever devotion Erasmus had to the new faith was put to the test in 1546, when imperial armies attempted to return the region around Hall to traditional Catholic practice. In December of that year, Hessian mercenaries under Spanish command burst upon Hall in search of its famous reformer Johannes Brenz, whom they intended to execute as a first step in the reconversion of the city. As a result of the assistance of an unknown nobleman, whom contemporaries and later historians have believed to be Erasmus, Brenz was taken to a hiding place near Crailsheim, where he successfully escaped the Hessian dragnet. A second attempt to capture Hall's reformer also failed, this time because then bürgermeister Philip Büschler (Anna's brother), learning of the new plot at a council meeting, immediately sent Brenz a note ("Brenz, flee as quickly as you can!"), which allowed him to escape again with his wife and six children to a safe refuge in Obersontheim or Gaildorf, this time unquestionably arranged by Erasmus.[17] Because of such involvement on the old reformer's behalf, both Erasmus and Philip have been remembered in local history books as champions of Hall's Reformation.

 Letters

THE ERASMUS ANNA BÜSCHLER KNEW AND LOVED IN HER YOUTH was neither a gentleman nor a hero. In place of the legendary figure of confessional history, where small favors can bring one everlasting fame, we find a young man of all too ordinary passion and spite, writing to a woman with whom he wishes only to have his way. Thanks to the survival of their correspondence, we can meet them both in their own words, unembellished by either contemporary or modern historians.

The first surviving letter in the couple's four-year correspondence is dated New Year's Day, 1521, a scant eleven days after the death of Anna's mother, when Anna was again living in her father's house. The exact date of her departure from castle Limpurg is unclear, but it was most likely in the weeks before her mother's death. By this time, she and Erasmus were surely lovers. During the years they corresponded (1521–1525), Erasmus was in his late teens and early twenties and constantly traveling, as he made contacts with his royal peers and superiors, perfected the skills of a cavalryman, and learned the duties of a Schenk. He was a frequent visitor to Würzburg, the seat of the imperial court, and Bamberg, where his uncle Georg was bishop.[18] He undertook numerous police actions and administrative assignments in imperial lands at the command of the lords he served.

Anna's New Year's Day letter indicates that she was under instructions not to write to him too often while he was away from castle Limpurg, as he then was in Würzburg, lest a steady stream of messengers between them draw suspicion. With this letter, however, Anna threw caution to the wind, compelled by worry to write much sooner than was advisable. As would often be the case in their correspondence, her worry was over local gossip about her. In Erasmus's absence she attended festive events at castle Limpurg and other places, where she sometimes allowed her exuberant nature to get the better of her. She confesses to having been naive, by which she probably meant that drinking and flirting had been the worst of it. She feared, however, that a more virulent gossip about her behavior on such occasions would reach Erasmus, if it had not already done so, and damage their relationship.

Since Anna's father was very well-to-do, and because of his legendary reputation and prominence in the city government, the Büschlers had enormous political influence in Hall. The economic and political fortunes of the Limpurg Schenks, by contrast, were sagging at this time. Indeed, townspeople, particularly merchants attempting to collect outstanding debts, knew Erasmus's father, Schenk Gottfried II, as "Geoff with the empty wallet."[19] Castle Limpurg had fallen into disrepair, parts of it already in ruins, its lamentable condition attested to by Erasmus's later unsuccessful effort to sell it, along with its attached properties and privileges, to Duke Ulrich of Württemberg for the bargain price of 26,000 gulden, thereby keeping it among the royals. That the city of Hall bought it for almost twice that sum (45,700 gulden) had nothing to do with its intrinsic worth. Buying the castle enabled the city to end its ancient boundary disputes with the Schenks and to gain control over the tolls that came with the property.[20] The Haller actually viewed the castle as a menace to public safety, both because of its decrepitude and because of its ability to provide the city's enemies with a convenient citadel should they wish to besiege Hall. So although the city initially refurbished parts of it, within three decades of the purchase, castle Limpurg was intentionally demolished.[21]

The Limpurg Schenks' hard times were, however, those of royalty. The family experienced some deprivation and self-denial, but nothing remotely approaching impoverishment as ordinary people knew it. Erasmus remained the scion of a centuries-old dynasty of imperial Schenks, whose future still seemed bright. For this reason he probably never entertained the thought of marrying Anna, either out of love or for money. In an age acutely conscious of class and rank, Anna was not a realistic match for a royal Schenk. She was a good catch for a man from the lower nobility, but not for royalty. If the thought of a permanent relationship with her had ever crossed Erasmus's mind, such a union would have been completely unthinkable to his parents and peers. Anna, on the other hand, may have accepted this fact of social reality more slowly and only after some embarrassment and pain. As her involvements with Erasmus and Daniel Treutwein indicate, she preferred the company of noblemen and greatly valued her contacts with royalty.

Was this also true of her doting father? Had Hermann Büschler dreamed of a royal match for his daughter and placed Anna in the household of the Schenks with that possibility in mind? Perhaps this was the reason he had found all of her suitors unworthy. Perhaps Anna was driven from her father's house because she had spoiled his own ambitious plans for her and for himself. Perhaps the most devastating realization for Hermann Büschler came not when he read Anna's letter to the Schenkin indicating her affair with Erasmus, but when he read the Schenkin's letter to him terminating her contact with the future Schenk and thereby closing for both father and daughter alike a perceived golden gate into the world of royalty.

That is a plausible scenario for a modern romance, but not at all for one set in the sixteenth century. It was one thing at this time for a burgher to have political equality with local nobility and even greater wealth than minor royalty, but quite another for him to leap into the ranks of princes. Again, it was a matter of origins and honor, which Hermann Büschler's noble colleagues had already impressed upon him during the taproom battles of 1509–1510. Anna lost her father's devotion not because her behavior ended a dream he had to catapult them both into a higher social world, but because she had lessened his stature within his own world.

Throughout the correspondence with Erasmus, Anna acknowledges the divide separating the two families. Following the expected epistolary etiquette of the age when addressing royalty, she remembers, with a few notable exceptions, Erasmus's greater social standing and accepts the inequality of their relationship as a condition of its continuation. This accounts for the formality, strange to the modern reader, that attends the talk of love on both sides. Despite their intimacy, Erasmus often writes to her in the royal we, as ruler to subject, and she is careful to acknowledge his eminence in even her angriest letter. While not always successful in doing so, both also attempt to cloak their emotions in the proper attitude of a superior and an inferior, he by restraint and seeming indifference, she by apparent subservience and self-effacement. On the other hand, Anna is no passive playmate, even for a royal Schenk. She is quick to remind Erasmus of the sacrifices she makes on his behalf and of what she expects from him in return.

1. ANNA TO ERASMUS (NEW YEAR'S, 1521)

Most darlingly radiant, gracious, and honorable sir. From the bottom of my heart, I wish your grace a good and happy new year and send my heartfelt greetings; and I offer your grace every good and obediently willing service that a poor burgher's daughter can perform for a high lord . . .

Most darlingly gracious sir, I have both dreamed and heard told through my informants something I can well imagine to be true, namely, that someone has slandered me in your presence. Your grace will certainly know whoever does or has done so. Most darlingly gracious sir, your grace should not believe a word of it, for it does me an injustice in many respects. Although this misfortune has been beyond my control[22] I do know a little about the ways of the court, and I truly have not deserved [such slander] from anyone.

Most darlingly gracious sir, it is my heartfelt wish that your grace write to me when it is possible. Of course, if it is just not possible, then your grace should by no means do so. If [however] I am unable to write your grace anything about my well-being, your grace may well know a good bit about it already.[23]

Honorable and most gracious sir, your grace's bracelet[24] is now finished, but there is no way I am going to send it to your grace. Your grace must come and fetch it himself, either on his next visit or at another time; it is all the same to me.

Most darlingly gracious sir, do not be angry with me because I have written to your grace. Although it is not at all proper or fitting for me to do so at this time, I don't know when there would be a better time for me to write, since the messenger is now at my service.

Most darlingly gracious sir, I commend your grace to God; may God give your grace much luck and joy in whatever is good and useful to your grace. I pray that God grants it. A thousand good nights. Written on New Year's Day.

Most darlingly gracious sir, because I know well that I am not your grace's equal, I would do nothing to harm your grace. That would only lead to a lot of trouble.[25] Anna Büschler.

Kind, kinder, dearest sir, after your grace has written to me, believe it, your grace. O, one so dear and good, return to me honorably; touch me and make my waiting short. I have no peace; peace will not stay.[26]

Erasmus responded from Würzburg, where he had ridden with his new lord. After knightly training, which began at seven at the court of a lord, continued after fourteen in the field as an esquire, and ended in knighthood at twenty-one, the sons of minor dynastic families like Erasmus's performed military or custodial services for princes of the larger territorial states, who also had their place in the imperial hierarchy. Between 1521 and 1525, Erasmus, in the company of his father, was serving the princes of Württemberg as counsel and sheriff in Laufen.[27]

2. ERASMUS TO ANNA (MARCH 30, 1521)

Our warm greeting, dearest Anna. We are letting you know that by God's grace we are well and hardy. Know that it is also a special joy for us to hear of your good health.

Dear Anna, you write to us about how you are supposed to have been slandered in our presence. We cannot understand this, for truly nothing bad has ever been said about you to us. And you need not be surprised that we have not written to you for so long a time; it is due simply to the lack of a messenger. So stop worrying; I still have the old love for you!

You write about the bracelet, that we should come and fetch it ourselves. That is something we truly cannot do, because Father will not allow us to ride [to Hall]. So do what you think best about the bracelet. We appreciate your gift, dear Anna, and when we have the opportunity to return the favor, we will gladly do so from the heart.

We would have liked to write more, but we have not had the time. Be happy and of good cheer. Written in haste in Würzburg on the Saturday after Good Friday [30 March], 1521.

Whatever Erasmus's professed love for Anna may have meant to him, it did not necessarily include attentiveness and fidelity. Through mutual friends and acquaintances, Anna received eyewitness reports of his carousing and womanizing in the town of Schesslitz (letter 4), about which she wrote to him in a now nonextant letter requesting an explanation. Her ardor, too, was cooling by this time. We know about the letter only from Erasmus's surviving response, as he tersely declined comment on the episode: "Anyone can of course think what one wishes," he tells her, "but whatever one wishes is not reality, so we are at a loss to know how to answer your letter."[28] Anna, however, did not doubt the reports, and she knew exactly how to answer Erasmus's flippancy.

3 [4]. ANNA TO ERASMUS (N.D.)

. . . Your grace writes me that he is not completely pleased by my letter. I am rather alarmed to hear this and cannot understand what your grace means to say, whether your grace thinks that I have made it all up myself, or whether your grace means that other people have. If I knew that your grace meant [to accuse] me [of fabricating], I would write your grace everything [I have heard] chapter and verse, for I am well acquainted with all the stories people have told about your grace's behavior in Schesslitz.

But why should I write at length about this, when I can see that your grace does not like to hear it, and I do not want to dwell on it either, for truly this matter bothers me more than anything else in my life at the moment.

May God grant me luck so that I may come to your grace sometime in the future, although such a visit is still far off.

Gracious sir, I have carefully thought it over and I will send the bracelet to your grace, even though your grace already has many better and more beautiful ones.

Three letters from Erasmus, written in April and early May 1521, separate this letter from Anna's next. In them, he protests his love for her with apparent tenderness and even vulnerability. Had the arrival of the bracelet she had made for him and her willingness to drop the subject of his carousing touched him? The more likely explanation is jealousy. He writes to her, seemingly in the throes of self-doubt, from Herzogenaurach, where they had planned to rendezvous on May 1.

His distress stems from the knowledge, not yet shared with Anna, that
he is not going to be able to keep their date. For the first time in the
correspondence he begins to drop the royal we, addressing her directly
in the first person singular, as if she were an equal.

4 [5]. * ERASMUS TO ANNA (N.D.)

Our warm greeting, dear Anna. I thank you most sincerely for
the gift you sent. When I can return the favor, whether by day or
by night, I will gladly do so from the heart.

Dear Anna, you have thanked me much for the concern I have
for you. However, know that I am have been concerned about
you in a way I could do without. For as I hear it, there are good
strong fellows (*khappen*) in Herzogenaurach, who might be better
able than I. I ask you to keep my goodwill and concern for you
in mind, and I mean it sincerely when I ask you to do so. Please
don't scorn my good opinion of you.

May God give you no fewer than many thousand good nights.
I will do what I have said as soon as I get back.... Written in
Herzogenaurach.

The term *khappen* (or *kappen*) literally means "cap." But it also
designates the comb of a rooster or a hen, and as a verb describes a
rooster's pecking in mating—slang for sexual commerce. Erasmus
worries about the "good strong fellows" of Herzogenaurach and Anna
in his absence, especially now that he must (in her mind inexcusably)
break their date.

Erasmus's second letter blossoms into romance, as he now breaks
the news that he cannot keep their date, which Anna, perhaps provoc-
atively, had set for St. Walpurgis or May Day (May 1). In medieval
culture, this day was preceded by St. Walpurgis Night, the great occasion on which witches' sabbaths supposedly occurred, and both days
were associated with unrestrained sexual behavior. Erasmus had to
break their date because he had been ordered to depart on that very
day for the city of Worms to attend the first imperial diet of Emperor
Charles V. That convocation of Germany's political elite, in session

*See p. 201, no. 26.

during April and May, was of unusual importance, both because it was the new emperor's first and because on April 17 Martin Luther made his famous stand there, declaring in the presence of the emperor that he would retract none of his teaching, unless convinced of its error by the clear statement of Scripture. Arriving in early May, Erasmus missed this famous scene, which, had he been there, would likely have weighed less heavily on his mind at the time than his standing up Anna. Hoping to console her for what he knew would be a big disappointment, he promised a gift upon his return.

5 *[6]*. ERASMUS TO ANNA (N.D.)

My friendly greeting and willing service, dear [Anna]. I have read with joy the letter expressing your desire to come to me on St. Walpurgis Day [May 1]. That would have been a joy to my heart. But I must tell you that I now have to ride to Worms on that day. But as soon as I return, in ten days, God willing, I will bring you a present, if you will still accept it from me. There would be no greater joy for me than to be alone with you at last and to open my heart, for in my heart, I am well disposed toward you. I ask you from the heart to write me back. Just give the letter to Vogeli's women [for delivery to me], so that when I return home from Worms I may discover your feelings in a waiting letter. And wherever you write from, there I will gladly come. I ask you to do no more than to love me as I love you, no more than that. I want your friendly answer.

As Erasmus had feared, Anna took the breaking of their date in Herzogenaurach hard. As usual, however, she is both ingratiating and indignant. She will not be pushed around, but she also recognizes that their relationship must continue if it is to develop. So even as she accuses him of breaking faith with her, she writes a pleasing letter and sends along another gift. Her initial response to the canceled meeting survives only in Erasmus's brief description of it in which he again addresses her with the royal we.

6 *[7]*. ERASMUS TO ANNA [LIKELY MAY 1521]

Our friendly greeting, dear Anna.... We have read your letter, which pleases us and brings us much joy. Therefore, dear Anna, be of good cheer and don't let anything upset you. We also thank you for the gift you have sent us, a favor we will gladly return when we can.

Dear Anna, you perhaps think that our heart is false, but we are telling you that our intentions are good and that the old love for you is still there. So we ask you again not to let anything upset you, but to give us credit for much good. May God give you many hundred thousand good nights. Written in a hurry. Erasmus, Lord of Limpurg.

By now, Anna was finding it difficult to be patient and forgiving with Erasmus, as he requested. On top of everything, they were now quarreling over discussions he was then having with his mother, apparently pertaining to Anna, who by this time was becoming a subject of Hall's rumor mills: Anna found herself increasingly alienated from the Schenkin, and she knew she could not count on Erasmus to be her advocate with his mother. Anna describes herself as helpless and resigned in the matter.[29]

The suspicions of Erasmus's mother, whose protective instincts with regard to her son should not have been unexpected, were unfortunately not the only unhappiness Anna had to bear at this time. An even ruder shock was a surprise encounter with the royal competition for Erasmus's heart and hand. Anna might survive the young Schenk's aloofness and womanizing by protest, sufferance, and even infidelity of her own. But suddenly to find herself being interviewed, as one close to Erasmus's family and presumably privy to his innermost thoughts, on the subject of whether he might agree to marry the sister of counts Albrecht and Georg of Hohenlohe left Anna feeling like a woman about to be scorned. She recounts the interview for Erasmus in such a way as to make it memorable for him as well.

7 [8]. ANNA TO ERASMUS (MAY 9, 1521)

... Dearest sir, I am letting your grace know that as soon as I returned from [Herzogenaurach], Frau Elisabeth of Hohenlohe [1495–1540] sent someone to question me about the kind of gentleman your grace is. As was fitting and proper, I praised your grace to the full. Then, within two weeks I was interviewed again, and this time asked if I could find out if your grace had any desire or interest in her, and, because Schenk Friedrich [of Speckfeld] is dead, if anyone still wanted to discuss the matter.[30] They also were concerned to know if your grace might be put off by the hump.

I did not have much to say in answer to these questions. I told them that I was not now in regular contact with your grace, but that when I was with your grace again I would discuss these matters with your grace, but that such a time was still far off. Furthermore, I said that I did not know whether your grace knew that she had a hump. But should your grace meet with her, do take note of the high coat she wears.

Should I find myself in her presence in the near future, what answer should I give her? Do let me know what your grace wants me to say. She also has a prospect of marriage with Herr von Hag, and there is talk as well of giving her to von Löwenstein, Count Ludwig's son . . .[31]

Despite the fissures now so clearly pulling them apart, Anna again could not write to Erasmus only about the things that threatened their relationship. Having had her say on Elisabeth of Hohenlohe's husband-hunting, she returned in the remainder of her letter to the playful small talk that must have bound the two together lovingly in the beginning of their relationship, and that now kept them together in the worst of times.

7 [8]. (CONT.)

Would your grace let me know whether he will be staying on with the lord of Bamberg[32] or going to [the court of] the emperor's brother [Archduke Ferdinand]? I ask your grace to take the time to write me a letter, and not a hasty one. Tell me who teased your grace about me at dinner and asked if I was pretty. Your grace writes that I should be of good cheer. But whom should I be cheerful with?

Gracious sir, please have a sketch made of the emperor for me, one that portrays him as neither more handsome nor any uglier than he really is, for such a sketch would be worth something.

And have such a sketch made of your grace as well, which I will display.

May God bless and keep you, and whatever I can do that is dear and good to your grace, your grace should by all means let me know. Kind, darlingly gracious sir, may God give your grace's heart a hundred thousand good nights.

Do not in any way reveal to the questioner of Hohenlohe [Countess Elisabeth] that I have spoken to your grace about her. I am writing to your grace about this in confidence. Written on Ascension Day [May 9, 1521].

By August, Anna was completely downcast, and not only because of her bumpy relationship with Erasmus. There had been a new round of nasty gossip about her, and over the summer she had fallen out with Erasmus's mother, who now accused her of petty thievery. The accusation is believable, given Anna's well-reported thievery at home. But the continuing gossip about her may have triggered it, as it could reasonably have led the Schenkin to conclude that the time had come for the family, and most of all Erasmus, to distance themselves from the increasingly notorious Anna. While Erasmus did not share that sentiment, he did very much want his amorous relationship with Anna to remain secret, a concern increasingly expressed in his letters. For this reason, he repeatedly urges her to destroy his letters immediately upon reading them, lest one inadvertently find its way into his mother's hands and she discover the true nature of their relationship.[33]

This was not an unrealistic fear. As a friend of the family, Anna continued to go back and forth on an informal basis to castle Limpurg. Erasmus's sister, also named Anna (1500–1524), was virtually the same age as Anna (the two had to a degree grown up with each other), and Anna made a point of being at the castle on the festive occasions she enjoyed so much. And as we also know, she continued to do some sewing for the family, in particular, to make Erasmus's shirts. So a lapse in vigilance, or an indiscretion on her part, with unhappy consequences for them both, was not inconceivable.

Against this background, Anna wrote to Erasmus in mid-August 1521, more pessimistic than ever about their relationship. Her courtship with Daniel Treutwein may already have been budding at this time, providing a fresh source of gossip about her in Hall. On the other hand, later reports by those who observed her behavior during these years suggest that she was a spontaneous flirt and able to set tongues wagging simply by her dress and manner.

8 [9]. ANNA TO ERASMUS (AUGUST 15, 1521)

... Your grace is always writing to tell me to be of good cheer. But [I again ask] with whom? That your grace's letter doesn't say. The one I want to be cheerful with is not nearby.[34] If only things could be as they once were, then I would gladly be of good cheer! But now I know only sadness.

Dearest, gracious sir, I live in constant fear that someone has slandered me to your grace, and it deeply troubles me. Should anyone actually do so, I beg your grace to believe it neither a little nor a lot; people are simply making up things about me.

Dearest, most gracious sir, although I said I would not write again about [your mother], I truly cannot let it pass. After she went off, she instructed the bailiff to come to me and get back a coach button, which I am supposed to have taken. Now that would surely be a poor settlement of accounts,[35] should I revenge myself on her by stealing a coach button. I am not her enemy, and I would rather give to her than take from her, although she seems to have no trust in me. But what's done is done; it is a wrecked relationship. I cannot salvage it.

Dearest, most gracious sir, how shall I overcome my heartfelt sorrow now that I am in a hailstorm with your grace? What can I possibly say when every fool wants to make fun of me, although some of them are the [true] simpletons. They also gossip to their heart's content about me. I don't know who is telling these stories about me, but there is nothing I can do about it.

Dearest, most gracious sir, I am sending your grace a small feather. Please accept it for the time being until I can send something better. I have instructed the servant to bring it to your grace as a gift on my behalf. Please treat it as dearly as your grace would, if I had personally brought it to your grace ... And do be a little kind to my servant Michael; he is very dear to me.

I ask your grace to make the best [of what I write] and not to be angry with me, for my intentions are heartfelt and good.

Therewith be commended to the grace of God, the virgin Mary, and the holy St. Anna. Written on the eve of Assumption Day [August 15].

Anna Büschlerin

Both affection and deception have a place in Anna and Erasmus's relationship. Being both unmarried and unable to consider their relationship either as exclusive or as having a future, the two could only behave toward each other in the ambivalent fashion they do. Never expecting anything more from Anna than friendship and sex, Erasmus accepted the limits of the arrangement more readily than Anna, who seems at times to have hoped for more. While the possibility of that happening was not wholly preposterous, Erasmus had been destined by birth to marry at his rank, as the encounter with Elisabeth of Hohenlohe abruptly reminded Anna.

Both Anna and Erasmus understood the situation well enough when they pondered it realistically, and each knew that the other was not being faithful during their separation. For these reasons, their efforts to console each other often turn into self-defense and implied suspicion, as happens when Erasmus responds to Anna's despair over the gossip then threatening her reputation in Hall and trying his own patience with her.

9 [10]. ERASMUS TO ANNA (1521)

Our warm greeting, dear Anna. We have your letter, in which, among other things, you tell us [still again] of your worry that someone is slandering you to us. You truly should not be concerned about this or have any doubts about [us], for we are not that easily turned against you. For us to act otherwise would be neither kind nor fair.

Dear Anna, recall the letter we wrote you when we were last in Worms. In it, we told you to be of good cheer and to believe nothing that anyone tells you about us. Do not doubt, dear Anna, that we wish to hold fast, to believe no slander, and to allow you to vindicate yourself.

Know also, dear Anna, that I will be going to the court in Heidelberg before winter sets in and while I am there, we will be nearer to each other and able to communicate [more easily]. Believe us, if our father would allow us, we would long ago have joined you in Hall. You can see yourself how I feel.

Lastly, dear Anna, we thank you for the feather you sent us. We will return the kindness on another occasion. God bless and keep you and give you many hundred thousand good nights. Written in 1521.

Erasmus, Lord of Limpurg

If Erasmus had doubts about Anna's character at this time, he did not allow them to end the relationship; nor was he was in any position to throw stones. His own very public carousing and womanizing had made him the object of much irreverent gossip as well. From a modern point of view, his behavior is reprehensible. Yet because of the class and gender double standard of the age, contemporaries did not view it that way.[36]

For her part, Anna was ready to forgive and forget, and she vows to "cherish to the end" the assurances Erasmus gives her.[37] Managing the rumors and gossip circulating about Erasmus proved emotionally difficult for her, however, suggesting again that her involvement had been deep and her expectations perhaps too high. When she received new reports of his drunkenness and whoring in the town of Speckfeld, she could neither ignore them nor take them philosophically in stride. Erasmus describes the episode and its emotional aftermath in a letter written probably in early 1522. Anna had greeted the initial reports of his new decadence with sarcasm, for which Erasmus now reproaches her. Yet in his own crude way, he also attempts to apologize for his behavior.

10 [13]. ERASMUS TO ANNA (N.D.)

Dear Anna, I am not a little taken aback by the letter you have written, which I must assume you wrote in a whimsical mood. If the "Speckfeld pigs," as you call [me and my party], have made a lot of work for the maids [here], I believe they have more power to do so than the mother pigs of Hall [Anna and her suitors], who have also left quite a lot of work for the maids. So how dare they reproach us! Also, I have heard it said before that where drinking is held in honor, vomiting is no shame.

But I rejoice in God on your behalf that He has heard your plea and given you a mind capable of engaging in witty conversation.[38] I just spent some time in Nürnberg, where [at meetings of the imperial diet] Archduke Ferdinand awards the wittiest person a prize or a ten-piece, the greater of the two going to the winner. I see that God has enlightened you so that you too are now ready to enter such a competition; and I have no doubt that you would outdo all the ill-tempered here.

As for what you wrote about the New Year's [gift], it was not without reason that I told you earlier, as you will recall (if you really want to), that I was preparing to travel to Nürnberg and spend some time there, and that if you wished to do so, you were to write to me there, and I would respond appropriately. As I became busy with my father's affairs, however, that did not happen, and I also forgot about the New Year's [gift]. I swear to you now that I have no goldsmith in Speckfeld, so I still cannot send you anything. But I will keep my promise to send you something when it can be done.

Dear Anna, as you mean what you say in your letters, I mean what I say in mine. If what I write is good, I intend it to be good, if angry, I intend it to be angry, grain for salt. God willing, I will speak no false or untrue word to you as long as I live, unless you first give me reason to do so. But I must entrust myself to God in this. A doctor may be as learned as he will, but if he has no practical experience, his knowledge is worthless. This has also been the case with me. But with injury also comes wisdom, for one then knows to watch one's step all the more.

Written between Pfingsten and Esslingen, when they are bringing home the manure.

Erasmus had an ulterior motive, soon to be made apparent, in writing this letter. Nonetheless, his grudging apology for the spectacle he had made of himself in Speckfeld, together with his promise henceforth better to conform his deeds with his words, had the desired effect on Anna. She renewed her efforts to reassure him of her worthiness and to make peace with his family. Through his trusted secretary and their loyal go-between, Hans Kitzinger (also known as Hans of Heidelberg), she delivered a love toast to Erasmus—a bottle of wine to be drunk in Kitzinger's presence, accompanied by the latter's conveyance of her fondest wishes of luck and well-being. For Erasmus's younger brother Philip, Anna embroidered a fine collar,[39] which Kitzinger presented to the boy in his mother's presence, later reporting that the Schenkin had found it "very agreeable and pleasing" and instructed him to tell Anna so. Anna even made a bracelet for Kitzinger, who was so elated by the gift that he promised to wear it as long as it could be tied.[40]

Anna, however, never believed that Erasmus properly recognized her generosity, much less returned it. She accuses him of writing to her less regularly and warmly than she to him. The fact that more of his letters to her have survived than of hers to him supports her claim of deeper involvement in and loyalty to the relationship. Contrary to his instructions, she did not destroy his letters, while there can be little doubt that he destroyed hers. Her surviving letters are surely drafts of her own, which she kept along with his, which was normal epistolary practice at the time: to send a clean copy and to keep the first draft for one's own records. Erasmus's letters meant enough to Anna for her to risk their discovery and her own undoing.

Despite Erasmus's assurances, his deeds never did catch up with his promises. It is over just this issue—the one-sided nature of their relationship—that Anna complains in her next letter. For the first time in the correspondence, she drops epistolary convention and addresses Erasmus as an equal. Also for the first time, she writes explicitly about sex, accusing Erasmus of avoiding her out of fear that she, in her new anger at him, might let herself get pregnant by him. The comment suggests that they had been using a form of birth control, successful up to now, which Anna managed—possibly sponges or an acidic ointment, which were available contraceptives for women.

11 [15]. ANNA TO ERASMUS (N.D.)

Noble, kind, and most darlingly gracious sir. I should write your grace a long letter, but I am now so confused that I don't know what I should do. This is because I have no idea what your grace's wishes are. You send me messages every day, one saying you are coming, the other that you are not. The messenger reminds me of a cat I send off in the night to Limpurg that both licks my face and claws my back.

My dear sir, when you concern yourself with me so much, yet confide in me so little, you might just as well not contact me at all. Perhaps you fear that if you came to me I would give you a little bastard.[41] I swear I can do nothing like that. But take care that another woman just as mad [at you] as I does not one day come along and do just that. I myself am still too young and inexperienced in such matters, although I am learning. I leave it to God and to time. You are perhaps worried that it [still] might happen to you one day. But you are much too handsome for me to do that to you,[42] so don't worry about it. I am happy that it is not true.

Dear sir, could you have given me no other answer to yesterday's letter than that you have ridden off with Georg von Crailsheim and [are not coming here because] he had no need to be in Hall today? Dear sir, if you do not come to me as gladly as I see you, then it is best for us to forget it. I still would liked to have seen you, had you been invited here. But it's turned out differently. Either your grace has not been here, or your father has not been here, or my father has not been here.[43] But I believe your grace would as soon not have come, even if I had made a great fuss about it. That is how I see things. No matter how it turns out, I only end up making a fool of myself.

Despite Anna's ability to joke about it, she and Erasmus had reason to fear a pregnancy. They lived at a time when unwed mothers and fathers were being met with increasing intolerance and harsh treatment. And Hall had its own reputation for strict justice. Since the thirteenth century, it had possessed among its executionary devices a crude guillotine, made by implanting a sword blade in an oaken block, and executed criminals were hung in public view until "dry." Even the council treated its members roughly, fining those who came late to meetings, while firing and possibly imprisoning those who spoke disrespectfully and defiantly to the council, broke the law, or acted without the council's permission, and, after 1525, opposed the Reformation.[44]

An unwed mother faced loss of employment, a fine, corporal punishment, public disgrace, and/or exclusion from her community. According to a contemporary chronicle, Hall confined pregnant maids with accused witches as soon as their pregnancies began to show, and when the time came for their delivery, they were placed under guard in the "purgatory" of the hospice. After their recovery from the birth, the new mothers were whipped out of the main town gate with newborn babes in arms by guards and willing townspeople. Clergy entered the names of illegitimate children into the baptismal books in red ink, their bastardy thereafter shadowing them lifelong, making it difficult for them to gain honorable work and to enter an honorable marriage. So frightening had the prospect of unwed motherhood become by the seventeenth century that some pregnant women resorted to infanticide when a marriage could not be arranged.[45]

In seventeenth-century Hall, known illegitimate births were extremely rare. Of 146 baptisms registered in the parish church of St. Michael's in 1637, only two were of infants born to unwed mothers. One of those was to a woman named Ursula Gräfin (1606–1660), whose experience as an unwed mother might conceivably have been Anna's. After losing her parents at twenty years of age, she had worked as a maid in Hall's neighboring villages. While employed at a local mill, she got to know a man there and became pregnant by him. She had every expectation that a marriage would result, and when by the seventh month of her pregnancy it had not, she filed a paternity suit against the accused father, charging him with breaking his solemn promise of marriage.[46]

For his part, the alleged father confessed to having had sexual relations with Ursula, but denied ever having promised to marry her, and he countered her charges with a defamation suit of his own. The case remained under consideration for almost a year, from January to November, during which time (in March) Ursula delivered a daughter.

In the end, the city council could not prove conclusively that the accused man was guilty either of paternity or of breaking a marriage vow, and so it did not order him to pay child support. However, the council did fine him fifty gulden for immoral conduct (fornication), and he did spend some time in jail, while the council debated the case.[47]

In dealing with Ursula, the council prescribed a more severe penalty, but one which, uncharacteristically, it did not in the end enforce. Ordered in November to leave Hall lands immediately with her six-month-old child, she became the recipient of a groundswell of support from a number of citizens, both men and women, who had known and respected her parents and had watched her unsuccessful litigation sympathetically. At their request, the council reviewed her case and modified her punishment, banning her only from the city proper and not from the neighboring villages as well. This comparatively mild banishment would have allowed her still to come and go in the villages familiar to her, and since winter was imminent (the new ruling had come in early December), the council further permitted her to postpone her departure from the city for two months. However, as these two months passed, she remained in the city without protest from either the magistrates or the populace and continued to support herself and her daughter there by sewing. At her death in 1660, the entry in the Registry of Deaths (*Totenbuch*) praised the honesty of her life and work in the years after her transgression. Her daughter, who was now twenty-three years of age, continued to live and work in the city as her mother had done.[48]

Whether Anna and Erasmus would have fared better or worse than Ursula and her lover in a paternity suit is a moot question. Given Erasmus's position and Anna's reputation, the outcome would surely have been happier for him than for her. Still, if Anna is to be believed, Erasmus feared the prospect of a pregnancy more than she. The reason for his fear would doubtless have been the reaction of her father as much that of his own. Erasmus might have his way with barmaids, prostitutes, and ordinary maidservants with impunity, but Anna's father was a powerful man and in a position to give him and his family real grief. It was very much in the interest of the Limpurg Schenks at this time to maintain the best possible relations with the Hall city council. So Erasmus wanted not a hint of scandal, much less a fine or jail time, and as the gossip about Anna and her suitors increased in Hall, he became obsessed with the secrecy of their relationship.

Although the inference may be entirely too speculative, it may have been the case that Erasmus already at this time suspected that Anna was pregnant and he sought to abort the fetus. That may be the hidden subject of a letter, unfortunately undated, that he wrote to his mother about settling his affairs with Anna. In the letter, he tells his mother to instruct Anna to be bled without delay in a very specific way for an unspecified malady.

12. ERASMUS TO HIS MOTHER (N.D.)

Dear Mother. I hope to put all my affairs in good order when I come home, especially one matter that still needs to be straightened out. I must pay Anna Büschler everything she is owed and tie up all loose strings with her, for she truly deserves this much from me . . . Greet her for me and tell her that I propose that she have a good bleeding[49] next Saturday, [and that she do so] from the median vein just under the navel. If she has no servant to assist her in this, she should let me know, and I will arrange for friends to help . . .

Erasmus, Lord of Limpurg[50]

If Anna had been pregnant at this time, which is extremely speculative, and had followed this instruction, she would most likely have induced an abortion. All the major medical authorities of the age advised against bleeding pregnant women at any time, but especially during the first and third trimesters. This was true even if the woman in question had a history of safe, regular bleeding.[51] Bleeding from the median vein, which Erasmus here recommends, provided a general evacuation of the body and required several days' recuperation. It was the major treatment for diseases of the heart and chest cavity, and was also highly recommended for the cure of headaches.[52] One actually bled this vein from the lower arm near the elbow, not from beneath the navel, which Erasmus appears erroneously, but understandably, to instruct, if he then feared Anna to be pregnant. Of course, he might just as well have recommended the procedure in the belief that it might also have prevented a pregnancy, which, as Anna indicates, was also a subject very much on his mind.

In the sixteenth century, phlebotomy was the vastly popular cure-all for virtually every internal disease or illness, and physicians alternately recommended it to their patients and warned them against its overuse. Reigning medical science treated most disease and illness as the result of accumulating foul matter in the body, the sloughing off of which by bleeding might prevent illness in the still healthy and reverse it in the already stricken. Bleeding thus kept, or restored, the body's natural equilibrium, thereby maintaining, or strengthening, a person's natural resistance to disease and illness.

Because of its reputation as a panacea, women with a history of miscarriages and stillbirths desperate for a child might well have been tempted, against the advice of the medical authorities, to turn to bleeding as an aid to a successful pregnancy. That is exactly what the famous scholar-diplomat Christoph Scheurl and his wife, Katharina, a well-to-do Nürnberg patrician couple, appear to have done. Katharina had repeated stillbirths between 1522 and 1527; the couple buried six fetuses, each of them properly named, prayed over, and buried: Christoph in 1522, Helena in 1524, Ursula in 1525, Katharina in 1526, and Albrecht and Hieronymus in 1527—noteworthy behavior in light of the widespread belief that parents in the past neither loved their children nor were able even to recognize them as such.[53] Then, in 1530, while in the town of Forchheim on business, Christoph met a woman who, like his wife, had also had a history of stillbirths, but had finally managed to deliver a healthy child by bleeding herself before and during pregnancy; at least that was what she attributed her good fortune to. Christoph had hardly told Katharina the story before she was bleeding herself as well, and eventually with similar success. She gave birth to a son on April 19, 1532, the first of three healthy boys she delivered before her childbearing years ended in 1535.

For his part, Christoph believed his son's birth to be a miracle of God, not a work of medicine, and compared himself and Katharina to Elkanah and Hannah in the Bible, who also had been childless for many years before getting their Samuel by fervent prayer (1 Samuel 1).[54] Katherina, on the other hand, was impressed by the instrumental role bleeding had played in the divine outcome. From a contemporary (and modern) medical point of view, she and the woman in Forchheim she imitated had been very lucky.

Anna, of course, could have been suffering from any number of legitimate illnesses, which bleeding from the median vein was believed to cure, in which case Erasmus's directive to her via his mother would have been for the times both caring and sound. Also arguing against a pregnancy, either true or false, is the fact that no hint of such appears in the trial records. Since exposure of Anna's allegedly immoral character was her enemies' main tactic, had she ever been rumored to have been pregnant outside of marriage, that information would most certainly not have been withheld by them in court. Finally, the fact that Anna remained childless through two later marriages raises the question whether she could have children under any circumstances.

Be all this speculation as it may, the next time Erasmus wrote to Anna he was back in castle Limpurg and as eager to see her as ever. Through Kitzinger he informed her that his father would be departing Limpurg and away for an extended period of time, and that she should take advantage of the situation at her will and pleasure, requesting only that her journey to Limpurg be as discreet as it was quick.

13 [16]. ERASMUS TO ANNA (N.D.)[55]

My heartfelt greeting. I am letting you know that I went crazy [while I was away from you] and was unable to do virtually anything. But as I see from my father's posted orders that he departs today and won't be back for two weeks or more, I am letting you know it so that you can come to me when you wish. Only above all, travel inconspicuously; otherwise it will be obvious who you are. So if you have something in mind, don't ride your horse through Hall, because as soon as you dismount and leave it behind, someone will notice it.

But I leave this up to you. Do what pleases you and do it your way; just be discreet. A hundred thousand good nights.

Anna responded to Erasmus through Kitzinger on August 14, 1522, mocking his letter. Evidently still angry over his aloofness and seeming taunting of her, she informs him of *her* father's absence and her availability in Hall, if he wishes to meet her there. If anyone was going to come to anyone, it would be he to her.

14 [18]. ANNA TO ERASMUS (AUGUST 14, 1522)

My humble, obedient, and kindest greeting, most darlingly gracious sir. I am letting your grace know that I went crazy [in your absence] and was unable to do virtually anything. As your grace thinks that we are in the same situation, I am letting your grace know that my father is now away and won't return before St. Michael's Day [September 29] or later. So I leave it up to your grace to act. If your grace has something in mind, send Hans to me and I will give him instructions.

Most darlingly gracious sir, [let] everything [proceed] accord-

ing to your grace's pleasure, and not in malice, but in faith and
trust. I wouldn't worry at all at this time, but I leave it to your
grace to do what he wants. A hundred thousand good nights.
Written on Assumption eve [August 14], 1552.

Erasmus absolutely refused to come to Hall, understandably fearing
the scandal that would result if a rendezvous between the two in her
father's house became known. His point was surely well taken. If one
or the other were to be seen, better that it be Anna entering castle
Limpurg, where she had legitimate reasons to go, than he entering her
fatherless house on market square in Hall, which could only be taken
for what it was. That was especially true now that her neighbors were
giving her the fisheye because of the gossip circulating everywhere
about her.

15 [17]. ERASMUS TO ANNA (N.D.)

Dear Anna. I see that you are completely indignant, which I don't
deserve from you and I cannot look on kindly. If you would just
consider the situation carefully, you would not be advising me to
come to you, for that will mean scandal for us both, but especially
for you. So I hope you will just as quickly cool off and put aside
your anger, and if it is possible to do so, I still hope you will come
to me here. If you can't come to church, I hope you will consider
other possibilities.[56] I have always believed that you would not
forsake me lightly.

    Please respond. May God fill your every hour with many thou-
sand good times. Dear Anna, if I were [there] with you, I would
explain fully why I dare not come there [to Hall]. Again, I ask
for a reply.

Erasmus sent Anna still another plea during this small war of wills
over who should visit whom, begging her to remember the good times
they have had together and to keep the promises she has made.[57] Did
the two finally meet? The next letter suggests that they did, although
it leaves unclear on whose turf. The conditions of their visits would
continue to be an issue between them, because where and when they
met said something about the terms of their relationship.

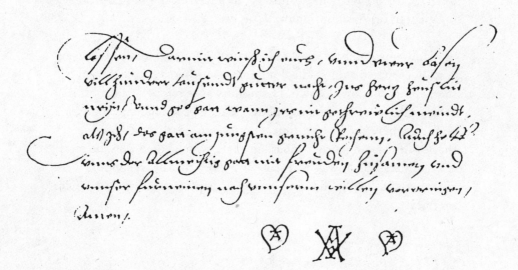

*E*rasmus concluded letter 16 with this ornamental signature, preserved
in court copies of their letters prepared for the imperial commission.
Between the two hearts, each of which contains an "A" (for "Asmus,"
short for Erasmus, and Anna), are placed two large "A's," also indicating
their names. One is upright, the other inverted, but now merged and
entangled with one another and no longer apart, indicating the way
the two once were, not what they had now become—a frequent
theme in Erasmus's letters. This novel signature appears in only one
other letter, in which Erasmus again begs Anna not to allow herself to
be turned against him.

A more serious development, threatening to destroy the bond of affection between them altogether, soon rendered this issue petty by comparison. Erasmus suddenly had in hand a credible report of Anna's amorous involvement with Daniel Treutwein. He shared his discovery with her in his next letter, magnifying the effect by holding its revelation until letter's end, and then delivering it to her as if it were just another piece of casual information. He even sends along with it a gift, apparently a piece of family jewelry then in his possession and at his disposal. That a volcano had in fact erupted beneath them becomes clear when he invokes God's wrath upon her.

16 [20]. ERASMUS TO ANNA (N.D.)

Dearest Anna, I herewith send you the New Year's gift I promised long ago. I ask you most kindly not to scorn it, but to consider my situation, which you know well. I also ask you, dear, kind Anna, not to let my mother or sister see this gift when you visit them, because they know it well. I have learned, dear, kind Anna, that you are to be invited there. You know well how to react. And even if my sister approaches you, don't say anything to her [about us], because she knows nothing from me.

Dear, kind Anna, I ask you most sincerely to behave as we agreed you would do when I left you last, and to let me know [just what you are doing], as you also promised to do. My own behavior will be such that you shall have no reason to be unhappy with me, notwithstanding my [present] illness and [future] royal service, which I expect to begin very soon. I will let you know exactly when.

Dearest Anna, I have received a completely reliable report that you have taken up with that man I don't like [Daniel Treutwein]. I don't want to give it any credence whatsoever and hold it against you. In light of my feelings for you, I expect you will let me know exactly what is going on.

Dear, kind Anna, I have placed my hope and trust in you so completely that I have no doubt whatsoever that you will abide by what we have many times agreed [namely, to maintain the secrecy of our relationship]. Herewith I wish you and your cousin[58] many hundred thousand good nights in the little chamber of your hearts. And if you have not been as honest with me as I have been with you, may God take His vengeance upon you at the Last Judgment. May almighty God now help us come together joyously and fulfill our wishes. Amen.

If Anna ever answered Erasmus's demand for an accounting of her relationship with Daniel Treutwein, the letter has not survived, nor is it one either party would likely have been inclined to keep. On the surface, the issue appears to have disappeared in the remaining correspondence; Erasmus brought it up again only once in his surviving letters (see following), while Anna never comments on it again in hers. Between the lines, however, the affair with Daniel Treutwein hereafter haunted their correspondence, especially after it became public knowledge and Anna once again the subject of widespread gossip.

Whether it was due to Daniel Treutwein's presence in her life or just another sign that the relationship with Erasmus had run its course, Anna began to speak her mind to Erasmus more freely than ever after his discovery of her "infidelity." Already before Daniel had come on the scene, Erasmus's distance from her, both physical and emotional, together with his all too public carousals, had taken their toll on her feelings for him—just as the gossip in Hall about her penchant for self-display and coquetry had shaken his confidence in her. To remind Erasmus bluntly of his shortcomings may have helped Anna cope with her own duplicitous behavior, as she now proceeded to have simultaneous affairs with the two men, despite the protests of each. Both desire and convenience appear to have influenced that decision. She manifestly liked both men, and inasmuch as one or the other was almost always away on some military errand or at some political conference, the opportunity to see them both could only have doubled her pleasure.

If the affair with Daniel emboldened Anna in her dealings with Erasmus, it increased Erasmus's determination to maintain a lower profile with her. Now more than ever he begged her to keep their pledge of confidentiality. Despite these warnings, he also wanted her as much as ever to be his occasional lover. In this regard, the new competition for her affection had only increased his desire. So while his excuses for not coming to her multiply, his distress over her reluctance to meet secretly with him on his terms also intensifies.

17 [22]. ERASMUS TO ANNA (1523)

Dear Anna. I am taken aback not a little, but a lot by your wanting me to come to you there [in Hall], when you know well that my father is now here [in castle Limpurg]. Whatever reason could I think up for going to town? For I would have to explain to him what my business there was. And as long as he is here, it is even more impossible for me to come by night. But were he not here, I would think further about how I might come to you.

I can only think that you have made an issue of this to dash all my hopes. In the past, to please me, you came to me. But now you are being difficult, even though I have not deserved this from you and am not willing to give in to it. I also trust that you will not [continue to] be so rash, but will remember how often I have acted on your behalf in the past. I do want an answer from you on this matter.

Please wish [your cousin] Margrethe and your sister [Agatha] many thousand good nights on my behalf; and I wish you the same as well. Dated in 1523.

Although Anna's response to Erasmus's plea has not survived, his next letter to her, written in response to her continuing insistence that he come to her in Hall, makes clear the changing terms of the relationship. By standing her ground and rejecting his excuses, she elicits the most fervent outpouring yet of his good intentions. Evidently she had accused him of avoiding her out of fear that public disclosure of their affair might occasion his disinheritance. Still, he remains as adamant as ever that castle Limpurg, not her Hall home, must be their rendezvous.

18 [23]. ERASMUS TO ANNA (N.D.)

Dear Anna. When you write a letter that takes me so completely aback, I can only respond by asking you to consider what would have happened had I come there with [the others], then separated from them [to go off and find you]. Everyone would of course have said that I was with you. Ask yourself whether I am right or wrong about this. Also, dear Anna, when you write that you think it ignorance on my part to consider coming by night, I of course recognize that. You have misconstrued my letter; it was not intended as you have understood it. My concern was whether I might come to you [in Hall at any time] without harming the both of us.

I am also taken aback when you write that you can't believe that I place my hope in you. Just consider how I have behaved toward you for such a long time, even incurring misfortune because of it.[59] If you have the will to look at things differently, you can judge for yourself whether I place no hope in you. For that reason, I had not expected such a letter from you.

As for your coming here to me, I hope and trust that you will reconsider and still do so. I continue to believe that my hope and confidence in you have not been misplaced.

Dear Anna, God knows there are no grounds for your writing that I would not trouble myself [to come to you] even if I could do so in front of my father and the other people who would see me going there. Also what you write about my trust fund[60] doesn't bother me. I feel no obligation there, and I truly don't believe what you write about it anyway; I thought you to be more high-minded[61] than that.

Also dear Anna, when you write that I should advise you how in this matter demanding such secrecy you might come here [unseen], that is something you can best judge for yourself. God in heaven knows that if I were in a position to help, I would do so gladly and count it a pleasure. Also in the matter of the locksmith.[62] I would gladly kiss you, but unfortunately it cannot be. So I just have to live with the situation until things are better. . . .

Dear Anna, let me know what you are planning to do. To tell you a secret, I expect my lord to send me away soon, but not to go with me. I have already ridden [alone] to Vellberg with all kind of difficulty at first (God's will). I should be back here today, so you might answer me as soon as you can.

Dear Anna, I do want to talk with you, but you know well that I cannot arrange it. God bless you. I would like to send you something so that you would think about me; but I truly have nothing to send. But as for a color for you, I give you ashen, brown and white; I ask you to wear it for my sake.[63] God bless and keep you and give you many thousand good nights.

E[rasmus], L[ord] o[f] L[impurg]

Over the next six to eight months, suspicion and complaints increased on both sides as the affair now progressively soured. Still, the desire for stolen moments together remained irrepressible.

19 [25]. ERASMUS TO ANNA (JUNE 13, 1523)

My warm greeting, dearest Anna. I have understood clearly from your letter how I was supposed to have been in Hall recently and to have had my horse shoed there. Despite what you say, God knows that I have not been in Hall since I received the money from you.[64] Whoever told you I was, spared you the truth. If you are going to believe everything people tell you, then you are a foolish woman. The rumor mongerer who told you I was in Hall wishes neither of us much good.

Kind, dear Anna, I also understand clearly from your letter that the gossip further alleged that I cursed you and swore you harm. Dear Anna, the things you were told appal me.

I also understand clearly that you think I have written to you with a false heart. God as my witness, that is not true. I wish to God that you could know my heart and how [sincerely] I have meant what I write. . . .

Kind, dearest Anna, I would like to send you a gift, but I dare not trust this messenger; I fear mischief might be the result. But I have promised myself to be with you soon and to act as my own messenger.

Dear, kind, beloved Anna, may God bless and keep you always into eternity. If there is a service I can honorably render you, you shall find me always willing; I shall place it above service to my lord. The Saturday before St. Vitus's Day [June 13], 1523.

Anna had of course heard such talk before, and she knew that Erasmus's behavior belied his pledges of loyalty. Two months after this outpouring of his devotion, she found herself writing to rebuke still another episode of public carousing and womanizing. However, this time, through no fault of her own, her rebuke went astray and ended up in the wrong hands, producing a small comedy of errors within this tragedy that was building. Erasmus's secretary Hans Kitzinger confused Anna's letter to his lord with one she had written to him at the same time, and he mistakenly opened and read the former.

Because the letter was of a very personal nature, an embarrassed and fretful Hans delayed in telling Anna about his error, by which point he required her forgiveness as well as a clarification. Realizing that Hans's error could mean trouble with Erasmus for them both, a sympathetic Anna quickly wrote a consoling note to the penitent Hans.

20 [21]. ANNA TO HANS OF HEIDELBERG [AUGUST 14, 1523]

My warm greetings and assurance that you should expect only good things from me.

Since you have written to me about the letter, I am letting you know that it did not belong to you, but to your lord, and the young lass mentioned in it also belonged to him. The *other* letter was yours.

My dear, kind, loyal friend, I did not know that you had opened the letter, and I became quite upset with your lord for not responding to me for so long. So I wrote briefly to him again. If the messenger has not yet delivered my [second] letter, he will be coming. Had I known what had happened, I would not have written to him again about it. Do settle the matter as you think best, so that no harm comes to yourself, my dear, kind, true friend.

I had written to your lord about a matter that he should take up directly with me. If he is now angry because of what has happened, please be a good mediator, and I will repay you for your efforts when I can.

Although I would have liked to write you more, I could not make the time. But answer me as soon as you can, for I am deeply worried about what has happened. . . . Written on Assumption Eve [August 14, 1523] as the clock strikes midnight.

Poor Hans soon lost his usefulness as a courier between castle Limpurg and the Büschler home, but not because of this unfortunate blunder. His frequent goings back and forth to Hall during the periods when Erasmus was at home had begun to draw unwanted attention, and Erasmus felt moved to dictate new arrangements lest the affair be discovered and publicized.

21 [26]. ERASMUS TO ANNA (OCTOBER 28, 1523)

Our greeting, dear Anna. We have read your letter in which you indicate that if we can do so, we should send Hans to you [with mail]. We would like to oblige you in this, but as you can judge for yourself, that is not possible because Hans is too well known in Hall. So we ask that you select another place where he can find you and have your messenger tell us where it is. If you think about it, you will agree that no matter how secret our affair is now, it would become very public [if we did as you suggest]. So please consider another arrangement that is less obvious and does not subject us to more gossip than we deserve.

Dear Anna, you have written us a long letter, and we would like to send Hans to you with our answer, if only you would choose a place where he can meet you in secret and there safely convey to you whatever message we would then entrust to him.

May God give you a hundred thousand good nights and bring us together in joy. Written on St. Simon and St. Jude's Day [October 28].

1524 was not a good year for women in special situations in Hall. That year, as we know, saw the demolition of the Franciscan cloister, the closing of the public house, and an order to clergy living in concubinage to separate from their female companions. How appropriate, then, that Anna's secret as a woman with two lovers should also begin to be disclosed, as both Erasmus and her father took steps to distance themselves from her because of her affair with Daniel Treutwein.

Early in the year, Anna had presented Erasmus with still more, by now tedious, accusations of carousing and womanizing. In two letters of self-defense, Erasmus directly blamed Daniel for troubling their relationship and alienating Anna's affection. More ominously, he informed her that her father now knew about the things she and Daniel were doing behind his back, thanks to her new lover's loose tongue.

22 [28]. ERASMUS TO ANNA [1524]

Dear Anna. God give you a happy New Year. I thank you for the [New Year's] gift you made for me.

As you write about several [personal] matters, let me say that I am an honest and honorable man and that what is being said about me is entirely unjust. I would have thought by now that you would not listen to such talk so readily but seek more information [before drawing conclusions]. I have also heard from my servant how someone is telling lies about me. On my word of honor, whoever is saying such things about me is a desperate, cowardly scoundrel, who lies openly.

You also have asked me [again] to come to you [in Hall]. You know that is impossible. However, if you can do so, come here to me. Think again about when you can come and let me know. May God give you many hundred thousand good nights. If we do get together, I will tell you things I cannot write.

23 [29]. ERASMUS TO ANNA (1524)

Dear Anna. I am very disappointed that you do not write and tell me how you are and let me know if you have received the New Year's gift I sent you. I can only conclude that that man I do not like [Daniel Treutwein] has displaced me in your affection, so that I must now have the scandal, while he gets the fruit. If you are wondering how I mean that, I can only say that I know it for a complete truth that he has been with you secretly in your father's house for several days and nights. There is nothing I can do about it now, and I know for a certainty that you will not admit it to me. But he has been such a loudmouth that even your father knows about it now.

With that I drop the matter. Many hundred good nights. Written in haste in 1524.

 Daniel Treutwein

ALTHOUGH ANNA COULD NOT HAVE FORESEEN IT AT THE TIME, nor controlled the consequences of her action, when Daniel Treutwein entered her life, forces were set in motion that would destroy her relationship with both her father and Erasmus. Of these three men, Daniel

Treutwein is the most intriguing, but perhaps only because his story is far the most difficult one to tell. Contemporary chroniclers describe his father, Daniel, Sr., as a chronicler himself and the last Treutwein to reside lifelong in Hall.[65] Another Daniel Treutwein appears in the city's records as a young noble mercenary hired by the city in 1474, for 120 gulden per annum, to fight the city's feuds and perform its military obligations to the emperor in the company of other young noblemen. That the two are the same man is a most appealing thought, but lacks proof.[66] It is clear, however, that earlier in its history Daniel's family had been Jewish. Its coat of arms, which he continued to display, portrays the bust of a man wearing a wide Jew's hat tied with a string under the chin and set against a red background.[67] The colors (white head on red background) may indicate the family's earlier "purging" and conversion to Christianity, an indication perhaps of their having been washed by the blood of Christ and thereafter made pure.

Jews had been in Hall since the mid-thirteenth century, working as salt-makers and as money-lenders. The name Treutwein, in one variation or another, appears in the city records only a few times in the fourteenth century, and then only early and late. By the 1430s and 1440s, however, several families of Treutweins were settled there.[68] Their near total absence from the city after midcentury can be explained by the persecution and exile of Jews almost everywhere during the peak years of the Black Death (1347–1350). Although there had been earlier expulsions of Jews from Christian towns (for example, in France in 1182 under King Philip II, and in England in 1290 under Edward I), the unprecedented horror of the Black Death inaugurated an equally new and nasty relationship between Christian and Jew in medieval Europe.

For centuries, forces, many subterranean, had prepared the way for that change. In their sermons and at festivals, Christian preachers routinely portrayed Jews as betrayers of Christ. From making great loans to princes to renting books and clothing to students, the practices of Jewish moneylenders provoked both envy and hatred among Christian borrowers.[69] And leaders on both sides adopted policies of virtual segregation—Jewish leaders because of the exclusiveness of their religion and the Christian penchant for proselytizing among and persecuting Jews, Christian leaders out of fear that Jewish culture and religion, if allowed to flourish on their own in too close proximity to Christian, might overwhelm the latter with their antiquity, richness, and wisdom.

Already the tens of thousands of aristocratic Christians who made up the armies of the First Crusade (1096) had attacked Rhineland Jews while en route to the Holy Land; and in 1215, the Fourth Lateran Council, which promulgated such lasting features of medieval Christianity as the dogma of transubstantiation and mandatory annual confession, also set discriminatory guidelines for Christian contact with Jews that might also be considered something of an assault. The council wanted Christian relations with Jews to be limited to the necessary economic dealings between merchants on each side. It forbade sexual relations between members of the two faiths, and Jews could not be placed in positions of authority over Christians. The council also restricted Jewish worship (basically keeping it out of sight) and discouraged the building of new synagogues in Christian cities. And while not exactly recommending ghettos, the great Church council proposed segregating Christian and Jewish communities within the same town.[70]

By the sixteenth century, major pogroms had occurred in Spain. Between the 1390s and the 1480s, perhaps three-fourths of the Jewish population there chose to become Christian converts (*conversos*) rather than be exiled from their homeland by a determined Church and crown. But having converted, they were then suspected, not without reason, of being Christian in name only, and the converted Jew became more feared and hated by his Christian neighbors than the Jew who chose exile. Having greater security, power, and proximity to Christians than ever before, Spain's converted Jews suddenly became a Trojan horse within Christian society, a situation that resulted in the expulsion of the *conversos* as well in 1492.[71]

The history of Hall's Jews is the European story in microcosm. There, too, the terror of the Black Death combined with centuries of religious prejudice and hatred of Jewish moneylenders to make the Jews scapegoats for the city's misfortune. A sizable community existed in the city in the first half of the fourteenth century, living on their own street. The appearance of the plague in 1348 gave rise to accusations that the Jews were poisoning the city's wells and committing unspeakable crimes against Christians. The crisis peaked in 1350, when some Jews were accused of ritually murdering a Christian child.[72] A group deemed responsible were herded into the Neuburger tower on a hill by the Langerfeld gate at the southeastern wall of the city, where, after being tortured, they suffocated and burned to death as the dilapidated tower was burned to the ground. In the aftermath, the city expelled its Jews and confiscated their property and goods.

Because imperial law forbade pogroms, the emperor fined Hall eight hundred gulden for the action, but in a manner that may baffle a modern reader. Dukes Eberhard and Ulrich of Württemberg received the commission to collect the money, which they deposited in their treasuries. Not a single pfennig was given to Hall's exiled Jews, whose confiscated properties and goods became, by imperial decree, the city's "to keep and enjoy as its own."[73] The intention of the fine had been to punish the city for breaking imperial law, not to compensate Hall's Jews for the injustice the city had done them; imperial law, not Jewry, had been the offended party and thus received the damages. Although a few Jews could be found in Hall in the 1370s and 1380s, and more lived in the surrounding countryside, there would not be a true Jewish community in Hall again until the nineteenth century.[74]

By the time our story begins, Daniel's family had long since integrated itself into Hall and was a part of the city's Christian establishment. As a doctor of canon and civil law, Daniel's brother Eitel (d. 1536) was as learned as a man could be in the late Middle Ages, and he occupied important ecclesiastical and civic positions: canon in Worms, prior in Neuhausen, and dean of the nearby Comburg monastery, as well as a lower judge (*Assessor*) in the imperial supreme court.[75]

Daniel's career track, by contrast, had been strictly secular and military. Basically, he was a mercenary, and by all reports exceptionally good at his work, gaining his reputation as a crack cavalryman during service with the Swabian League in the 1520s. The league was a confederation of princes, cities, counts, and knights created in the late fifteenth century to maintain law and order in southern Germany. It visited swift and harsh punishment upon both noble and plebeian lawbreakers. In the 1520s, it was particularly the latter whom the league confronted.

In Swabia and Franconia, the vast majority of peasants rebelled against their secular and ecclesiastical landlords in 1525, culminating decades of determined but lesser protest. They did so in the name of some of Martin Luther's most popular teachings, particularly the freedom and equality of all Christians and the right of local congregations to choose and depose their own (Evangelical) pastors. Although the peasants' own goals were far more material than spiritual—it was a political and social revolution, not a religious one—peasant leaders opportunistically seized upon Luther's spiritual egalitarianism to further them. Still, Luther's teaching gave the peasant cause a new dimension, enlarging its goals beyond the mere restoration of traditional privileges and property, which the German princes' policy of territorial centralization had been eroding for decades. Inspired by the Reformation, the peasants envisioned their release from serfdom, "because Christ has set all men free," and demanded the right to renegotiate their contracts with their lords as virtual equals, again in accordance with the alleged teaching of Christ.[76]

Such notions were, however, completely contrary to Luther's theology and anathema to sixteenth-century rulers, and both condemned them as dire threats to what civil peace and order society then possessed. The peasants had virtually no supporters outside of their own ranks (only a few farm-oriented city dwellers and artisan dissidents), and once they had rebelled, the call for their suppression was both loud and nearly unanimous in south German cities and territories.[77]

In the region around Hall, peasants first revolted on April 2, 1525, in the village of Braunsbach north of the city, just as the men there were fetching their pregnant wives from a traditional fish meal prepared by the local miller. There the assembled peasants learned that the peasant militia had revolted in Rothenburg, whereupon they, too, decided "to lend a hand to divine justice" and formed their own units. Marching through the surrounding villages that evening, they called upon their neighbors to join with them in the fight for their rights.[78] Area peasants particularly resented having to pay a percentage of their produce (fruits, vegetables, milk, cheese, butter, and flax) and livestock to their lords in so-called "small tithes." A variety of church taxes vexed them almost as much.[79] Inspired by local leaders, prominent among them Johann Waltz, a Franciscan preceptor turned revolutionary preacher, peasants were soon plundering and burning the castles of noblemen in the countryside around Hall, setting the stage for a major confrontation with the Swabian League.

To their great regret and misfortune, the lords who had for so long taken such advantage of their peasants had also given them arms and taught them basic military strategy and tactics. They did so with the intention of using peasant militias as emergency forces in lieu of standing armies, whose provisioning was expensive and behavior often unpredictable. When the peasants now revolted in the lands around Hall, their lords found themselves confronted by armed men who knew something about making war, not the helpless but freedom-loving rustics sometimes portrayed in modern history books. When they besieged an area village or town, peasant bands first stormed the churches to silence the bells and to seize the small cannons in the steeple, which were the first line of defense against external attack. Thereafter, they occupied the parsonage and the bürgermeister's house, incapacitating the local leadership and breaking the chain of command. By such tactics, a number of local pastors were forcibly conscripted into the peasant army, among them Hall's contemporary chronicler of these events, Lutheran pastor Johann Herolt (1490–1562), who had little sympathy for the peasant cause, despite incessant peasant efforts to win him over during his captivity.[80]

By the time Hall's walls were threatened, its militia of four to five hundred men faced a besieging peasant army nine times their number. In the weeks before the assault, the city became a beehive of activity, as every strong-bodied person joined in a hasty repair of the walls, digging the trenches around them deeper and stockpiling stones for the catapults, sulfur and pitch, lanterns, and gunpowder along the walls and in their several towers. Culverins (long guns) and other artillery were strategically placed at every street gate and tower, places where the city was most likely to be penetrated.[81]

On the day before the assault (April 1), members of the city council went out to the peasant leaders to warn them not to revolt, promising to help them reach their legitimate goals peacefully, if they put down their weapons. The die, however, had been cast, and neither side was disposed to compromise. The peasants proclaimed their defiance on their clothing and banners, displaying white crosses in taunting imitation of the soldiers of the Swabian League, with whom they knew they were destined to clash, and on whose uniforms and guidons red crosses were emblazoned. What Hall's militia lacked in numbers, however, it more than made up for in field guns, which the peasants lacked. Attacking in the dark of night on April 23 as the church bells pealed the Ave Maria and their five cannons lit the night sky, Hall's militia routed the peasants in an easy initial victory.[82]

The war, however, was not to be so short. With its numbers soon increased by fresh recruits from Limpurg, the peasant army regrouped and besieged the city a second time. After a two-month standoff, during which the city was supplied by the Swabian League and able to build up its forces, the besieging peasant army was crushed. In the aftermath, the city punished peasant households throughout the region with fines of between six and sixty gulden, depending on the size of a holding. Seven of the peasant leaders were beheaded, four had fingers severed, and holes were burned in the cheeks of two—maimings marking them as rebels and warning off future imitators. In Oehringen and Neuenstein to the north, the peasants were more successful in the short term, defeating both those towns and forcing the two Hohenlohe counts to swear allegiance to them. The counts were invited to think of themselves as the peasants' "brothers," as they would no longer their lords.[83]

A contingent of surviving peasant soldiers from the Hall region fled north, eventually to join a massive peasant army then besieging Würzburg. En route, they made an early detour to Weinsberg in Württemberg to participate in a massacre of Duke Ludwig of Helfenstein and his knights. In vain, the duke had tried to buy his life before he and twenty-three other noblemen and their servants were herded into a field and executed. Also rushing to Würzburg at this time was the 25,000-man army of the Swabian League, with Daniel Treutwein very likely in its ranks. This great force also stopped in Weinsberg to revenge the massacre of noblemen there. The occupying peasant army was annihilated, and its captured piper, who had piped the killing of the noblemen, was tethered by a chain to a stake encircled by a fire and left slowly to roast to death, as the league marched on to Würzburg to slaughter still greater numbers of peasants.[84]

Such was the violent world of Daniel Treutwein. He served his lords with distinction, killing rural noblemen for Duke Ulrich of Württemberg—a man of so many crimes and atrocities that it took his enemies a thousand lines to memorialize them in rhyme[85]—and rebellious peasants for Count Palatine Ludwig. While aide and secretary to Duke Ulrich, Daniel wrote a locally famous vernacular poem in the duke's defense (1519)[86]—perhaps the only kind words the duke received from a contemporary after his abortive attempt to subjugate the imperial city of Reutlingen had brought about the occupation of Württemberg by the Swabian League and the duke's own humiliating exile.

In the first days of Hall's peasants' revolt, Daniel's cavalry unit led the assault on the peasant militia in the woods around Königshof, and Daniel got the credit for the first kill. After the war, Count Ludwig appointed him lifelong bailiff (*Amptmann*) in northern Boxberg, forty-five kilometers from Hall, in recognition of his distinguished service. Boxberg was a castle town with a particularly bloody history. It was the home of a famous renegade nobleman, Thomas Absberg, who feuded with the Swabian League throughout the 1520s. In 1521, he killed a league member, in retaliation for which the league razed over twenty castles in Franconia, Swabia, and elsewhere that were either associated with him or suspected of similar banditry. Castle occupants who resisted such "purging" faced loss of life. Boxberg was among the castles targeted for such disciplinary action, and while it was well fortified and provisioned, its militia surrendered to league soldiers without a fight. Those soldiers thereupon burned the castle and sent ashes from the fire to Count Ludwig, its titular lord, as documentation and to allow him to savor the victory.

This was the castle, rebuilt and refurbished, that became Daniel's residence. The transition to the new post did not, however, go smoothly, as Daniel's name turned up on a list of people suspected of supplying the Absberg faction there with food, shelter, and arms during the years of the feud. In the summer of 1527, the league ordered Daniel, along with fifteen others also suspected of collaboration, to appear at its annual meeting in Ulm and take a purgation oath.[87] That ceremony required a public hearing of the charges against one and a sworn denial of them in the name of God and all the saints, upon pain of death and eternal punishment. Daniel, however, did not appear for the ceremony, citing "pressing business," and begged the league's indulgence. He was among several penitents the league excused for what it deemed to be a legitimate reason. At its scheduled meeting in Ulm, it referred his case to his patron, Count Palatine Ludwig, for a private purgation at a later date.[88]

It was at the height of Daniel's military career, between 1522 and 1524, when he was so efficiently killing factious noblemen and rebellious peasants for the Swabian League, that he tenderly courted Anna. Like Erasmus, he corresponded with her often and over an extended period of time. While none of her letters to him has survived, nineteen of his to her exist as undated copies made by notaries for the hearings held by imperial commissioners at midcentury. The original letters were among those found by her father in the fall of 1525. At his death, Hermann Büschler passed them on to his son Philip, who later (1550) submitted them, together with Anna's correspondence with Erasmus, to the Machtolff commission in an effort to discredit his sister's character during the Büschler family dispute over inheritance. Even though there are no surviving letters from Anna to Daniel, Daniel almost always writes in direct response to Anna, so his letters also tell us something about what was on her mind at the time.

Daniel's letters vividly document Hermann Büschler's reaction to the pair's behavior and his low estimate of Daniel. They also document Daniel's promises to stand by Anna and not abandon her to the mercy of her father—this despite his own dread of a confrontation with the fearsome bürgermeister, whom he recognized to be capable of doing them both a great deal of harm.

Daniel had an equally great dislike for Erasmus, and not only because of the jealousy created between the two by their sharing of Anna. They had other things in common that divided them as well. In their different ways, each was a mercenary, Erasmus at a more glamorous and commanding level, befitting his higher social rank as an imperial Schenk, Daniel at a somewhat grubbier and more subservient one, corresponding to his as an ordinary cavalryman.

For all of Daniel's ferocity on the battlefield, as a lover he was far the kinder and gentler of the two men and was a better companion to Anna. That he was in his early forties and almost twice as old as Erasmus (then in his early twenties) when he courted Anna in her mid-twenties, probably had something to do with that. He did not, of course, have the close personal associations with royalty that made Erasmus so fascinating to Anna. He did not, like Erasmus, attend dinners at imperial diets where royal guests teased him about his secret love and asked him how pretty she was (no doubt after much boasting by Erasmus). Nor was Daniel ever in a position to send Anna real-life sketches of the emperor. In these regards, Daniel and Anna had something in common that favored their relationship: neither of them was royalty. They wrote to each other in the same language, without separate forms of address designating superior and inferior. She could approach him comfortably as her social equal, and even act as his benefactor when he ran short of cash, as he frequently did. Whereas in time of need she went begging to Erasmus—

who was a none too willing creditor, despite his taking money from her in her better days[89]—Daniel easily sponged off her. One of the reasons for her stealing from her father may have been to assist her new love. Daniel also frankly shared his personal failings and ambitions with her, something Erasmus rarely did, and then with perhaps ulterior motives. If the testimony of witnesses can be believed, she and Daniel were natural comrades in mischief, each ready to throw caution to the wind and defy respectable society.

Nonetheless, Anna came to doubt the sincerity of Daniel's profession of love as much as she did Erasmus's, although in Daniel's case her doubts were more easily assuaged. This was because Daniel stuck with her through thick and thin when the relationship with her father began to deteriorate. He arranged a consultation for her with the city secretary on her legal rights as a dependent daughter. Like her father and Erasmus, he begged her in his absence to mind her conduct and not allow herself to become again the subject of gossip. Still, by comparison with her relationships with the other two men in her life, Anna's relationship with Daniel was one of greatly diminished criticism and tension.

This was true even though Daniel knew about her continuing involvement with Erasmus, whose presence in her life he resented every bit as much as Erasmus did Daniel's appearance. On three separate occasions, he asked her to stop seeing Erasmus, threatening in the end to abandon her if she did not. Because Erasmus looked on Daniel as his inferior, his jealousy was apparently a matter more of hurt pride than of a broken heart. Daniel, on the other hand, seems truly to have cared about Anna, despite once threatening to "smash her big mouth" if she did not break off the relationship with Erasmus.

Hermann Büschler, of course, knew about his daughter's cavorting with Daniel before he discovered her affair with Erasmus. After he learned that she and Daniel were raiding his wine cellar and carousing late into the night in his absence, Daniel had a more difficult time seeing Anna than did Erasmus. Thereafter she and Daniel were under her father's watchful eye, and he fumed at them both privately and publicly, all the while completely unaware that Anna was also deeply involved romantically with Erasmus. Not until he found Anna's private letters did he realize the variety, and overlap, of his daughter's amorous activities.

Daniel's letters to Anna appear to have commenced after her father discovered the full extent of their nocturnal life and barred Daniel from the house. That would most likely have been in late 1523 or early 1524. Shortly after New Year's Day, 1524, Erasmus, who had known about Anna's relationship with Daniel for at least a year, wrote to inform her that her father now knew what she and Daniel were really doing, courtesy of her new lover's big mouth (letter 23). Several letters comment on what are described as Hermann Büschler's false accusations and near vendetta against them. As the Büschler home was now off-limits to Daniel, he, much like Erasmus, had to arrange secret rendezvous elsewhere. Quite a few letters are written from nearby Leofels, just northeast of Hall, where Daniel was apparently stationed in the castle of Georg von Vellberg, a knight who was then organizing area forces against peasant rebels in Rothenburg and for whom Daniel now rode.[90]

Outside of Hall, Daniel and Anna seem to have met most often in Leofels, especially when she traveled north to her maternal home of Rothenburg, just over the border in Franconia, which was another meeting place for them when both were in that region. And Daniel also intercepted her along the road when she traveled to other destinations.

In addition to the absence of letters by Anna to Daniel, this correspondence differs from that between Anna and Erasmus in its narrower preoccupation with arranging secret meetings, surviving Anna's father, and making ends meet. There is small comment on the larger world around them and little information about what each is doing. Daniel takes quick aim at Anna's heart, not at her head. The letters convey caring, devotion, and passion, and seek assurance of her loyalty and love in return. Save for planning rendezvous, he does not instruct her, and his only criticism is leveled at her continuing contacts with Erasmus.

 Letters (late 1523–1525)[91]

[1]

Kind, dear Anna.
I have read your letter and if there is some way I may successfully help you with your father, tell me how and I will spare no effort.

As for the other matter, if you are going to Rothenburg as planned, you may find me at your will in Leofels next Tuesday, Wednesday, or Thursday morning, and on these same days every week. If you wish, let me know when you are leaving and who is traveling with you, and I will catch up with you along the way between Kirchberg and Krefftelbach [in the district of Crailsheim]. But this must be done quietly, because Heinz Traub[92] will be watching me.

Should your father send for me, I will conduct myself in such a way that no harm shall come to you. Trust me in this and don't worry; and be assured that I will act the same way around everyone else.

Nisin[93] is not here with me now, but I expect him to come to Hall a week from Sunday or Monday. Until then you will have to await news [from me there]. You must not think that I am giving up [on us] as I delay here for a while. My hope is that we can still find a way to meet often. Be consoled by that.

I will spare no effort to do whatever good I can on your behalf. May God bless and keep you. I am riding away tonight and won't return before Tuesday.

[**2**]

Kind, dearest love.
I want you to know that I sent my servant to a nobleman who owes me thirty-five gulden. Unfortunately, he did not find him at home, and I still must have that money. Much is riding on this for me. So I beg you most sincerely to lend me eight or ten gulden and not leave me in the lurch. You can send the money to me with the next messenger to Leofels. You have my word that I will repay you soon. Please don't abandon me. I place a special trust in you, which I sincerely intend to earn. If you do not have the money, you will know how to get it.

May God bless and keep you and give you what you desire, but nothing, I hope, that is dearer to you than I. Alone yours.

[3]

Kind, dear love.

Believe me that my heart's desire is to be with you. It has been such a long time since we were together that I cannot describe in writing how much has happened to me now that I am no longer near you. God willing, I will be with you in a week and take my leave from you.

Would you make a bracelet for me? I have one too few.

I cannot write any more at this time because the messenger is ready to go. May God bless and keep you and give you what you desire, but nothing that is dearer to you than I.

I ask you please not to make the pilgrimage to St. Erasmus again.[94] I cannot be at peace with you, if you go to him again. Act as I trust you to do. Alone yours.

[4][95]

Kind, dearest love.

I am letting you know that in four days [no one] will be at home, so this is a friendly request that you come to me, if you can. But reconnoiter first. I know what your nearest neighbor has said about you, so cover your trail carefully behind you.

Looking ahead [to our meeting], I should ask how kindly you meant it when you wrote in your letter, "The stronger my love grows, the weaker yours becomes," and accused me of not truly loving you. I would like to know exactly what my failing has been. You still have the power to bid and forbid me, and I will gladly do whatever you ask.

O, crown of my heart, the things you do for me still make me feel truly loved. By God's will, I ask you not to deny me. But I leave it to you to come or not. Let your heart be your guide. A hundred thousand good nights. Written on Tuesday.

And [should God give you] something that is dearer to you than I? I think not!

[5]

Kind, dear [Anna].
I cannot come to you now because of a matter involving money. Nor can I send the Nis [Nisin] to you before Friday. Meanwhile, if you can wait until Friday, let me know where he can find you, and I will send him to you there. It is not good for him to come to you in Sulz. If you wish, I will have him there by next Thursday. Many good nights. Greet the margravine a thousand times for me.[96]

[6]

Kind, dear [Anna].
Having read your letter, I expected you to go to Rothenburg last week, as your friends were there, which would have suited me very well. I was about to let you know that [I might meet you there, but] I have promised to ride with Georg von Vellberg and there is no way I can break my word to him. So I cannot meet you on the way to Heilbronn. But Nisin will ride through Hall on Wednesday, Thursday, or Friday next and stop at Lienhard Mangolt's.[97] You can keep an eye out for him. There is just no place on the way to Heilbronn where we can meet, for I am afraid that Heinz Traub [will be watching me and] might notice something as long as he knows that I am in the area. But if you must go to Kirchberg, do so on Friday, and let me know your plans between now and then.

May God bless and keep you. In haste. If you will be coming on Friday, let me know as best you can whether you will arrive early or late.

[7]

Kind, dear love.
I wish you many hundred thousand good years[98] and everything else you desire. I want you to know that I am now in Leofels and

would gladly have ridden out to you. I have had little peace of mind since I was last with you. You are the object of all my desires. If your father is not going to be around, I would come to you next Sunday or Monday [if you wish]. Write me how best to do it, and the more secretly done, the better. You may instruct me through my servant, if you wish. But if you can't write so soon, then send your messenger. Just direct him to the chaplain's house in Leofels; there he will get the necessary instructions.

We have much to talk about. And I fear that I must smash your big mouth, for I hear that you are still making your pilgrimage to St. Giles.[99] I have been told all kinds of things [about you] that I do not wish to hear.

May God bless and keep you, and give you what you desire, but nothing dearer to you than I. Write and tell me what I should do.

[8]

Kind, dear love.
I have received your letter, and as you wish, I have delayed [my departure] until next Tuesday. This is a very inopportune time for me to be here and I cannot delay any longer. I am already being pressed to ride.

You have written that someone took you aside and spoke to you. Let me know who it was and what has happened to you since because of it. Let the priest know, or send him the letter. As you know, he is aware of our situation [and will serve as a messenger].

I ask you not to detain me here any longer [than Tuesday], for I cannot wait around. Send it[100] with the letter, for it is important to me. God bless and keep you and give you what you desire, but nothing that is dearer to you than I.

[9]

Kind, dear love.
Your messenger missed me last time, but I have understood from your letter that [your father] will be departing soon. If this is so,

would you let me know it again by your messenger at the [same] place he tried to find me last time. I will still be there until next Sunday or Monday.

I have longed to come to you, but there is a good reason why, for love's sake, I could not. I will tell you all about it when I do come. I have much more to write you, but I dare not entrust it to this messenger, who is still unproven. Write back immediately and tell me what I should do [to see you]. May God bless and keep you and give you what you desire, but nothing that is dearer to you than I.

Yours resolutely[101]

[10]

Kind, dear love.
I had expected your reply by now. I must assume that the matter [with your father] is now partly resolved. Do let me know how he is treating you. As I have promised before, I will not abandon you; have no doubt about that.

I am preparing to return to my lord next Thursday, since I don't have permission to be away any longer. But I will be coming back here around St. Vitus's Day [June 15]. So we will be together again in time. May the intervening period be kind to you. If you don't have a messenger going my way, just send the letter to the priest, who, as you know, can always deliver it. You can find me in Leofels on Sunday and Thursday until noon. Let me know what your plans are at this time. May God bless and keep you and bring us together again in joy. To Master Hannsen, pastor in Ramsberg.[102]

[11]

Kind, dear love.
I have read your letter, and you have understood well my complaint. As I told you yesterday, the way things now stand, I would bring much grief upon myself [if I said any more]. But let about

a year pass, and I shall behave so that you shall see in me a man who has done you a favor.[103] And don't get bored waiting, for I have great hopes for this year and expect much good to come to me in it. And don't take the conflict [with your father] too hard, even though he now denounces you to your relatives. I am not going to abandon you.

I am today off to Vellberg, where I will be until Thursday or Friday. As my servant will be returning [to Leofels], I will send him to you. Let me know what is happening to you; I don't want to lose touch with you. May God bless and keep you.

D[aniel] Treutwein

[12]

Kind, dear Anna.

I have read your letter and am letting you know that I must ride away today. It is quite important to me, and I can't cancel out on short notice, so I won't be able to meet you in Lendsiedel. The earliest I expect to return to Leofels is Sunday. Today I sent my servant to Dr. Mangolt[104] and indicated to him something of our situation, so if you want to pursue matters with him, I expect he will do his best for you for my sake.

I am not a little taken aback by what your father still accuses us of doing. If I had nothing but what you gave me,[105] I would not have gotten fat from it, so he does me an injustice when he says that I entered his house like a thief in the night. I will look into the matter, and if it is as you have indicated, he will know of my displeasure, for I have behaved all along as an honest man.

The messenger who delivered the letter from you reported that the chief bailiff had given the letters to him.[106] If the chief bailiff is agreeable, [send him] to me in Leofels next Sunday fully informed of the situation. Bare your heart to this man and let him know how you, who are innocent, are being hounded by your father because of me. I will have to think about how to deal with him.[107] I wanted you to know this. May God bless and keep you.

D[aniel] T[reutwein]

[**13**]

Kind, dear love.
I have read your letter and was completely unprepared for such sharp words, because as far as I know I have done nothing dishonorable. Nonetheless, I must endure this.

Please help me find a way to bring us together, so that we may be alone with one another. I need to talk with you about things I cannot write. If we can't be alone together, I don't want to come at all. May God bless and keep you and give you what you want, but nothing dearer to you than I.

Yours resolutely

[**14**]

Kind, dearest love.
I have read your letter and I am letting you know that there are serious reasons why I can't come to you. I will tell you what they are when I do come. God willing, that will be soon.

I don't have my servant with me now, but I expect him to be in Hall on Thursday or Friday. Through him, you can write me all your concerns and tell me how I can help. You will find me willing.

My heartfelt desire is to be with you, but, honestly, I cannot arrange it now. May God bless and keep you and give you what you like, but nothing that is dearer to you than I. Alone yours.

[**15**]

Kind, dear love.
As you know, when I left you, you said that you would send it to me last Friday.[108] [Had I known otherwise] I would have ridden off and not have waited for it here. Please reply through this messenger and let me know the reason for the delay. I will not and cannot wait beyond next Sunday.

I am also letting you know that I am still ill. I wish I were well and with you, for I still have much to tell you. I must write this in a hurry, as the messenger has to be off. I hope we will be together soon. May God bless and keep you and give you what you like, but nothing that is dearer to you than I.

Yours resolutely

[16]

Kind, dear love....
I am writing now, as I did last time, to ask you to believe that it is my heartfelt desire to be with you. But I now must do escort duty, as the messenger who brings this letter to you can explain more fully. God willing, I will come to you after Easter. I still have many things to tell you that cannot be written.

Please conduct yourself so that you do not become the object of people's gossip. May God bless and keep you and give you what you like, but nothing that is dearer to you than I.

Please have some more crackling [fried pork rinds] made for me. Alone yours.

[17]

Kind, dear Anna.
I am letting you know that I am not yet in Würzburg, but I am preparing to depart Wednesday morning, so herewith I take my leave from you. Please don't forget me and allow me suffer because I must be far away from you. Would to God that things were such that I might always stay with you! I would have preferred to have said goodbye to you in another way, but unfortunately it cannot be.

If there is something of particular concern that you need help with, you need simply send old Hans[109] to the chaplain in Leofels, and he can always send your letter or whatever else I can help you with on to me. Whatever is troubling you, you shall find me unsparing in body and possessions.

So my dear Anna, make the best of this humble letter. And please don't go again to St. Erasmus, for if you do, our friendship is over. May God bless and keep you and give you what you like, but nothing that is dearer to you than I. Alone yours.

[18]

Kind, dear love.
Your letter only arrived late yesterday, so I have not been able to come to you. Please help me find a way for us to meet as soon as possible, for I have much to tell you. But don't let too many people know; the quieter, the better. May God bless and keep you and give you what you like, but nothing dearer to you than I.

Yours resolutely

[19]

My dear Anna.
Would you do me a favor and lend me a gulden, or half a gulden? Dear Anna, I am in great distress for want of this money. If you have it, please send it. I will repay you within four weeks, of that you should have no doubt. I beg you, dear Anna.

 The End of the Affairs

ERASMUS'S DISCOVERY OF ANNA'S RELATIONSHIP WITH DANIEL slowly turned him against her, as he believed that relationship had earlier turned her against him. But Daniel's intrusion into her life indicates that her passion for Erasmus, who was so often far away, had cooled before Daniel arrived on the scene, while Erasmus's professed love for her may always have been opportunistic. Still, even after both recognized that their relationship had run its course, neither wanted to end it completely. Anna especially had good reason not to break it off. Increasingly estranged from her father because of Daniel, she could still find a powerful ally in Erasmus, whose advice and financial assistance she continued to seek.

Erasmus, however, now had less reason to be loyal to Anna. If the affair with Daniel did not break his heart, it did take its toll. What he liked to call "the old love," whatever that may have been, was now clearly gone. Although he continued to protest his good faith and to offer her his good offices, he had in fact washed his hands of her, as she was slowly and painfully to discover.

Two letters by Erasmus, dated 1524, indicate that they had stopped writing to each other for a long period of time, probably the peak period of Anna's romance with Daniel. Judging by Erasmus's warnings against rash actions on her part, she seems to be on the verge of taking preemptive legal action against her father before he strikes at her, something Daniel's letters also indicate. At the very least, Anna was now informing herself about her legal rights as a dependent daughter. In the sixteenth century, a woman in her late twenties, unmarried and dependent on a widowed father who thought her a tramp, was in an extremely vulnerable position. The specter of physical violence, abandonment, and disinheritance could not have been far from Anna's mind.

Erasmus now professed an earnest desire to meet and plan her best course of action. He was, however, prevented from doing so at this time because of illness.

24 [30]. ERASMUS TO ANNA (1524)

Dear Anna. I am very disappointed that you have not written to me for so long. Apparently you write now because you see things differently. But what you are preparing to do now, God knows, does not please me, and I still hope you will reconsider so that no harm comes to you.

Dear Anna, [I know that] you want me to come to you, but so that you may see that it is you who should rather come to me in Birklingen,[110] I am letting you know that I am still in a very bad way with a bad leg and, almighty God as my witness, neither able nor daring to ride. Two days ago I sent all my servants to Ansbach to answer for me and await instructions there from my gracious lord, since I cannot yet ride. I fully expect my servant to return in a week, at which time I will endure the pain and meet you secretly in Birklingen, where few people will know we are together. So if God wills that I can ride, I will come to you then and discuss all the pressing matters with you.

So dear Anna, let me know by return mail if you can be in Birklingen in a week and I will meet you there, for I have many things to tell you. Many hundred thousand good nights. I gave the messenger a quarter gulden [so you needn't pay him anything]. God willing, I hope you will still find mercy.[111] If only God will give me my health! I hope your situation shall become better. Written in 1524.

25 *[31]*.   Erasmus to Anna *[1524]*

Dear Anna. Inasmuch as you want me to depart immediately for Birklingen to meet you, I must tell you on my word of honor that I dare not ride or travel at this time, and tomorrow I will be completely confined. I beg you not to be annoyed with me, for I would like to come to you, but by God and all his saints I cannot. I will send my servant to you and he will tell you all about it. May God make me better!

Dear Anna, think the best [of me] and if at all possible, do not depart [Birklingen before I can come there], for I still have a great many things to tell you. Many hundred thousand good nights.

Erasmus's next letter indicates that a diseased leg may have been the least of his maladies, for he now reveals that he is also striken with syphilis. For Europeans, syphilis was then a frightening new epidemic disease, although not quite as baffling, wanting in prophylaxis, or lacking in treatment as infection by *Yersinia pestis*, the bacterium of the bubonic plague, which lived in the digestive tracts of fleas. One knew that the infecting agent of syphilis lurked in the vaginal secretions of prostitutes and that one should avoid the baths and other places where prostitution occurred. By the 1530s, the disease might be treated with a mercurial ointment, the invention of the Swiss alchemist and physician Paracelsus [1493–1541] and the standard treatment until the nineteenth century. Still, its prevalence and fast pace in the first half of the century made it a topic of conversation between parents and children, especially children departing home to study, work, or "wander" abroad. Among the advice Leo Ravensburg, an Augsburg patrician and associate of the famous Welser banking and mercantile firm, gave his fourteen-year-old son when the boy departed Augsburg in 1539 to begin an apprenticeship in Lyon was a warning to "stay away from dishonest women, so that you do not get the pox and the other maladies that flow from them."[112]

Erasmus, however, was now beyond warnings and prophylaxis. The bad leg from which he suffered may have been a result of the syphilis. He writes to Anna from Würzburg, where he is about to begin the "wood cure,"[113] a prolonged drinking of large amounts of a tea brewed from a species of myrtle popularly known as "poxwood."[114] For Erasmus, it was to be the last in a series of remedies he had tried without success. He is also financially strapped and unable to lend Anna the modest sum of money she then urgently sought from him.

26 [32]. ERASMUS TO ANNA [SUMMER 1524]

Dear Anna. I have read your letter and among other things you ask me to lend you twenty gulden. I swear on my soul's salvation that I do not have it. In addition, I must take the wood cure in Würzburg promptly on Wednesday or Thursday at the latest. I have been trying many cures, but have been unable to get well, so I will try once more to [regain my health] by this cure.

After my last trip, I didn't know where I should get money, because my brother doesn't have any.[115] He had to use what he had to pay the interest that came due on St. Peter's Day [June 29]. Also, I borrowed a hundred gulden from him last summer, which I now on my faith and credit must repay him in a week. But I don't have a heller on me and, God as my witness, I don't know where I will get the money I need. My confinement in Würzburg is going to cost at the very least thirty gulden, wherever that will come from.

So, dear Anna, please don't be angry with me because I am not helping you. Believe me, I don't have the money; if I did, I would give it to you unasked. But if God helps me get well, I will use all my cunning to see if there is a way to make your life better. But God as my witness, I cannot ride now. It has been eleven

weeks since I was last on a horse, and since then I have been in no shape to do anything. But as soon as God restores my health, I will deal honestly with you, although [I know] you don't believe me.

Many thousand good nights. Please don't let yourself be angry with me. Write to me now and then.

E[rasmus]

The next time Anna wrote, it was again in search of money and advice, and Erasmus again excused himself because of illness and insolvency. However, he made it clear that even if he were solvent, as he soon expected to be, he would not be the generous patron she required.

27 [33]. ERASMUS TO ANNA (N.D.)

Dear Anna. You write me to come to you, but God knows it cannot be done, for I am disabled and there is reason to fear that I won't be able to ride anywhere for three or four weeks. And as soon as I am well, I must go to the [royal] court in Ansbach. So be in touch with me again in three or four weeks, and I will then come to you, so that your situation may improve. I will give you further notice [first].

Dear Anna, since you ask me to send you three gulden, I must tell you on my soul's salvation that I don't have them. But as soon as God helps me reach Ansbach, I will have my own money, and then I will remember the trust you have placed in me and not abandon you. So dear Anna, don't worry so much. There is a God who wills you good fortune and salvation.

Dear Anna, I also have much that I want to complain to you about. So send a messenger to me in three or four weeks at my expense, for as soon as God helps me reach Ansbach, I hope to assist you with two gulden. However, on my last trip my father gave me nothing inasmuch as I was so close to home, and the time before that also nothing. Many hundred thousand good nights.

Anna might well have read this letter as a hollow promise, for Erasmus had now denied her thrice. In addition, the conflict with her father was fast peaking, and she needed to chart a new life for herself outside

the Büschler house without delay. Erasmus still remained her most immediate influential friend, and certainly few knew more about her troubles than he. He was also in a position to arrange a temporary safe haven for her outside of Hall in the custody of someone powerful enough to shelter and protect her from her father. That person was to be the margravine of Hohenlohe, whose niece Elisabeth had earlier sought Anna's opinion of Erasmus's marriage prospects.[116]

The county of Hohenlohe occupied much of the land to the north of Hall, and the royal family had castles in the northwestern towns of Oehringen and Neuenstein within easy traveling distance of Hall. Anna and Erasmus, whose great-great-grandmother Elisabeth was a Hohenlohe, probably met there in happier times. Like the Schenks of Limpurg, the House of Hohenlohe was an old enemy of Hall, with major feuds going back to the fourteenth century, and certainly not ill disposed toward helping Anna and Erasmus. Now that Anna's father had read their correspondence and knew of their affair, Anna was of the opinion that Erasmus, like it or not, had become part of her destiny and was obligated to assist her.

As Erasmus had made it clear that he neither could nor would come to her at this time, she now proposed, in the most agreeable manner, to meet him on his terms. Her closing words may, however, reveal her true feelings about doing so: whereas in previous letters, she had wished him "many hundred thousand good nights," she now speaks only of "many good days."

28 [35]. ANNA TO ERASMUS (N.D.)

Noble, gracious sir, here is my humble request. I am astonished to think that I have done something to cause your grace not to want to come to me. But it is up to God whether I shall now lose my life, honor, and property on your grace's account.

Gracious sir, it is my sincere request that your grace come to me whenever you wish. But if your grace doesn't want to come here, then I ask that you let me know how I can get to the margravine's, should the devil, my father, and [his] relatives catch up with me.

Dear sir, I have pleaded with you, and although you have told me that you will help me when your situation improves, I can't

understand why you should want to do so then [if you aren't doing so now]. . . .

Dear sir, let me know this moment how I should get to the margravine's, for, dear sir, I have a great need to know that. Many good days.

Two final letters from Erasmus address Anna's new fears and conclude the correspondence. Never before had he been more reassuring, nor, ominously, more theological than he is now. Amid his vague promises, he also delivers, at last, his promised solution to her troubles.

29 [36]. ERASMUS TO ANNA (N.D.)

Dearest Anna. As I have written to you before, just relax and be patient. If God wills it, things will change.

I wanted to write you a long letter, but I have not been able to do so. The only advice I can give you now is that you trust almighty God to work everything out according to our wishes. That is why I will try to think of ways to help things turn out for the best.

So be of good cheer and think only this: after sadness comes every joy, and things do turn out as God wills. May God give you a hundred thousand good nights. Written in haste.

30 [37]. ERASMUS TO ANNA (N.D.)

Dearest Anna. I have read your letter, and God knows it doesn't please me much that things now go so badly for you. I know that you place your hope in me and want my advice, and I do hope your intentions are good and honest when you do so. On the other hand, you also complain, as far as I can understand you, that I do not really want to help and advise you. Would to God that I knew some good advice to give you, for I would do so with a glad heart.

Dear Anna, although it now goes badly for you, don't worry. Whatever I come up with to help you out of this situation, I will share with you. On my word of honor, you needn't worry that

I will deal with you dishonestly, as I also hope you will not do with me. So just take hope and ask your family if you might come back home.

Dearest Anna, I will not abandon you even if, as you have said, the devil should care less if I did, and I don't make this claim falsely. Many hundred thousand good nights. Take hope and don't lose heart. I mean well and I hope you do too. Written in haste.

Erasmus's advice—to trust God and beg her father to take her back—was no realistic solution to Anna's problem. She and her father had long ago reached the point of no return; neither of them could now abate their anger at the other. Anna desperately needed a home elsewhere. For while her behavior may not have exceeded the mercy of God, it was certainly beyond the ability of her father and most Haller to let bygones be bygones. But then, neither was Anna prepared to forgive and forget the treatment she had received at her father's hand and, by omission, from the city council of Hall. In advising her to crawl back to her father, Erasmus simply abandoned her to her own devices.

As for Erasmus's own personal life, he married the countess Anna of Lodron (d. 1556), daughter of a wealthy south Tirol family and widow of field general Georg von Frundsberg, commander of mercenary armies. The two are memorialized with their children in a stone picture epitaph in the chapel of the Schenks in the monastery of Comburg. They kneel facing each other under the crucified Christ, Erasmus on the back of a lion, symbol of power and authority, Anna on that of a dog, symbol of loyalty and fidelity. Their son, Friedrich, is with his father, their daughters, Maria and Katherina, with their mother. Four coats of arms, two at the base of the sculpture and two framing the cross of Christ, proclaim their paternal and maternal origins. The legend beneath reads:

On February 25, 1553, the noble lord Erasmus, lord of Limpurg, freeborn and hereditary Schenk of the Holy Roman Empire, died. May God be kind to him.[117]

What of Daniel Treutwein, a man of seemingly less fickle heart, who had been a help and consolation to Anna in other times of need? No longer was he foursquare at her side, as he had promised always to be. His activities can be traced at least until 1527, and there is some evidence that Anna went in search of him in late 1525.[118] By the end of that year, however, or certainly the next, he, like Erasmus, had quietly disappeared from her life. Perhaps her father had succeeded in convincing him that Anna was not worth the grief he intended to put them both through should the two of them continue to see each other. Perhaps the dual affair and the scandal it threatened had become too much for him, as it had for her father. More likely, Daniel acted on his repeated threat to abandon her if she persisted in seeing Erasmus, which she clearly had done. The "pilgrimages to St. Erasmus" had so upset this otherwise seemingly caring lover that he threatened a beating, if they continued.

Circumstances also strained the relationship almost as much as Daniel's fear of her father and jealousy of Erasmus. Throughout their courtship, Daniel's military service forced him also to become another rendezvous man, not a steady presence in Anna's life. The relationship, for this reason, may simply have run a natural course for them both by 1525. Certainly after Daniel became the bailiff of Boxberg, he had a full life of his own apart from Anna. Whether that new life ended shortly after it began (perhaps on a military mission, perhaps as a suspected traitor at the hand of the Swabian League), or Daniel lived long and ruled well in Boxberg, is presently unknown.

*T*he Büschler house on Market Square is today the western part of the Hotel Adelshof, Hall's plushest. The lower floors were originally the residence of the imperial mayor, the emperor's representative and watchdog in Hall since the twelfth century. Attached to them and carefully maintained was a modest royal court, which the emperor occupied during his infrequent visits. In the fourteenth and fifteenth centuries the building was the domicile of Hall's bürgermeisters. It became Hermann Büschler's private home in the sixteenth century and was the residence of later bürgermeisters as well. Thereafter it was the Ratskeller before becoming a hotel.

CHAPTER
THREE

On the Run

HERMANN BÜSCHLER DID NOT HAVE TO READ ANNA'S ENTIRE stash of private letters to have his worst fears confirmed. He was not, however, the kind of man who allowed disappointment and grief to occupy him for long. Anna soon confronted a father whose anger would light the legal skies of Hall until his death eighteen years later and keep them burning bright until her death nine years after his.

The sixteenth century was a time when everyone had his or her place in society, and certain kinds of behavior were expected and enforced in accordance with a person's rank in life. Townspeople lived on pre-assigned streets, according to their trade or profession, and they dressed in clothing appropriate to their social class. To reach above one's station in life or to act contrary to it unsettled one's neighbors and was viewed as a threat to public order. The elaborate sumptuary laws of contemporary Nürnberg, a model German city, equated such behavior with the deadliest of sins. Entitled "Regulation and Prohibition of PRIDE by the Knowing Council of the City of Nürnberg," those laws proclaimed a renewed version of the city's traditional dress code in 1618: "What Its Citizens . . . in Their Various Classes . . . May and May Not Wear."[1] Dressing out of one's class, or decorating one's house beyond the permitted embellishments, was deemed to be the first sprout of more dangerous forms of willfulness and self-indulgence, which, if unsnipped, might well grow into open disobedience and rebellion. For the same reason, Nürnberg laws threatened harsh and indelible punishment for insidiously threatening the social order, taking two digits from the finger of a perjurer and the tongue of one who dared to blaspheme against God and civil authority.[2]

After studying the city of Nürnberg for four months on behalf of his government, the Englishman William Smith concluded that the honesty, civility, and security of its citizens were closely associated with their city's cleanliness and orderliness and the wisdom and vigilance of its law enforcement.

[The cittie] hath 528 streets and lanes that are paued . . . which streets are . . . alwais . . . cleanely kept. For they haue no doung hilles in all their streets, but [only] in certayne odd by corners. Neither is it the custome there to make water in the streets or the throw out of any vrine or others, beffore tenne of the clock at night. The punishment whereof is 20 dollers besydes emprisonment. Yea so precyse are they in the sweet keeping of their cittie that although a man haue a yard or backsyde in his house . . . yet may he . . . kepe . . . but only one pigg, & yet that no longer, till it be half a yeare old. . . .

The cittie is gouerned by a prudent and sage Counsell of the gentility . . . through whose politik & wyse gouerment, the people are kept in quyetnes, dew aw, & obaysance. For I think there is not a cittie in the world, where the people are more ciuill. . . . I haue read that about 100 yeares past, one of the cheiffest potentates in Germany came to this cittie & demanding of . . . one of the cheiffest gouernors [there] how he could kepe his people so quyet, being so great a multitud, he answered, with cherishing of the good, and punishing of the evell. . . .

It is not the maner there as it is in England, that in purchasing or convayance of landes or tenements, contracts of matrimony or such lyke matters of importance, that any man maketh a wryting and setteth to his hand and seall, but [it] is sealed by two of the Comon Counsell. And so it is effectual in their law, or ells not. Therefore need they not many lawyers or scriueners. For except the clarkes of the chauncery and their procurators, I know not aboue two notaries publike in all the cittie. So trew and just are they in their dealings, that their word is as much as an obligation. . . . So trew and just are they, that if you lose a purse of mony in the street, ring, bracelet or such lyke, you shalbe sure to haue it againe. I would it were so in London.[3]

Basic virtues and physical order understandably become sacrosanct among people who find themselves theatened easily and often by sinister forces (famine, feuds, plague, revolts) that are beyond their control and understanding, as was the case in Anna's lifetime. A family's security in time of need and success in everyday life might then depend on nothing so much as what their neighbors think about them. For this reason, the harm done to Hermann Büschler's honor and reputation by his daughter's behavior would have enraged any sixteenth-century parents who found themselves in a similar situation. For contemporaries, no greater sin of childhood and youth existed than the public humiliation of one's family, a maxim drummed into the young in school, church, and home.[4] Such an act not only revealed ingratitude for the many things a parent gave a child, from life and sustenance to education and inheritance; still worse, it invited gossip about, ostracization of, and predation upon the child's family. For this reason, the majority of the witnesses who later recalled Anna's expulsion from her father's house identified with the bürgermeister and thanked their lucky stars that they had been spared the shame of so willful and disobedient a child.

For Anna, however, her father's actions against her were not expressions of justifiable anger, but the deeds of an "unfatherly heart" incapable of parental love and duty.[5] Until the end of her life, she would insist that he had cast her out of his house without just cause.[6] The fatal flaw, she believed, was in his character, not hers, and the fatal act was his as well, namely, the spurning of his paternal responsibility to provide her a proper marriage. "If Hermann Büschler's daughter was acting improperly against him," her earliest legal brief declared, "or if he knew of any disgrace, depravity, or wrongdoing on his daughter's part, then as a parent, he should have taken it to heart and disciplined her by marriage, or in some other honorable way."[7]

Denied shelter and protection by her father, Anna turned initially to her immediate relatives in Hall for support so that she would not have to beg on the streets or turn to prostitution.[8] For three days, she stayed with cousin Conrad Büschler, Sr. But her father soon discouraged such aid and comfort, as he informed her kin in both Hall and Rothenburg of her moral failings and threatened to punish any who assisted or sheltered her. According to her cousin and Rothenburg mayor Hans Hornberger, Anna's relatives had little desire to associate with her after her father effectively "banned" her from the two cities.[9]

Thereafter, Anna had few options for lodging and board. Her father's maid, Barbara Dollen, recalled how she had taken shelter for a week in a Junker manor where her (Dollen's) father worked.[10] Finding both family and friends in the immediate area hesitant to take her in,

Anna recognized that she would have to depart the region altogether to escape the hounding of her father and begin a new life elsewhere.

Before she did so, efforts were made on her behalf by others to persuade her father to take her back into his custody and care,[11] as Erasmus had advised her to do in his last letter. But among the forty witnesses, only Barbara Dollen, who had good reason to dislike Anna and to curry her father's favor, said that he was willing to have her return home and live with him again.[12] If in his heart of hearts that sentiment was true, there is no record that Anna ever walked voluntarily through his doors again.

Departing Hall with only a few possessions, Anna now wandered far from the city. She accepted shelter and assistance where they were offered, associating with what witnesses, both hostile and friendly, would later describe as "all kinds of unsavory folk."[13] Under the circumstances in which she now found herself, shelter was shelter and a helping hand a helping hand. As she still maintained her Catholic faith at this time, she might have taken refuge for a while in a cloister, as battered and homeless women were then known to do. However, such a retreat was clearly not what she had in mind.

 New Friends and Enemies

ONE PERSON WHO TOOK HER IN AS SHE MADE HER WAY NORTH TO her relatives in Rothenburg was the blacksmith of Weissenbach.[14] Her father learned of her presence there and of her future plans from the wife of the mayor of the village of Blaufelden, Apollonia Prenner, who was at the time visiting in Weissenbach and whose husband was then befriending Anna by seeking support for her among influential relatives in Dinkelsbühl. The intention was to bring Anna's plight before the imperial supreme court (*Reichskammergericht*, or imperial cameral tribunal), then sitting in Esslingen, so that she might win that high court's assistance in gaining a hearing of her case in Hall, the jurisdiction in which the conflict with her father would ultimately have to be resolved. The kindly mayor's intervention in the Büschler family scandal, however, upset his wife, who was recovering from childbirth. She apparently feared the consequences for her family once Hermann Büschler learned of her husband's efforts on his daughter's behalf, espe-

cially if those efforts led to effective action against him in Hall.
Inasmuch as Anna's reputation, like her father's warnings, had preceded her to Blaufelden, the woman may also have had misgivings
about her husband's close proximity to the notorious maid of Hall.
Here is how the anxious Apollonia expressed her concern to Anna's
father.

> After your daughter left you, she came here to Weissenbach and
> has been living at the smithy's. I wish that she would leave me
> and mine alone. She says she is going to do your honor [Hermann
> Büschler] a lot of harm before the imperial supreme court (*Cam-
> mergericht*).[15] I am a poor woman recovering from childbirth, and
> I truly regret that this is happening. But if your honor will not
> take precautions against her, then I must do so myself in a way I
> would prefer to avoid. So I ask your honor to prevent that, to
> think of my poverty and get her out of here.[16]

 A Hearing in Hall

THE INFORMATION HERMANN BÜSCHLER RECEIVED FROM APOL-
lonia Prenner proved to be completely accurate. Not long after his
receipt of her letter, Anna, aided by maternal relatives and friends,
formally petitioned the supreme court's assistance in gaining a safe
hearing before the city council of Hall, the city's supreme executive,
legislative, and judicial authority, before which she hoped to win fair,
even generous, financial support from her father. She now had legal
counsel (*beystand*), evidently paid for by her maternal allies, who
might certainly expect to be reimbursed, as there was clearly money
to be gotten from Hermann Büschler. In addition to the immediate
support she was seeking from her father, she was now also due a share
of the estate left the children by her deceased mother. In her petition
to the Esslingen court, she described her father as a man consumed by
"inflexible, harsh, unforgiving anger" toward her.

> To the best of his ability [he has] belittled, reviled, and raged
> against me in a way that is not at all befitting or proper for a

father to do. He should rather shelter, care for, and protect me from scandal and disgrace, as natural fathers are obligated by both divine and human law to do.[17]

The imperial supreme court in Esslingen was one of three in which Anna and her father—and after his death, she and her siblings—did battle over her fair share of the family's wealth. Founded at the imperial Diet of Worms in 1495 by the German princes and other dignitaries, the court was intended to be a tool to resolve conflicts among the German estates lawfully and peacefully. It was to be both the empire's highest court and one that might act independently of the emperor, who had a penchant for weakening the jurisdiction of the existing imperial courts by granting exemptions to favored clients or intervening on their behalf in other ways. For the first thirty-five years of its existence, the court was itinerant, sitting in no fewer than ten cities before finally becoming more or less stationary in Augsburg in 1530. During the 1520s, it resided in Nürnberg (1521–1524), Esslingen (1524–1527), and Speyer (1527–1530).

The court had original jurisdiction in cases where the imperial ban (the power to outlaw subjects) had been defied, and in criminal cases where the peace of the land had been broken by rebels, outlaws, and feuding imperial estates. In civil cases, the court held original jurisdiction over complaints against governing persons or corporate bodies, like city councils, and it had appellate authority over the rulings of both urban and territorial courts. Whereas the rulers of the larger states did not permit their subjects to appeal decisions made in the territorial courts, the cities were not so fortunate. Before the supreme court, a citizen of an imperial city could challenge the legality of a local court's ruling, or protest the latter's refusal to hear, or delay in hearing, a complaint, all of which Anna would do.[18]

At the time of its creation in 1495, the new imperial supreme court had a keen rival in the older imperial court of Rottweil, which held jurisdiction over the duchy of Swabia and a great part of Franconia. Still active at the time of our story, that court would prove to be Anna's best hope. Unfortunately for her, the emperor had granted so many exemptions from Rottweil's authority that it was a court in decline by the turn of the century. All of its rulings could now be appealed to the supreme court, and in most instances such appeals proved successful.[19]

Finally, there was the city council of Hall, with its legislative, judicial, and executive powers all rolled into one, and governing by customary laws dating back centuries. Its relationship with outside courts may be described as unfriendly, if not hostile, a result of a long history of intrusions into its jurisdiction, particularly on the part of the territorial court of Würzburg, which had long attempted to maintain judicial supremacy throughout the region.

As a dependent single woman claiming wrongful abandonment and impoverishment, Anna had a right to request financial support from her father, who technically still had legal custody of her, and she was also legally due at this time a share of the maternal inheritance. In the summer of 1525, the Esslingen court sent the city council of Hall a copy of Anna's petition for a hearing there on the question of her support, expecting in return either compliance or an explanation. The council shared the petition with her father, who declared that he had "no desire whatsoever" to discuss money with his daughter.[20] That being the case, the council informed the Esslingen court on August 14 that its hands were tied and it considered the matter closed.

Thus finding the "gentler way of direct negotiation" blocked by the intransigence of her father, Anna asked the city council of Hall through the Esslingen court to set a date certain, on which she might come to Hall and present her case against her father. Nowhere in Germany at this time did the appeals of citizens to courts of higher authority please city councils, which looked on them as virtual betrayals of one's "homeland." In the fifteenth century, Hall had declared it a punishable breach of citizenship for any Haller to turn to a foreign court against a fellow citizen, insisting that local disputes be settled in the home court, whose decisions were to be received as final.[21] In turning to Esslingen against her father and the city council, Anna had positioned herself for bitter conflict with both.

Before Anna and her counsel would venture a single kilometer into territory under Hall's jurisdiction, where the city council, Hall's high court, might serve process on her, they wanted the council's firm assurance of their safety. So together with their petition for a hearing in Hall came also a request for a letter of safe-conduct to and from the city. This procedure addressed several concerns. At this time, Anna was deemed still to be within the household and under the custody of her father, who was a powerful official in Hall, and also one who might reasonably be expected to take action against her, either private or legal, once she entered Hall territory with the intention of suing him.

It was a courageous and difficult undertaking for a child at any age or of either gender to challenge a parent in a court of law. Even though Anna was now technically in her majority (over twenty-five), being unmarried and without means, she remained a dependent child seeking support, and as such she still could not proceed against her father without prior court consent. Her petition for safe-conduct was also a request for the city council's forbearance and willingness to stand *in loco parentis* on her behalf. In a word, she wanted the council to protect her from her father until it had heard and adjudicated her case, and she had safely in hand that portion of the family wealth then rightfully due her, by which means she could, at last, lead an independent life. The Esslingen court's acceptance and forwarding of her petition to Hall had already been a step in that direction.

In addition to being a dependent child in the eyes of the law, Anna was also an unprofessional single woman, and as such she could not act legally in a court of law without an accompanying male counsel or representative, normally a woman's father or nearest male relative. This was only one of several restrictions on the legal status of women that resulted from the general rule of male guardianship. In Germany, a widow also could not act independently as the guardian of her children, but had rather to make all decisions affecting their education and welfare, including testamentary dispositions, under the guidance of one or more male guardians appointed either by her deceased husband or by a court.[22] And whenever an unprofessional woman spoke in court, her word always carried less weight than a man's.

Roman and early German law based male guardianship of women on women's comparative physical weakness and their limited experience in worldly affairs, the latter a self-fulfilling deficit, as women were excluded from politics and formal higher education. The original intention of the practice had been to compensate vulnerable and disadvantaged women by providing them with male guidance and protection in the public forum. In this sense, the practice, so prejudicial from a modern point of view, actually served social order and provided women a greater degree of justice than they might otherwise have received at law given then prevailing attitudes and circumstances.

By the sixteenth century, however, restrictions on a woman's rights at law were also being justified by womankind's alleged mental inferiority and emotional instability.[23] The revival of these unflattering classical and clerical stereotypes accompanied changes in the workplace that reduced employment opportunities in urban trades and sparked a new level of competition between men and women for the available positions. During the high and later Middle Ages, and especially after the Black Death had depleted the ranks of skilled artisans in the cities, women's labor had been much in demand in urban shops and businesses. As a result, women gained increasing prominence, equality, and economic strength in urban trade and industry, and their new status and respect moderated the rule of male guardianship. By the sixteenth century, however, that rule was staging a comeback in urban society. The demands of the new export markets opened by the voyages of discovery and the need to keep pace with the rapidly expanding and labor-intensive publishing industry forced urban industries to reorganize. Those industries now turned increasingly to the more flexible countryside and away from the guild-heavy cities for their labor force. With the flight of employment opportunities from the city to the countryside, the competition for urban jobs increased, along with the determination of males to monopolize them. Under the protests of male apprentices, women were now progressively squeezed out of male-dominated and mixed-gender trades. At the same time, the trades women had traditionally dominated—textiles and food processing—stagnated with the development of the new industrial world, shrinking further women's opportunities to learn a craft and shifting their work increasingly back into the household.[24]

As a rule, married women at this time might litigate in court only through their husbands, as Anna would do after she married. Indeed, she would later shock the citizens of Hall by declaring a talent for litigation to be the quality she most desired in a husband.[25] Unlike mere wives, professional women with marketable skills, whether married or single, and whether sharing a husband's business or operating one of their own, were recognized as having a proper legal status and thus able to speak for themselves in a court of law just like any professional man. Otherwise, it would have been impossible for them to be held liable for the promises and transactions they made in the normal conduct of their businesses.[26] The maintenance of social order, always the highest priority in premodern society, had required both the appointment of guardians for unprofessional single women and the endowment of professional women with a proper legal status exempting them from such guardianship.

Prodded by the Esslingen court, the city council of Hall agreed to hear Anna's complaints against her father on September 12, 1525, and promised a quick decision. Anna and her lawyer also received a comprehensive safe-conduct for the journey to and from the hearing.[27] When the day of the hearing arrived, the two of them faithfully appeared, documented Anna's need, and made the case for immediate paternal support (*forderung pro alimentis*).

Present also at the hearing was, of course, her father, who, having come prepared for a fight, was eager for one after hearing his daughter denounce him in his own chambers. Immediately upon the presentation of her case, he asked his colleagues for a delay of forty-five days to prepare a response. Given the urgency of her situation, Anna strongly resisted the delay, but the council deferred to its leader and granted it over her protest.

Not to be so easily outdone, Anna countered with a request of her own. Inasmuch as she was then without means and the council's decision would now be at least seven weeks in coming, might the council order her father to arrange room and board for her in the city, or failing that, give her the money to do so herself, thereby enabling her to await the ruling in Hall, comfortably sheltered? The council refused to issue such an order, and it also denied her subsequent request to lodge at city hall during the interim. That left Anna with no choice but to return to Esslingen, which she did with the council's permission.[28]

 Surreptitious Capture

HAVING GAINED VALUABLE TIME, HERMANN BÜSCHLER TOOK A leaf out of his daughter's book. Unknown to her, and also to the vast majority of his peers in the city council, he hastily journeyed to Esslingen and petitioned the imperial ruling council (*Reichsregiment*) on his own behalf against his daughter. That body had only recently, and reluctantly, been revived (1522) by the emperor and was destined soon to disappear (1529), because it competed with his authority, notwithstanding the presence of his deputy at its meetings. Composed of rep-

resentatives of the German princely estates and imperial cities and
chaired by one of the seven electoral princes, the council claimed full
authority in ruling the empire, including the enforcement of the decisions of the imperial supreme court.[29]

Because of the pending action between father and daughter in Hall,
Hermann Büschler's colleagues in the city council could not properly
have condoned this action had they been aware of it in advance. But
even if they had known about it, it remains an open question whether
they would then have taken measures to block it by directly informing
the Esslingen court of the status of the process in Hall.

Hermann Büschler now asked the imperial ruling council for a special order permitting him by his rights as a father to take his willful
and disobedient daughter, who had since returned to Esslingen, into
his paternal custody and return her to her home in Hall, if necessary
by force. To justify his request, he portrayed her character and behavior to the council in terms Anna would later dismiss as wholly slan-
derous. And as she and her lawyer would also point out after the fact,
he neglected to inform Esslingen of the litigation then pending with
his daughter in Hall. Clearly, Hermann Büschler had found Anna's
case against him to be a compelling one, which she might conceivably
win even in Hall. So he now sought to neutralize it by a new, super-
seding legal action of his own.

How is Esslingen's seeming negligence in allowing Hermann Büschler to gain the upper hand in so devious a manner to be explained?
According to Anna's lawyer, her father was able to work his will on
the council thanks to the assistance of powerful cronies in Hall (particularly syndic Jacob Kröl) and Esslingen, where authorities made no
effort to investigate the circumstances of his petition or to check the
accuracy of the facts of the case as he portrayed them. Nor did they
consult Anna on the matter, something they might have been expected
to do, inasmuch as Esslingen had originally directed her case to Hall.

There are, however, other possible explanations for Esslingen's jux-
taposed and seemingly contradictory orders. Honest oversight is one.
Different lower judges (or assessors) might have staffed the two preliminary hearings, and since both Anna and her father presented what
the imperial supreme court would have considered routine petitions,
the judges could have granted them both without the high court's actually meeting to hear either. That is, judge A could have heard Anna

and judge B her father, and since many such preliminary actions were not recorded, neither might have known of the other's order.[30] And even if the imperial ruling council had been aware of the two petitions, it might still have concluded that the court had done its duty to Anna once it ordered the city council of Hall to hear her case.

Be all this as it may, on October 11, 1525, Hermann Büschler got exactly what he wanted. On that day, the imperial ruling council issued in the emperor's name an order permitting him, by whatever means necessary, to take his daughter back home to Hall—a so-called "mandate for surreptitious capture."[31]

> We Charles V, elected Roman Emperor . . . publicly acknowledge with this letter and declare to everyone, that in response to the complaint and argument officially brought before our imperial government in the Holy Empire by our and the empire's loyal [servant] Hermann Büschler, we grant and allow him, as is proper and in strict accordance with the law, to take, place, and hold in fatherly custody and imprisonment his mischievous, insolent, and disobedient daughter, who is still under paternal authority, and who has in many ways done harm to him, her true legal father, having remarkably often stolen from him secretly and against his will, and in addition disgraced him, and in still other ways behaved in a completely bad and dishonorable way, contrary to maidenly discipline, thereby setting a bad example and giving offense.[32]

The decree also ordered all authorities under imperial jurisdiction, of whatever rank and station, "and especially those of Schwäbisch Hall," neither to delay nor to hinder Hermann Büschler as he passed through their lands, nor to give any heed to the plaintive cries of his captive daughter.

Thus empowered, Hermann Büschler, assisted by a servant, presumably Lienhard Vahmann, located and seized Anna in Esslingen, bound her and placed her in a cart, and transported her back home to Hall. There she remained a prisoner in her father's house for over six months, chained by a foot to an oak table.[33]

Public transport in chains and imprisonment at home was at the time a medically approved and legal procedure for dealing with the mentally ill.[34] Anna, however, was a healthy woman in full possession of her faculties, and one can only imagine the terror and humiliation inflicted on this proud, spirited woman by her seizure, transport, and captivity. The experience left her wounded lifelong, but like a tiger, not a lamb.

In later trial testimony, no one disputed the basic facts of her case as Anna alleged them, not the servants who had been directly on scene, nor the members of the city council who had learned of her distress in the comfort of their taproom. All agreed that she had been taken from Esslingen to Hall against her will and kept as a prisoner in her father's house for half a year, without any protest from or intervention by city officials. Barbara Dollen, who was present in the house during these months, confirmed that Anna had been chained there.[35] Anna herself describes the experience as "a harsh, unusual, unspeakable captivity."[36] The only recorded kindness shown her throughout the ordeal was Vahmann's professed effort to provide her with better wine than he had been ordered to give her by her father.[37]

Anna escaped from her father's house in April 1526, climbing out a high window that had inadvertently been left unlocked. Within days of the escape, however, Hermann Büschler had in hand a new mandate for her recapture—impressive testimony to the emotional ferocity of their relationship and her father's political connections. This time the order came from the court of Margrave Casimir of Brandenburg-Ansbach, the electoral prince then chairing the imperial ruling council, and into whose territory Hermann Büschler believed his daughter had fled. That a new mandate was needed suggests that the first had been specific to place and/or time and carried no weight within the margrave's territory, or if it did, had by this time expired. Again, it was obtained with the help of a well-placed ally, Hermann Büschler's brother-in-law Wolf Oeffner, then the margrave's chancellor.[38] The new order, issued on April 11, 1526, gave Hermann Büschler a free hand to hunt for his daughter in the margravial lands of Werdeck and Bamberg. Nobleman Wilhelm von Vellberg, in whose service Daniel Treutwein at this time rode, was Werdeck's bailiff, and her father possibly suspected that she had fled to that area in search of Daniel.[39]

Anna, however, was not about to fall into her father's clutches again. Far from having been broken by his cruelty, she had been transformed into a warrior by the ordeal in Hall, and while she would never know real victory in the contests that lay ahead, she, not her father, would henceforth be the aggressor in their legal battles.

 Fighting Back

MAKING HER WAY TO HEILBRONN, ANNA TOOK REFUGE WITH MAternal relatives there. Around this same time, she married a poor nobleman and reputed compulsive gambler, Hans von Leuzenbrunn. If the rumor of his gambling is as true as it appears, he and Anna may have been kindred spirits, for she too had a penchant for taking chances. She also found in him a man who, again like herself, could take inspiration from outrageous fortune and subsist on righteous anger.

On June 7, 1526, the pair asked the imperial court in Esslingen to hear her case against her father, who was still hotly pursuing her.[40] When that highest court declined, ostensibly because of its previous rulings in the dispute, the Leuzenbrunns turned to the lower imperial court in Rottweil, which had both original and appellate jurisdiction over Hall. Historically, the relationship between the two had been a special one. In the late fifteenth century, Rottweil had come to Hall's defense after the territorial court of Würzburg attempted to extend its jurisdiction over the city. Thereafter, Hall looked on Rottweil as a friendly court, partial to local jurisdiction.[41] That perception began to change, however, after Anna successfully filed suit against the city there.

Anna's new charges held the city council of Hall equally responsible with her father for the treatment she had received at his hands, and she now demanded compensation from the city as well. Despite the council's safe-conduct and promise to process her complaint against her father with dispatch, it had postponed a decision for seven weeks, before the passage of which she had found herself taken captive, imprisoned, and "cruelly tormented"[42] for half a year by her father, while the councilmen of Hall had stood silently by. Her new brief further alleged that she had been forced to endure ridicule, shame, illness, loss of jewelry and clothing, and treatment "contrary to her maidenly modesty" while in her father's house.[43] She was convinced that had God not inspired a sympathetic old woman to assist her escape out a high window, she would have grown old and died in the prison created for her by her father.[44]

As her lawyer described them, those experiences had been her worst, but they were by no means the last of her father's cruelties. Hermann Büschler's successful appeal to the imperial ruling council had also interrupted the legal action she had brought against him in Hall. After her imprisonment in his house, the city council had simply allowed that action to die, thereby compounding the injustice done her by her father by denying her due process as well. For this too she held the city as responsible as her father. Once the council had learned that her father had taken her captive, did the city not have an obligation to inform the Esslingen court that she was under its safe-conduct and that a litigation was pending with her father in Hall? And knowing that she was in her father's house against her will, had the council not been obligated by the safe-conduct and the pending litigation to rescue her immediately and place her in its protective custody?[45]

In suing the city as well as her father, Anna demonstrated not only her determination to pursue justice for herself, but her enterprise as well. One of the conclusions of her petition to the Rottweil court reopening the case reads: "Anna would much prefer to lose or never to have had five-thousand gulden, if such could be hers, than to endure again the disgrace, insult, and loss she suffered at the hands of her father by such imprisonment." Inasmuch as the loss or denial of five-thousand gulden seemed to her a comparable experience to the one she had gone through, that very sum was what she now asked the court in Rottweil to order the city of Hall to pay her in damages on pain of outlawry.[46]

The shock of that ruling was clear in the city council's response. It hastily delivered to the Rottweil court a thickly documented reminder of the city's historical rights and protections from outside interference, replete with copies of letters from emperors Frederick III, Maxmilian, and Charles V. Ironically, this was exactly the kind of protest the Rottweil court had made in the past on the city's behalf, when foreign rulers and courts intruded into Hall's internal affairs.[47] This time, however, the city did not have the court's ear, because Rottweil viewed a breach of safe-conduct by an imperial city as a grave offense, and one well within its jurisdiction to punish.[48] On such assurances the very order of the empire hung. Persuaded that Anna should be compensated for the shame, insult, ridicule, and bodily injury she claimed to have suffered in Hall, Rottweil directed the council to hear her complaint.

Finding itself overridden in the lower imperial court, the council, like Anna and her father before, fled to the higher, asking Esslingen again to intervene in the case. The decision of the Rottweil court, it argued, had been based on false information, which, when corrected, would render its decision "invalid, or at least wrong and contrary to [imperial] law."[49] In making its case, the city presented two winning arguments. First, as a father, Hermann Büschler had a sovereign right to punish a disobedient child for shameful public behavior. The time had not yet come in Europe when children were deemed to be as much the wards of the "state" as of their parents, although the Lutherans were then beginning to make such claims in their school ordinances and catechisms. Urging princes and magistrates to provide compulsory secular and religious education for all boys and girls, Martin Luther informed parents that their children were "more God's than theirs," and hence they also "belonged" to magistrates and teachers, who shared with parents the responsibility to raise them up to be the men and women God required.[50]

While the councilmen of Hall did not necessarily approve of everything Hermann Büschler did in his capacity as a parent, they believed they had no power to intervene on Anna's behalf, once Esslingen had awarded her father a custodial mandate permitting her seizure and return to the parental home. By that order, not only did Hermann Büschler have the emperor's leave to take his daughter, but all of his actions pursuant to the mandate remained outside the city's jurisdiction. Indeed, the mandate had made a point of instructing "the bürgermeister, city council, and imperial mayor (*schultheiss*) of Schwäbisch Hall" *not* to interfere.

If that were not enough to tie the city's hands legally, the council had itself earlier placed clear limits on its responsibility for Anna's welfare and safety in Hall. The safe-conduct originally given her, and in the name of which she was now suing the city along with her father, had been strictly occasional and of limited duration, and it had already expired by the time her father seized her in Esslingen. Never, the council maintained, had the city intended its safe-conduct to be construed as an open-ended, lifetime guarantee; it applied only to Anna's travel to and from the city on the day of her hearing. When her father took her captive in Esslingen, she had already returned there safely from Hall, as the city had in good faith promised she would do, thereby fulfilling its promise of safe-conduct.[51]

Anna, of course, did not find the council's rebuttal of Rottweil's ruling persuasive, and she begged the court in Esslingen to reject it as well. Having succeeded in giving the councilmen of Hall a good scare, she did not want the process to end there. As far as she was concerned, the only pertinent condition for any action on her behalf by the city council of Hall was the fact of her incapacitating poverty.[52] When Esslingen now overruled Rottweil, denying her the damages the latter had proposed and returning the case to Hall for a new hearing, Anna could not have mistaken the loss of the best opportunity she would have to get even with her father.

In December 1526, a subpoena to that hearing was prepared for Anna. A note scribbled on the extant court copy by an unforgiving scribe tells of his attempt to deliver it to her at a prearranged place at the Esslingen town wall. According to the scribe, when the two met at the site, Anna informed him that the subpoena did not belong to her and refused to take it. The annoyed scribe claims that as she walked away he deposited the spurned summons "in a shit hole" on the wall where the two had met. When he departed, he noticed from a distance that Anna returned to the spot and took it.[53]

The return of the case to Hall's jurisdiction could only have brought joy to the council. Painfully aware of their vanishing opportunity, the Leuzenbrunns protested that Rottweil was a celebrated court from which no issue of law or safe-conduct could properly be released or redirected.[54] But their arguments accomplished nothing and must by now have seemed even pitiable. The overturned ruling of the Rottweil court would remain the most favorable Anna received during nearly three decades of litigation with her family. She had gotten in her licks, to be sure, but the opposition had escaped unfazed.

This particular episode was now finished. Neither Hermann Büschler nor the city of Hall would be punished for Anna's six-month imprisonment in her father's house. Of the original demands in her Rottweil petition only that for parental support still remained viable,[55] and she and her husband would soon pursue that request by another route.

Incest?

THE RELATIONSHIP BETWEEN ANNA AND HER LOVERS IS STRAIGHT-forward enough. It is that with her father that remains bizarre and begs further explanation. Here was a man of local prominence who freely allowed, and may even have encouraged, his daughter to dress in a provocative way, thereafter to reprimand her when, predictably, as he himself must have known, she caused a public scandal. If Anna is to be believed, her father also prevented her from marrying when it was more than fitting for her to do so, and when her behavior with suitors was making them both subjects of gossip. Having endured her thieving and cavorting with Daniel Treutwein, Hermann Büschler must have considered the discovery of her long-hidden affair with the future Schenk of Limpurg the last straw, and he drove her from his home and eventually out of Hall as one would a common criminal. But he then brought her back against her will, holding her in his house under conditions she herself described as "cruelly tormenting" and "an unspeakable captivity," during which captivity he allegedly also abused her "maidenly modesty." And no sooner did she escape that terrible prison than he began hunting her down again.

While the citizens of Hall had no liking for willful and disobedient children, and to this extent sympathized with Hermann Büschler, there were also those who considered his treatment of Anna unacceptable, even unparental and unnatural, as Anna herself described it. His conduct was sufficiently disgraceful in the eyes of his peers to cause his premature retirement from the city council—although his skirting of the council's authority during a pending litigation probably played the larger role in this. Why had he acted in so self-destructive a fashion? How is his hostility toward Anna to be explained?

So intense and persistent was the hatred between the two that it raises the suspicion that something profoundly disturbing to them both had occurred in their relationship. A modern reader may even detect a hint of incest in Anna's allegation that her father treated her "contrary to her maidenly modesty" while she was a prisoner in his house. He had been married to her mother for twenty-five years when she died in 1520, and one may wonder how easily he might have seen

the mother in the now grown daughter, after Anna returned from castle Limpurg to assume her place within his household. The main reason
he alleged for not wanting Anna to marry and leave the paternal home
was that she would nowhere have it so good as she would there with
him.[56]

There is also evidence that Hermann Büschler's relationships with
women after the death of Anna's mother were troubled. He had two
brief marriages after Anna left his household in 1525, one of which
ended in divorce. The first, in 1528, was to a local woman, Elisabeth
Krauss, who appears to have died within the same year. In 1529, he
married Barbara Eitelwein, a native of Heilbronn,[57] forty kilometers
to the west. After two years, she left him "in anger" and returned to
Heilbronn. Hermann Büschler refused to send her some clothes and
furniture she had left behind in Hall until she agreed to pay taxes on
her part of the marital property. Only after the city council of Heilbronn made a formal request on her behalf to its counterpart in Hall
(September 1531), pledging that she would pay her fair share of taxes
in due course, were her belongings sent.

Hermann Büschler had been Barbara Eitelwein's third marriage as
well, and she, like him, had a reputation for toughness and double-
dealing in family matters. After her first husband's death, his nephew
had contested her right to an inheritance, alleging that she had conspired with his Franciscan confessor to coerce the poor man into
changing his will to their benefit on his deathbed.[58] In Barbara Eiten-
wein, apparently, Hermann Büschler had met his match. After her
departure from Hall, he declared her no longer to be his wife,[59] and
their marriage was evidently annulled. He did not marry again.

Whatever suspicions of incestuous feelings or actions between father
and daughter might be extrapolated from such relationships, to indulge
them would be to speculate well beyond and against the evidence.
Certainly if anything of the sort had ever occurred, Anna could and
would have used it against him to very good effect. She gives a far
more plausible explanation of her father's behavior when she describes
him as an all too proud man who acted out of anger and greed. Hermann Büschler had liked the idea of having his eldest daughter return
home and replace her deceased mother in his home as his housekeeper.
She was to be both a loyal servant and an ornament of his power in
Hall. That contemporaries thought the arrangement strange and that

Anna believed it to be against her best interests were of no importance to him. He expected her to be grateful and to perform her duties with the same self-discipline and skill that he performed his. As the daughter of a legend, she had a lot to live up to. When she instead brought him embarrassment and shame, "inflexible, harsh, unforgiving anger" was the result, and he thereafter stalked and punished her as if she were an animal.

From Hermann Büschler's own reported comments, the discovery of his daughter's secret life had deeply shaken him. The realization that she preferred keeping house for the Schenkin to being the "mistress" of his own only confirmed her disloyalty. And it was a dagger in the parental heart to hear her wish him dead. That she should think of him as the obstacle to her happiness rather than as its generous source was ingratitude beyond the pale. Why else had he brought her home to live with him? Why had he indulged her so and given her so much slack? Had he not trusted her to run his grand house and look after his affairs in his absence? Could she not have known of the pride he took in her beauty and industry?

In the end, both father and daughter believed they had been betrayed by the other in the most unkind and unprincipled fashion—Anna by the denial of marriage and by physical abuse, her father by disloyalty and loss of reputation. From that sense of mutual betrayal sprang life-long enmity.

The major structure of the manor Lindenhof, as it exists today in the small, three-building farm a few miles north of Hall. After the family house in the city, Lindenhof was the major piece of fixed joint property in the Büschler family inheritance. On the threshold can still be seen the green and gold coats of arms of the subsequent owners, Hans Ludwig Adler of Unterlimpurg and his wife Agnes (born Senfft), dated 1611.

CHAPTER

FOUR

Half a Loaf

IN THE OVERLAPPING WORLDS OF SIXTEENTH-CENTURY POLITICS and religion, the 1520s were a decade of new protests, failed negotiations, and discouraging prospects for peace and unity in the Holy Roman Empire. Deep fissures appeared in both the family of nations and the structure of the Church. In the rapidly changing political and religious climate, the animosities of old enemies were rekindled, and old friends were torn apart as well. Concerted efforts at reconciliation and reunion foundered on stubborn regional pride and inflexible tradition. In the conflicts that followed, the bullying of the victors and the humiliation of the losers seemed to reach new heights and depths. The foundations for a century and more of territorial and religious wars were being laid.

In 1525, Spain and France clashed in the first of four major wars over disputed territories (the Habsburg-Valois wars, after the ruling dynasties), which would not end until 1559. On February 4, at Pavia in northern Italy, Habsburg forces handed the French their most humiliating defeat since the battle of Agincourt (1433), even taking the French king, Francis I (d. 1547), who had been fortunate to survive the slaughter, captive back to Madrid. There, for over a year, he would remain a most unhappy prisoner of Emperor Charles V, who seemed not to know what to do with his prize catch. His English ally, King Henry VIII, did not doubt the right course of action: the emperor should immediately take off Francis's head and eradicate the Valois dynasty while the chance was there—an action more easily carried out against English queens than against a foreign head of state.[1] In the end, the emperor's inability to act decisively combined with the French king's willingness to capitulate utterly to win the latter's release. The enabling instrument was the Treaty of Madrid (January 14, 1526), by which the French king renounced all claims to the disputed territories, agreed to marry the emperor's eldest sister (the recently widowed queen of Portugal), and even left his two sons behind in Madrid as hostages. But as the treaty had been signed under duress, it could not legally bind either Francis or, much less, France. To no one's surprise, except perhaps the emperor, the French king joined other Habsburg foes in a new military alliance (the League of Cognac) within two months of his release.

Among the signatories to that ill-fated alliance was the Medici pope, Clement VII (d. 1534), who, with his Church, now also fell afoul of the emperor and, like the French king, paid dearly for his defection. Threatened by the Habsburg Italian army, the pope quit the alliance, but not soon enough to prevent the sacking of Rome by mutinous Spanish and German soldiers and his own subsequent imprisonment in San Angelo. The sacking of Rome on May 6, 1527, has since been remembered both as a day of infamy in the history of the Church and as marking the cultural decline of the Italian Renaissance. Two years later, Habsburg forces gained their second victory over the French in Italy, exacting as the price of the pope's rehabilitation in the settlement that followed Pope Clement's recognition of Spanish claims to Naples and his crowning of the triumphant emperor in Bologna, the last papal coronation of a Holy Roman Emperor.[2]

Similar bitter division, bullying, and humiliation were the order of the decade also on the religious front. In Zurich, the Swiss reformer Ulrich Zwingli (d. 1531) led a successful second Reformation, in place by 1525, that was more socially and politically ambitious than Luther's. The result was a new, powerful, competing Protestant confession in the south, which would eventually evolve into Reformed Protestantism and embrace both the Calvinist and Zwinglian churches. Contemplating a powerful alliance between German and Swiss Protestants, Landgrave Philip of Hesse—with the elector of Saxony, political and military leader of the German Lutherans—brought Zwingli and Luther together in his castle in Marburg for the first four days of October 1529. His hope had been that the two might thrash out their theological differences quickly and create a doctrinal statement around which the two churches and the two lands could unite. Not only did the two great reformers fail to agree on fundamental doctrine, but each departed the colloquy more bigoted than ever and the lifelong enemy of the other.[3] By 1530, Lutherans and Zwinglians had their own confessions of faith (the Augsburg Confession and the Tetrapolitan Confession respectively) and their own military alliances (the Schmalkaldic League for the Lutherans, the union of Swiss Protestant cantons for the Zwinglians).

Zwinglianism was not the only Protestant confession the Swiss created. The first Protestant sect was born there as well, a splinter of Zwingli's reform its critics called Anabaptism. It had hardly appeared when Zurich's authorities declared it a capital crime (March 1525), as the emperor would also later do (twice, in fact, in 1528 and 1529). Anabaptists were biblical literalists and pacifists who rejected Zwingli's reform because of what they considered to be its slow pace and conservatism. Their persecutors identified the movement with its rejection of infant baptism ("anabaptism" means rebaptism), and acceptance of only adult baptism, a point of view deemed to be both treasonable and heretical. That was because the centuries-old rite of infant baptism had been Christendom's way of welcoming a new generation into the community of Christians and citizens, a pledge to rear and teach the young from infancy the civic virtues and religious truths of the society into which they were born. For Catholics, Lutherans, and Zwinglians alike, the baptism of infants remained an essential part of the ecclesiastical and social order. Zurich gave Anabaptists one week to submit their children for baptism or face summary execution or exile.[4]

As Zurich's reform movement split into orthodox and heretical camps, the thirteen cantons (or states) of the Swiss confederacy also divided along confessional lines and armed for war. Righteous armies of Zwinglians and Catholics clashed for the first time at Kappel in the summer of 1529 and then again in October 1531. The latter engagement left Zwingli wounded on the battlefield, there to be tormented, quartered, and burned by his captors, his ashes dunged over and scattered about, so that no relics might be taken by his followers.[5]

By the end of the 1520s, it was already clear that there would be no quick or easy reconciliation between the Lutherans and the Church of Rome. When, at the imperial Diet of Speyer in 1529, the emperor ordered Lutherans throughout the empire to return their lands virtually to the Catholic status quo ante, the Lutheran delegation made its famous "*protestatio*," from which event and term the name "Protestantism" has derived. By mid-century, the division of Christendom along strict confessional lines, which had de facto been the practice in

Switzerland and parts of Germany since the late 1520s, became imperial law. After 1555, the ruler of each land would determine its religious confession (*cuius regio, eius religio*), and those who dissented might convert, emigrate to a land of their choice, be exiled, or simply die.

 A Deal on the Maternal Inheritance

THE LATE 1520S WERE ALSO A TIME OF NEW PROTEST, FAILED NEgotiation, and discouraging prospects for peace and unity in the Büschler family. According to witnesses, Hermann Büschler completely ignored his daughter and her new husband from the day of their marriage (sometime after April 1526); not only would he give them nothing, he refused even to meet and talk to them.[6] Such treatment combined with the pair's hard times to keep the litigation over Anna's support and maternal inheritance alive and fierce, beginning in 1526 with the suit in the Rottweil court. Then suddenly, in 1528, in a claimed effort to end the pair's "harassment" of him, Hermann Büschler offered them a deal.

Three major events combined to trigger this brief rapprochement: Anna's marriage to Hans von Leuzenbrunn, her father's remarriage to Elisabeth Krauss,[7] and the death of her brother, Hermann, Jr.

In German law, when a father or a mother died, the children of the marriage to a large degree took on the legal person of the dead spouse. Because of the law's strong bias toward the husband in property matters, that was a more difficult role for children to play with a surviving father than with a surviving mother. There were a great many German law codes, as each sovereign entity had its own; almost two hundred different systems of property law, combining elements of these many codes, exist today in the lands of the old German empire.[8] Most of these codes gave the husband legal control over all the goods and property a wife brought into a marriage or acquired during the marriage, regardless of whether they were to remain her sole property. Save in a dire emergency, he could not, however, dispose of them without the wife's consent, and the same was true of the joint property of the marriage. The same rule applied to the surviving children of the marriage after the death of *either* spouse. Neither a surviving mother nor father could legally dispose of the children's inheritance without the latter's express consent, especially when the inheritance in question was ancestral land (*Erbgut*), normally deemed untouchable.[9]

The surviving spouse, then, held virtual full power of administration, usufruct, and alienation over the joint property of the marriage, as well as over any property belonging to the deceased spouse. These properties were not, however, to be diminished during the surviving parent's years of stewardship, and were expected to increase in value. This was one of the reasons why male guardians or trustees were appointed to advise widows and oversee the education and inheritance of their children after the death of the husband and father. When a parent died, inheritable family property was "sequestered" for the children, who would eventually divide it, and who for this reason had a vital interest in its proper maintainance and successful management. The surviving parent could not alienate such property without the consent of all heirs, which often meant the consent of their guardians, nor, if that consent was given and inheritable property disposed of, without then also fairly compensating each of the heirs for the loss. For this reason, children's property came to be called "iron property"; children were to receive it undiminished in the value it possessed at sequestration.

Several events might trigger the awarding of a grown child's portion before the death of both parents: a child's reaching majority age, a daughter's marriage, a surviving parent's remarriage, and/or evidence of parental mismanagement of the family estate. Whether a child's request for his or her portion under one or more of these circumstances was actually granted still remained the parent's decision. Reaching majority age did not automatically release a child from paternal authority or entitle the child to an inheritance. If the child remained in the parental home and dependent upon the parent(s) for support, paternal authority might continue just as if the child were still a minor.[10] That had been Anna's situation as late as 1525: a woman of at least twenty-seven years living at home with a father on whom she was completely dependent for her livelihood. The ability of a mature child to depart the parental home and begin an independent life, which normally happened when a daughter married, ended paternal authority and occasioned the distribution of inheritance almost always without a fight. As would happen with Anna's brother Philip when he married, a major part of that inheritance might be a dwelling in which the newlyweds henceforth lived. Often the newlyweds resided initially in one of the parental homes, most often that of the groom, which eldest sons could expect someday to inherit.

The other circumstance that normally occasioned the distribution of inheritance without a fight was the remarriage of the surviving parent.[11] Remarriage could occasion a change in the living conditions of surviving minor children, those of remarried widowers normally staying with the new family, while the children of remarried widows might move in with the deceased father's nearest male relative, who was also likely to be the legal guardian.

Two of the above events occurred in the Büschler family between 1526, when Anna, having departed home, married Hans von Leuzenbrunn, and 1528, when her father, staying put in his great house in Hall, married Elisabeth Krauss. It was the death of her brother Hermann, Jr.,[12] apparently also in 1528, that now moved Anna to demand a full settlement of her maternal inheritance and a slice of her deceased brother's share of it as well. She and her husband acted with a sense of urgency at this time for two reasons: they had outstanding debts, mostly her husband's, of almost eight hundred gulden,[13] and they had reason to believe that her father was illegally rearranging family property and wealth to favor her brother Philip and to disinherit her.

Anna and her siblings were assured of a share of the maternal and joint family inheritance not only by statute. There also existed a prenuptial agreement or "marriage contract," as it was then called, between her father and mother. Agreement between the two families on the conditions of a marriage was commonplace at all levels of urban society, and of great importance to well-endowed families like the Büschlers, who had gotten rich as wine merchants, and among the nobility, from whose ranks in Rothenburg Anna Hornberger had come. At the time of their marriage in 1495, Hermann Büschler and Anna Hornberger carefully defined the distribution of property in the event of their deaths. Such contracts carried great weight and could significantly supplement or alter statutory law. "A contract breaks the law of a land" (*Gedinge bricht Landrecht*), as a popular saying put it.[14] The agreement signed by Anna's parents placed clear conditions and limits on the disposition of maternal and joint marital property by either surviving spouse. It would become Anna's major weapon in her fight for a fair share of the family estate, first with her father and then, after his death, with her siblings.

According to the marriage contract, a complete inventory of all family property would be made upon the death of either spouse. That inventory was to restate what each party had originally brought to the marriage and specify what the two together had acquired thereafter, thus carefully defining maternal, paternal, and joint family property.[15] When Hermann Büschler married Anna Hornberger in 1495, she presented as her dowry (*heyratsgut*) all her real property and fixtures.[15] As a return gift to her (*widerlegung*), he pledged three thousand gulden, which his mother guaranteed. On their wedding day, he also gave her a bridegroom's gift (*morgengabe*) of four hundred gulden, all intended for her support should she become widowed.

If Hermann Büschler predeceased Anna Hornberger, she had the right to occupy and enjoy their collective property and possessions conjointly with any children born of the union for as long as she remained a widow. From that wealth she would support herself and raise the children, and as they came of age, award each a fair share of the family estate (maternal, paternal, and joint). Should, however, the widow take a new husband, or for any other reason choose not to be with her minor children, who in such circumstances normally became the wards of the paternal family, she could take with her into her new husband's household only the four-hundred-gulden bridegroom's gift and her own personal items. In addition, she would receive a third of the joint family property if the union produced only one child, and an equal child's share if there were more than one.

Should Anna Hornberger predecease Hermann Büschler, as the case would be, it was his charge to manage the property faithfully on the children's behalf and apportion each child according to the will of both families when the time was right, the remainder being sequestered for the children.[16] Should he remarry, he could award his second wife a marriage portion no greater than one thousand gulden of his own property. Should he predecease her and there be children from the second marriage, the surviving wife would keep the marriage portion and whatever she originally brought to the marriage, sharing both with the children as she saw fit. Any surviving children from Hermann

Büschler's first marriage would at this time also receive any undistributed maternal inheritance from that marriage.

As for the conveyance of paternal and joint inheritance to the offspring of Hermann Büschler from any and all of his possible marriages, his children were to share and share alike, no one child, regardless of birth order, receiving any more than another.[17] This particular clause in the contract was designed more to protect the children of the first marriage than to foreclose altogether biased inheritance strategies that might keep the greater part of a family's land and property intact, as would happen with the Büschlers. Regardless of the surviving spouse, the marriage contract of 1495 empowered the nearest relatives, on behalf of the children, to monitor and evaluate annually the management of the family estate.

The contract carried a special instruction to Hermann Büschler. He was to "secure honorably" for his bride and their children his promised marriage portion and bridesgroom's gift,[18] which would appear to have created a tidy 3,400-gulden maternal estate to support Anna Hornberger in her widowhood, should he predecease her, and to provide an adequate stake for any children they might have, should she also predecease them.

What Anna actually received in maternal inheritance in 1528 fell well short of the above theoretical share of 3,400 gulden divided equally among the four then apparently surviving children, namely, Anna, her brothers, Philip and Bonaventure, and her sister, Agatha.[19] The agreement reached with her father gave the Leuzenbrunns only 397 gulden in two equal payments—and strictly on the condition that they solemnly promise never to ask him for anything else again. At the same time, the city council ruled that Anna should receive one-fifth of her deceased brother's share of the maternal inheritance, apparently a principle of division that gave the four children and their father an equal part.[20]

Bürgermeister Lienhard Feuchter personally conducted the negotiations, collecting the money from Hermann Büschler and delivering it to the Leuzenbrunns in the privacy of his own living room.[21] Both sides recognized these payments to be settlement in full of Anna's claim to both a maternal inheritance and a marriage portion, and as ending any further demand on her part for material support of any kind from her father. The key passage in the agreement reads:

Hermann Büschler shall convey to me, Anna Büschler, on the date of this letter, as my maternal inheritance and portion, [along with] jewelry, ornaments, and cockades, three hundred and ninety-seven gulden in current coinage. In return, I shall not approach or trouble Hermann Büschler, my father, for any dowry or portion, clothes or jewelry, either in or out of court, as long as he lives. Nor shall my father and his heirs have any responsibility for settling or paying any debts, legal costs, or other expenses I have incurred, and they shall in no way be held liable for them.[22]

By every measure, the agreement favored her father. For what was for him a very manageable sum of money, he had settled the matter of Anna's maternal inheritance and apparently silenced her for the remainder of his life. Her estranged brother Philip and sister Agatha would later attempt to give the agreement of 1528 an even broader scope by invoking it as a precedent for denying Anna a share of the family inheritance as well.[23]

The Leuzenbrunns, however, were not to be so easily bought off. Despite the sizable legal obstacle placed in their path by the agreement they now had signed, they refused to accept it as the last word on the maternal inheritance, much less as any precedent for excluding Anna from a share of the family inheritance upon her father's death. Turning again to the courts, Anna claimed in a new brief to have been cheated out of more than half of what was justly due her in maternal inheritance,[24] apparently calculating her fair share to be in the neighborhood of eight hundred gulden. Henceforth, she would describe the money given her in settlement of the maternal inheritance as only a "nominal" payment in lieu of a full share,[25] which, until the latter was received, left her right to inherit still intact and "unsatisfied."

That Anna and her husband signed the agreement without first having raised and satisfied such suspicions is an indication, first, of their pressing need to satisfy their creditors, and second, of an unfortunate tendency on Anna's part, which will be seen again, to grab what the moment offers and not to ponder what the future holds.

The New Son-in-Law

THE NEGOTIATIONS LEADING TO THE AGREEMENT OF 1528 CRE-
ated very bad blood between Hermann Büschler and his new son-in-
law. Because Anna was now out of home, over twenty-five years of
age, and receiving assistance from maternal relatives and friends, she
did not require parental consent to marry, and Leuzenbrunn had been
a husband of her choosing, not of her father's.[26] A nobleman fallen on
hard times, apparently of his own making, Leuzenbrunn lived well
beneath his titled station in life, and the affluence and power of Anna's
burgher father filled him with envy and resentment. In addition, he
and Anna had belatedly concluded that her father had cheated them
out of a fair share of Anna's maternal inheritance, something they must
already have suspected when they were eagerly taking what he offered
them. To make matters worse still, Hermann Büschler spared his son-
in-law's feelings no more than he did those of his daughter, treating
Leuzenbrunn with an arrogance and disdain the fallen nobleman found
unbearable. Add to this Leuzenbrunn's belief that his father-in-law
was illegally diverting joint marital property to son Philip while neither
consulting nor compensating Anna, a legal heir, as the law required,
and one begins to understand why the Leuzenbrunns pursued this
dispute all the way to their graves.

Although Hermann Büschler had all of the advantages in the contest,
he incautiously gave the Leuzenbrunns a sound legal ground for new
litigation in 1534. In that year, they caught him in a flagrant violation
of the marriage contract of 1495. Contrary to that agreement, he had
awarded Philip, as a wedding gift, a manor in Lindenau, north of the
city, variously referred to as Lindenhof or Lindenauer Hof, with an
estimated value of one thousand gulden. The manor was uncontestably
joint marital property and had possibly been brought into the marriage
by Anna's mother as part of her dowry. As such, it was legally destined
to be shared equally by the surviving children upon their father's death.

As Hermann Büschler's last will and testament would later acknowledge, Philip also received other properties and goods (so-called *prelegata*) in advance of his father's setting the formal inheritance, the
minimal "third" of his goods and chattels[27] which the law required be

shared equally by the surviving children as their due and proper portion. Among Philip's other gifts which might arguably be designated joint property were a twelve-hundred-gulden bond with a sixty-gulden annual income and the family house and courtyards in Hall, valued at one thousand gulden. Still other properties bequeathed in advance by Hermann Büschler were his vineyard and winepress, which were given to Philip's son, Hermann, his grandfather's namesake.[28]

In favoring Philip in these ways, Hermann Büschler neither consulted the other known surviving siblings (Agatha and Anna), who were equal heirs to this property, nor took any steps at the time to compensate them for this lost share of the family estate. Legally, the consent of the offspring was as necessary for the disposal of joint marital property as the consent of a living spouse. A major asset was thus taken from the testamentary estate and prematurely awarded to a favored son in a preemptive strike on the family inheritance. To add insult to injury, Hermann Büschler appraised the manor at roughly the price he and Anna's mother had originally paid rather than at its present market value, which the Leuzenbrunns claimed was more than double that appraisal, or in excess of two thousand gulden. In fact, the two major properties Hermann Büschler gave his son as *prelegata* (the Lindenau manor and the family house in Hall) at an estimated combined value of 2,000 gulden had originally cost him 2,200 gulden,[29] so Philip got these properties on exceedingly favorable terms. The arrangement increased still further his lion's share of the family estate, while at the same time lowering the value of the "third" the three would share after their father's death.

In most German lands in the late fifteenth and early sixteenth century, partible or equal inheritance was the rule, and it would continue to be such in most Protestant lands until the mid-seventeenth century. It was, however, modified in the direction of primogeniture, a practice more widespread in England and other European lands than in Germany, and in Germany more popular among Catholics than Protestants, for whom the equal treatment of children became something of a divinely decreed parental duty. Partible inheritance did not prevent favoring the eldest son in property inheritance. Not only could he inherit the parental home, as Anna's brother Philip would do, but he might also receive a disproportionate share of ancestral land. However, he did so legally only on the condition that he fairly compensate his younger brothers and sisters either by a direct cash payment or by providing them with a reliable stream of income (annuities) during their lifetimes.[30] In this way, a family home, or a disproportionate share of the propertied estate, might in fact be given to the eldest son and through him continue intact within the family without creating the division and resentment occasioned elsewhere by the strict practice of primogeniture. However, setting fair compensation for younger siblings within a modified system of partible inheritance could be as disruptive of family unity as strict primogeniture, as, again, would be the case with the Büschler siblings.

It was in search of such fair compensation for Anna that her husband now brought the example of the manor to the attention of the city council, citing it as only the more outrageous of his father-in-law's violations of his wife's testamentary rights. The marriage contract had carefully defined the possessions each party might call his or her own and dispose of as he or she pleased, denying one child and favoring another. Hermann Büschler held such power over his horse, clothing, and armor, while Anna Hornberger might freely dispose of her clothes, jewelry, embellishments, and cockades.[31] Nowhere did the agreement give either spouse such power over shared real property, which was destined to be divided equally among the surviving children upon the death of the last spouse. Until that day came, the surviving spouse had full use of such property, but no power to alienate any part of it from the common inheritance of the children.

To document further the charge that his father-in-law was improperly disposing of testamentary property, Leuzenbrunn submitted a letter Hermann Büschler had written to Philip four years earlier, in 1530. He had intercepted the letter at the time and had apparently been keeping it under wraps until the time was right to reveal it. In the letter, Hermann Büschler asks Philip's advice about selling "many outlying old houses," presumably minor holdings outside Hall's walls, to settle his growing indebtedness. He also mentions having been forced to give four hundred gulden "to the bad whore" (*der bosen huren*), the outlay of which he now wanted to recoup by selling the family silverware,[32] assuming Philip had no objections. The bad whore could only have been Anna and the four hundred gulden the share of maternal inheritance he had agreed to pay her in 1528. Could there now be any doubt that Hermann Büschler was illegally disposing of family property for his own gain, and favoring his eldest son to the detriment of his other children?[33]

In the same letter, Hermann Büschler further indicated that he had discussed both the marriage contract of 1495 and his last will and testament with key city officials, informing Philip that he looked forward to sharing the results of these discussions with him as soon as the two could meet privately—for Leuzenbrunn, further indication that his father-in-law had understood the legal restraints placed on family property by the marriage contract, and was actively conniving with his son and cronies in city hall to get around them, again at Anna's expense.

The upshot of Leuzenbrunn's protest was a twofold request in a letter to the city council asking that it require Hermann Büschler to make an annual financial report on the family estate, and that it also consider appointing independent curators to manage the estate in his place.[34] In the event of either spouse's death, the marriage contract of 1495 had originally bestowed oversight responsibility of the estate on family representatives. Leuzenbrunn, however, believed that his father-in-law's management of the children's inheritance had proved so untrustworthy that a more searching scrutiny was now required.

Had Leuzenbrunn had his way in this, Hermann Büschler would have been treated more like a widow than a widower. The curatorship he recommends was the rule for surviving mothers,[35] and while demonstrably incompetent fathers might also fall under it, such a ruling would have been out of the ordinary. Over the fourteenth century, the guardians appointed to assist surviving widows (or to act alone if there were none) in managing the estates of orphaned children were required to report twice annually to the city council, or to the local court of highest appeal, on the condition of their wards' inheritance. Whereas older practice had given the guardians the usufruct of a minor child's property as payment for their services, after the fourteenth century, guardians increasingly received set fees, and those who abused their position and power were removed and punished.[36] Passing on the estate of one generation intact to its rightful heirs was as weighty a matter in family law as a legitimate heir's succession to the throne was in royal politics. Civil peace and social order depended on both.

To have succeeded in subjecting his father-in-law to a greater degree of official scrutiny than other fathers having similar conflicts with their children over inheritance would have pleased Leuzenbrunn. In addition, he also hoped to force his father-in-law to restore to the inheritance pool all the joint property that had been illegally alienated, or, failing that, to compensate Anna fully for it, so that she would not be further despoiled by her father.

 A Father's Rights and Responsibilities

NEEDLESS TO SAY, LEUZENBRUNN'S SUIT DID NOT ENDEAR HIM TO his father-in-law. Hermann Büschler was particularly incensed by the submission into evidence of the apparently purloined private letter he had written to his son years before. In rebuttal, he defended his management of the children's estate, both actions taken and contemplated, as competent, prudent, and always intended to increase their wealth, not to swindle them out of it. And he proclaimed it just cause for a parent to disinherit a child, and/or deny a child support, when that child presumed to obstruct the parent's lawful testament or disposition of family property.[37]

This was actually one of ten legally recognized grounds for disinheritance, according to the influential Nürnberg law code of 1479.[38] The other nine were assaulting parents wantonly; plotting grave mischief against them; falsely accusing them of a capital crime, such as treason; a son's attempting to have sex with his stepmother; refusing to make bail for a captive or jailed parent; a son's being a *katzenritter*, or cat knight, that is, behaving like an animal, biting and fighting with cats and other animals (i.e., being insane); a daughter's refusing to take her portion and marry after her father has arranged a marriage for her; and, finally, becoming a heretic when one's family is Christian.

Responding to his son-in-law's request that his stewardship of the family estate be strictly monitored by the council or even taken away from him and placed in the hands of others, Hermann Büschler attacked his son-in-law as a foolish man:

> It has not yet been rumored of Hermann Büschler that he gives away a lot of gold for an egg, or gambles away and squanders his wealth.[39]

For a man all too aware of his fallen state, that accusation cut to the quick. "Had I been the hangman's son," Leuzenbrunn bristled in reply,

> he should not have spoken to me with such disrespect. I have always spared him and not thought that I am of honorable ancestry, a nobleman, and my parents' origins respectable [while his are not]. God willing, I have acted honorably with him, and I want to show [my good faith] as well as a Büschler, even better than any of them. . . . But that his sons sit on chargers and I go back and forth through thorns and fields [on foot], and other of his children have land and property [belonging to my wife], that is madness against God and all fairness![40]

Apart from this emotional outburst, Leuzenbrunn had little to add to his previous accusations. Having exhorted the council to enforce the marriage contract of 1495, he rested his case.

Invited by the council to reply at length, Hermann Büschler admitted to some wrongdoing. On the whole, however, he attempted to explain away his son-in-law's accusations. One of the properties (a garden) supposedly sold at his children's expense he claimed to have been the property of his then new wife,[41] and thus no part of the children's legal inheritance. Two other gardens belonging to them had fetched him only sixty gulden, hardly a huge loss to them, he believed. As for the manor awarded to Philip as a wedding present, that was an act of fatherly generosity, consistent with local custom when grown children married. He insisted, and surely believed in his own mind, that he had been equally generous to Anna when she married, having treated her then "as if she were a loyal, obedient child," and under circumstances that neither justified such kindness on his part nor made it easy for him to express it. He had, after all, given her and her husband a total of 477 gulden in maternal (397) and deceased fraternal (80) inheritance in 1528, more, he declared, than the marriage contract with her mother had required and the two families advised.[42]

In the end, the city council concluded that the old bürgermeister had violated the marriage contract of 1495 when he awarded Philip the Lindenau manor without prior consultation with or compensation for his siblings. The council admonished him henceforth to adhere to that agreement and to present to the council an annual accounting of the family estate. In addition, it saddled him with the Leuzenbrunns' legal fees.[43]

While no compensatory amount or timetable of payments is stated in the council's report, the clear implication was that a fair settlement for the Lindenau manor would be negotiated in the foreseeable future with the other heirs. Hermann Büschler might conceivably have done this by mere retrieval, that is, by undoing his gift and returning the manor to the inheritance pool. Although he had no legal right to dispose of any joint marital property destined equally to the children, he did have sovereign use of the manor and other joint property of the marriage as long as he lived. By that right, he could also have allowed Philip and his new wife to occupy (not own) the manor until his death, after which, if not before, a settlement with Philip's siblings would be determined, as Philip then became its only heir and true owner. Unfortunately for Anna, her father in the meantime remained free to attempt to do posthumously—by amending his last will and testament—all the good or ill he desired for his children.

To the Leuzenbrunns, the council's decision must have seemed a slap on the wrist. Hermann Büschler retained full control of the testamentary property. Philip and his new wife remained in Lindenau, its virtual if not actual owners, and showed every sign of staying there forever. The only thing the council asked of its old friend was a yearly accounting of his stewardship and the payment of some legal fees. And that little bit soon became smaller still, because Hermann Büschler now appealed the city council's ruling to the imperial court. When Esslingen agreed to hear the case, it set in motion a new round of litigation over the Büschler estate, now involving all family members.

*I*n 1546, Anna's brother Philip and sister Agatha appeared on the honor roll of nobility (no. 13) supporting schools and needy students. Married to Wolf Schantz, a Wertheim government official, in 1545, Agatha appears under his name and with his coat of arms: a raven with a golden ring in its mouth, set against a white and black background (bottom right). The Büschler arms—golden spades crossed on a blue background (bottom middle)—appear under Philip's name. Above (left and middle) are Hall's arms: a gold cross on a red shield and a hand (or glove) on a blue shield. Both were coiner's marks (the "Heller" bore a cross and a hand), symbols of the city's autonomy.

The roll is in St. Michael's Church, directly across from the Büschler house.

CHAPTER
FIVE

Siblings

AFTER TWO DEFEATS BY IMPERIAL FORCES IN ITALY, WHERE France and Spain had fought over disputed territories since the early 1520s, the king of France, desperate for a victory, signed a commercial treaty with the sultan of the Ottoman Empire, Suleiman the Magnificent (d. 1566), in 1536. Never mind that this same king bore the title "Most Christian King." Increased commercial contacts with the Ottoman Empire promised a Franco-Ottoman military offensive in Italy that might just give the French king the advantage he so desired.[1] That hope materialized only in his mind's eye, however. That it had been contemplated at all attests the embittered political history of Italy and the Holy Roman Empire during the 1530s and 1540s.

Christian did not need to join Turk against Christian, however, for one side to gain advantage over the other in the now white-hot doctrinal war between Catholics and Protestants in these same decades. The pope accomplished that single-handedly by crushing the fledgling ecumenical movement inspired by religious reformers on both sides. Meeting in the German cities of Worms and Regensburg, the leaders had reached tentative agreement on twenty-three controversial doctrines. Pope Paul III (1534–1549) had earlier pocketed the comparatively mild organizational reforms of his own self-appointed blue-ribbon reform commission (1537), and he was certainly not now going to countenance major doctrinal changes on the recommendation of "liberal" Catholic and Protestant reformers. By the mid-1540s, Catholic housecleaning was safely confined to the carefully controlled Council of Trent (1545–1563) under prominent Jesuit leadership.[2]

The concurrent military contest between Catholics and Protestants within the empire reached its conclusion as well on April 24, 1547, when imperial forces crushed the army of electoral Saxony in a victory that adversely affected all German Protestant cities and territories, including Hall. Suddenly the elector of Saxony and the landgrave of Hesse, the political captains of the Reformation, had become the emperor's prisoners. Carefully chosen surrogates took their places, with a mandate to maintain Catholic religious practice until a new Church council could resolve the doctrinal disputes once and for all. The only Protestant traces to be tolerated were clerical marriage and lay communion with cup and bread.

The emperor's "Interim," as the new arrangement was called, only repelled both sides, however, and gave the conservative forces on each a greater following and authority than before. Discovering that the Reformation was too deeply rooted in Saxony and Hesse to be supplanted by the old faith, even the emperor's puppets soon turned against him. By 1552, the Interim was effectively over, and the road to the permanent division of western Christendom, politically and religiously, stood clear and inviting, as each land was soon to possess the legal right to determine its own religion.[3]

Betrayal and permanent separation also characterized these decades for the Büschler family. By his last will and testament, Hermann Büschler disinherited Anna as completely as he could, thereby transferring the conflict she had pursued with him until his death in 1543 to one she would now have to endure with her siblings until her own death in 1552.

The last years of the old bürgermeister's life had been among his best, and the winter of 1541 was surely one of its peaks. On February 11 of that year, Emperor Charles V had visited Hall en route to Crailsheim and had been a guest in the Büschler house on market square. As the emperor approached the city, an official delegation rode out to meet him. In it were bürgermeister Conrad Büschler, city secretary Maternus Würzelman, and wine merchant Christof Haas, closely followed by forty horsemen. The welcoming committee wore black, as did the emperor, who was then mourning the recent death of his wife. Behind the welcoming committee rode other important civic leaders, each adorned with brightly colored plumes; among them was Anna's brother Philip.

The welcoming party escorted the emperor to the Gelbinger gate, riding directly in front of him, and was followed by a rival Hohenlohe delegation, which had escorted him through their land. At the gate, the emperor received the keys to the city before proceeding to city square. He was very simply dressed in a plain black coat and hat and wore no silk or gold. When he dismounted at the Büschler house, the city presented him with baskets of pike and carp, two wagonloads of oats, and one of wine. In addition, the council gave him a goblet filled with gold pieces. Thereafter, he entered the house of Hermann Büschler and dined.[4]

The lower floors of the Büschler house had originally been the official residence of the imperial mayor (*Reichsschultheiss*), the emperor's representative and watchdog in Hall since before 1212, the first recorded date of the imperial mayor's presence in the city. Attached to it was a modest and carefully maintained royal court, which the emperor and his party had occupied in centuries past during their infrequent visits to the city. In the fourteenth and fifteenth centuries, the building became the domicile of Hall's bürgermeisters. In the sixteenth century, Hermann Büschler acquired it as his private home, although it would later serve again as a residence of Hall's bürgermeisters before being transformed into the city's Ratskeller. Today, the modern Hotel Adelshof stands on the spot and embraces within its bowels the old Büschler house. A figure of the emperor, commemorating his visits to the city in 1541 and in 1546, still decorates the main entrance.

For the evening meal, Hermann Büschler served the following bill of fare, a gourmet's delight, which can still be ordered by parties of four or more at the Hotel Adelshof.

> Purée of smoked trout with a light caper sauce and caviar, delicately arranged on a bed of colored lettuce leaves
> Purée of green pea soup with sour cream, bacon, and coarse-grained rolls
> Pancakes filled with mushrooms, minced egg, and vegetables and fried in lard
> Bits and pieces of Schwäbisch Hall pork in a bacon blanket on grape sauce with steamed turnips and baked semolina dumplings
> Tepid rice paste boiled in almond extract with glacéed pears, sugared cinnamon, and wafer cake
> Honey mead[5]

The following day, the emperor rode east to Crailsheim. Before his death in 1558, he returned to Hall one more time, on December 16, 1546, and remained in the region for a week. He did not come this time, however, as the city's friend, nor was he there to be festively entertained. He arrived with 20,000 men and the duke of Alva (1507–

...se her father owned on Gelbinger Street, outside the old city wall, ... still within a short walking distance from the family house on ...ket square. Her siblings also committed themselves to pay up to ...lve hundred gulden of her indebtedness, which may have been gen-...us, for according to one witness, Anna's "credible and recognized" ...ts stood only at around one thousand gulden.[17]

...Anna also received three beds, three cushions, four pillows, one pair ...bed linens, four tablecloths, six hand towels, three trunks, two tables ...e rimmed with metal), fifty pieces of pewter, some kitchen tools, ...ee silver cups (one a twelve-penny weight), and an alder distaff (pre-...mably with a spinning wheel), or, if she preferred, ten gulden in its ...ace. Her siblings further pledged to provide her every fall with three ...d a quarter bushels of corn, ten of wheat, and two of oats, along ...ith a large barrel of cooking wine and half a barrel of Neckar (drink-...g) wine, none of which, however, she might sell for cash if unused. ...ave for her clothes, which she remained free to dispose of as she chose, ...verything given to her was to be returned upon her death to her ...earest relatives, who, if she remained unmarried and childless, as then ...eemed likely, would be her siblings. Finally, Anna was to receive an ...ighty-gulden annuity for the rest of her life, payable in standard cur-...ency at the rate of twenty gulden per quarter.[18]

Viewed against a possible sixteen-thousand-gulden estate, this was ...hardly an equal share, but it did exceed what her father's testament would have given her. By that document, Anna was to receive only a third of the "legal" third of the family estate in formal inheritance (*legitimata*), the remaining two-thirds of "the third" to be divided more or less equally between Philip and Agatha, who would then also share the remaining greater part of the family estate as well. To make matters possibly worse for Anna, her father's testament also designated a lost son Bonaventure—a cloth merchant who had been absent from Hall for over two years without any communication and was pre-sumed dead—an equal heir to the official "third," should he, by some miracle, return alive. In addition, Bonaventure was also to share the twelve-hundred-gulden bond with Philip. Only in the very unlikely event that the three favored children (Philip, Agatha, and Bonaventure) died without surviving offspring was Anna to inherit anything beyond her third of a third.[19]

In real terms, Philip was far and away the winner and Anna the loser

1582), the commander of the imperial forces then engaging the Lu-theran Schmalkaldic League in southwestern Germany and soon to become the Habsburg scourge of the Netherlands' Calvinists. The em-peror had come as an avenger, to punish the citizens of Hall for its participation in the Schmalkaldic League, and perhaps, to his great delight, to see its Protestant reformer, Johannes Brenz, burned. Again, he spent the night in the Büschler house, now hosted by Anna's brother Philip, then its new owner. He departed on the following day after demanding payment of sixty thousand gulden from the city for its betrayal of the empire by joining the Protestant alliance.[6]

 Disinherited

IN A LIFE AS TRAUMATIC AS ANNA'S, IT MIGHT BE EXPECTED THAT both her father and her husband would die within a month of each other—Hermann Büschler in July, Hans von Leuzenbrunn in August 1543. The unfortunate Leuzenbrunn spent the last weeks of his life in Hall's hospice, where he was admitted as a "poor man,"[7] an indication of his and Anna's impoverishment. Located between Froschgraben and Spitalbach streets a block from the river, the city hospice was a com-munity in its own right and a true social institution. Dating back to the thirteenth century, it provided charity and medical care for any and all in need, whether rich or poor, nobleman or commoner. Having grown rich over the centuries from generous endowments, it had by the sixteenth century evolved from a mere depository for the sick and dying into a caring hospital and sprawling home for the aged, the or-phaned, and the poor. Numerous personnel staffed its many services, which included a bakery, a butchery, and a school.[8] As fate would have it, Anna would soon follow her late husband there, entering as a "poor person" in an even fuller sense of the term, not only as one who was ill and impoverished, but as a prisoner of the city as well.

In removing his hostile presence from her life and reopening the discussion of her inheritance, the death of Hermann Büschler might have been a boon to Anna's fortunes. Hermann Büschler had a knack for saving the worst for last, however, and once again he would excel his previous acts of ill will toward his daughter. Although at the time he could only imagine the consequences of his action, by his last will and testament he managed to cast an even darker shadow over her in death than he had done in life. He virtually disinherited her, leaving her only the absolute minimum he believed the law required. By doing so, he tempted her to litigate as furiously with her siblings for a share of the family estate as she had twice been forced to do with him.

She had, however, one powerful factor on her side: absolute disinheritance of a child was repugnant to German law, regardless of the circumstances. Originally that law had recognized only communal succession to collective property; the entire clan inherited ancestral land. The law did not permit the deceased to alter the claims of his many kin by a personal testament singling out only a few favored individuals. By contrast, Roman law based the order of inheritance on the free will of the deceased and only secondarily on a communal right of intestate succession to the family estate by all kin. This allowed for greater individualism and favoritism in the disposition of family wealth and made possible a strategy of inheritance. Over time, German law also came to recognize a freely chosen testamentary order of succession, while still maintaining a moral bias toward the rights of the larger family. As a compromise between the principle of a testator's freedom, on the one hand, and the interests and well-being of all members of his family, on the other, German law borrowed from Roman law the notion of a "compulsory portion." The statutory right of all kin to inherit was thereby restricted, while the right of the children, the surviving spouse, and even the grandparents to a fair share of the estate was guaranteed.

It was this deep-seated principle of equitable inheritance or fair portion, particularly in regard to members of the immediate and the nuclear family, that gave Anna a fighting chance to gain more of the family inheritance than her father had decreed. In German law, when children were passed over or insufficiently remembered in a father's will, they retained a powerful moral claim to the value of what they had lost. The disinherited or deprived child was viewed as a kind of creditor of the heirs who now shared his or her lost or diminished portion.[9]

According to priest Arnold Engel, Anna's brother Philip and sister Agatha had at first not wanted their sister to receive any more inheritance than their father's testament allowed.[10] They quickly recognized, however, that protracted litigation would be the price of enforcing

their father's testament. So as their father before [ ] matter of the maternal inheritance, her siblings, t[ ] a deal, believing that they could make peace wit[ ] to themselves.

After much frank discussion among themselv[ ] spective advisers and city officials, the three chi[ ] tober 16, 1543, to award Anna a somewhat more [ ] the family estate. The preamble to the agreemen[ ] edged their father's preemptive bestowal of testa[ ] on Philip in advance of his death. At least one w[ ] "several thousand gulden" had been given illegally[ ]

In his testament, Hermann Büschler appropria[ ] Agatha for such favoritism to her brother, while ign[ ] the terms of the testament been strictly followed, t[ ] would have ended up sharing most unevenly in the[ ] which various witnesses put at between fifteen thou[ ] thousand gulden and the Hall tax list set at sixteen [ ] year of his death (1543).[14] According to Anna's most s[ ] ness, student David Schmidlin, had Anna received an[ ] the estate at her father's death, she would no longer [ ] vantaged by the cruel events of her life, and the long B[ ] feud would have ended then and there.[15]

The preamble to the October 1543 agreement describ[ ] allotted Anna by her father as "rather too harsh and un[ ] ularly now that she was a widow. That frank acknowled[ ] part of all concerned, including members of the city [ ] signed off on the agreement, was an unusual civic admissi[ ] Büschler's neighbors and colleagues did not believe him to[ ] a parent as he was a bürgermeister. Not only did the smal[ ] left Anna fall well short of what was required to pay t[ ] brunns' "remarkable debts"; it did not even establish a flo[ ] of minimal comfort during Anna's remaining years, which[ ] tories, with Anna's likely exception, expected to be few.[16]

In alleged recognition of her age (mid-forties) and faili[ ] ("the result of many adverse circumstances"), and surely al[ ] hope of deflecting any further legal action she might be conter[ ] her siblings proposed a fairer distribution of the family estate[ ] for their quarreling to end, the agreement gave Anna lifelong

by their father's arrangements. In an estate of 16,000 gulden, an estimated 3,400 had already been bequeathed to Philip. Only one-third of the remaining 12,600 gulden, 4,200 gulden, was to be shared equally by the three (and possibly four) children (the legal "third"). Ideally, in 1543, that would have meant 1,400 gulden for Anna. But the testament also called for "fair compensation" to be paid to the other siblings for the properties earlier awarded to Philip. That was to be done by "reckoning" a fair cash equivalent of the value of those properties to the "third," which all the children would then share equally, the infusion of new money apparently to come from Hermann Büschler's estate and possibly also from Philip's lion-sized share of it. Such payments would still have been a bargain for Philip. Inasmuch as his father had estimated the worth of the properties given him to be no more than their original purchase price, he would thus have gotten them for perhaps as little as half of their true market value in 1543. In other words, his father had made it possible for him to buy out his siblings at a very deep discount. And Philip also shared in the third he fattened. On such terms, he would have been eager to add to the communal pie.

Calculating fair compensation, then, to be at least 3,400 gulden (the sum of Philip's two properties, estimated at 2,200 gulden, plus his 1,200-gulden bond), Anna's share of the compensatory payment would have added another 1,134 gulden to her basal 1,400, assuming Bonaventure never returned. So ideally, a 2,534-gulden award may have been possible. These figures, however, do not take into account any outstanding taxes or other obligations on her father's estate, so the actual figures were certainly lower.

On the other hand, the deal offered her by her siblings in 1543 gave her a sure twelve hundred gulden in immediate debt abatement, together with a house and furnishings, annual allotments of staples, and an eighty-gulden lifetime annuity, the total value of which, according to her brother, amounted to three times what her father had left her and more than half of "the third" the three were to share.[20] So while far from an equal portion of the family estate, the settlement Philip and Agatha offered their sister could have provided a good livelihood for a frugal and disciplined woman.

The two had every reason to be pleased with the agreement. Two years later, in 1545, the Hall tax list put Agatha and husband Wolf

Schanz's taxable wealth at 6,400 gulden and Philip's at 7,837, while Anna appeared on the same tax list as a "citizen without property," and hence no tax obligation. Four years later, Anna still held that lowly status on the tax list of 1549.[21]

 Against Womanly Discipline and Honor

THREE DAYS AFTER ENTERING THE AGREEMENT WITH HER SIBLINGS, on October 19, 1543, Anna, in a separate document, formally renounced any further claim to a family inheritance, and she swore "knowingly, finally, and irrevocably" to abide by the terms of the agreement and under no circumstances to contest it.[22] Finality, however, can only be a relative term for one whose back was as flat against the wall as Anna's. At the time of the signing, she could hardly have done otherwise; the agreement was the only way to bide her time. Before half a year had passed, she was again in full cry and the agreement on the verge of collapse. As new charges and countercharges flew back and forth among the three, her siblings threatened her with arrest, and a new, embittered round of litigation loomed.

It had been the city council's responsibility to enforce the agreement. When it now reconstructed the events leading to its collapse, the finger pointed solely to Anna. Because of her indiscipline, it alleged, she became unhappy with the terms of the agreement, condemned it, and abandoned Hall for Neuenstein in the county of Hohenlohe. There, again, as she had done in the past, she found refuge with one of the city's major enemies, whose royal family she had evidently earlier gotten to known through her Rothenburg family and Erasmus.

Even without prior contacts, the counts of Hohenlohe would likely have welcomed a refugee from Hall in the early 1540s. Between 1538 and 1544, feuding between the city and the county, which occupied much of the land to the north, had increased, and the year 1543 was something of a watershed in this long, bitter conflict.[23] Boundaries and royal escort duty were the staples of that conflict. In 1538, Count Georg I (d. 1551) of Hohenlohe-Waldenburg sparked an armed confrontation after hacking through the Haller boundary hedge for a third time. Then, in 1542, his brother, Count Albrecht III (d. 1551) of

Hohenlohe-Neuenstein, triggered another series of confrontations when he approached the city with his knights to escort King Ferdinand I (d. 1564), then visiting in Hall, to the seat of the imperial government in Speyer and was rebuffed by the Haller when he reached their borders. The two sides thereafter raided one another's territory for months, Albrecht on one occasion occupying a church on Hall land and declaring it his own, the Haller on another attacking a Hohenlohe castle, and both sides sparing no opportunity to insult and threaten the other. In January 1543, the two sides held a two-week peace conference in an effort to resolve their differences. However, by mid-century, the accustomed cycle of feuding and negotiation had begun anew.[24]

Anna, however, did not remain long in Neuenstein, a place of mixed memories of times spent with Erasmus. Having mustered her resources, she was soon off to Speyer to explore afresh her legal options. As she did so, her Hall critics accused her of acting not only against "womanly discipline and honor," but against her duty as a citizen of Hall. Showing some of her father's flair for the dramatic, she denounced her brother and the city council both publicly and privately to any Speyer official who would listen, making something of a spectacle of herself. At the same time, she wrote contemptuous letters back home to both, which her brother and council members were later all too happy to share with the imperial commissioners adjudicating her complaints. Such provocative actions eventually moved Philip and Agatha to sue her for defamation[25] and the city council to summon her home to Hall to answer for her reckless behavior.

By a coincidence, Maternus Wurzelmann, Hall's lordly city secretary,[26] was also in Speyer at this time, and learning of her activities, he sought to calm her on Hall's behalf. Earlier he had been the major draftsman of the agreement with her siblings and was one of the two officials designated by the city council to advise her during the deliberations. It was he who had put the quill in Anna's hand when she signed the agreement.[27] Because of his political stature and the seemingly amicable nature of their previous relationship, he evidently believed he might influence her behavior.

To that end, he invited Anna, her new lawyer (Ludwig Ziegler), and an unidentified friend of her late husband to meet privately and informally with a delegation from Hall in his Speyer lodging. The meeting occurred in March 1544 and is described by Wurzelmann in a letter he sent shortly thereafter to the city council of Hall to warn his colleagues of a newly militant Anna.

As Wurzelmann remembered the event, he began the meeting by asking Anna why she was troubling herself and so many others over the agreement with her siblings. According to his account, she responded with "loud rude screams," attacking the leader of the delegation and declaring the agreement to have been a deception from the start, and one she now had no intention of honoring.[28] Specifically, she complained that her siblings had refused to pay her creditors, and that even as she spoke, the Jew Moses of Beihingen, a moneylender to whom she was much in debt, was hotly pursuing her. Because of such hounding, she felt like a cornered person, ready to flee on a moment's notice, lest she be thrown in jail for some delinquent debt.[29] As for her present plans, she intended to appeal the agreement to the imperial court in Rottweil, in the hope of having it overturned and the matter of her inheritance reopened.

That prospect greatly annoyed the delegation, as it would mean another intrusion by an outside court into the city's domain and still another public washing of its dirty laundry. Attempting to deflate Anna and console the delegation, two councilmen commented that since fleeing Hall, she had found a "fat bone" elsewhere (an apparent allusion to Neuenstein and her Hohenlohe friends and protectors), and so she would not be residing again in Hall anyway. It was further pointed out in her presence that her brother had said she was crazy, and as a crazy person, no pledge, oath, or agreement she made could possibly bind her. The delegation also threatened to destroy her Junker seal, that is, to debase her social standing, her credentials as the widow of a nobleman—an action her deceased husband's friend had come to warn them against.[30]

If such comments had been intended to take the wind out of Anna's sails, they rather filled them instead. She informed the delegation that could she relive the day in the council room when she signed the agreement with her siblings, knowing then all that she knew now, she would dispense with every semblance of womanly courtesy, and "in the presence of your honors, squat down in the middle of the council room and politely perform the coarsest bodily act."[31] And with that eye-popping declaration, she denounced the agreement as "a thing born of evil," which she assured the delegation was also her opinion of her father's vaunted property and his marriage to her mother.[32]

At this point in the proceedings, Wurzelmann, who was accustomed to deference, particularly from women, became unnerved. The agreement remained fully binding on all parties, he now informed Anna. She had entered into it freely and knowingly in the presence of her relatives. Its creation had been a kindness and a mercy to her on the part of her family and the city council. Had her inheritance remained what her father had prescribed, she would have been unable to pay her creditors and become a pauper. So if by her own petulance she now broke the agreement, her brother could not in the future be expected to intervene on her behalf when her creditors sued her, and much less could she blame the city when such misfortune befell her.

For all these reasons, her "rude and shameless behavior" before the delegation was condemned as completely inappropriate. She was, after all, talking to men who had shown her and her late husband "every favor, good will, and paternal consideration." If any honor still remained in her, she should rather be showing shame in the delegation's presence. Indeed, Anna's shaken host now proclaimed, "when one continues to show ruling authority such insult and offense, it is time for a rock around the neck and into the water!"[33]

What had never been a discussion now threatened to become a brawl, and Anna again rose to the challenge. She declared it her intention to take as her second husband "the most unprincipled man she could find, but one who also had a sharp and cunning mind,"[34] by which she meant a man capable of working her will through the courts and giving the councilmen of Hall grief.

That threat made a lasting impression on the delegation, as well it should. For a woman living in the sixteenth century, Anna Büschler had made a remarkable public confession, and one most prejudicial to her case. Such arrogance, vulgarity, and anger in a public forum were associated at this time with witches, not with honorable women and loyal citizens. Wherever she was found, the female witch had in abundance a quality the Scottish witch-hunters called "smeddum," by which was meant "spirit, a refusal to be put down, quarrelsomeness."[35]

After the members of the Hall delegation had returned home, Anna's words were soon on every Haller's lips. Here was a woman who would marry purely for revenge, who was prepared to call an unprincipled paladin "husband." And it was no foolish or deranged character in some play or carnival troupe who was making such declarations, but the bürgermeister's daughter, and she was doing so in the presence of the city's most honorable men. The damning phrase *spitzig in kopf,* "sharp and cunning of mind," subsequently appeared in the city's legal papers against Anna, and many witnesses remembered it as well.[36]

As for poor Wurzelmann, he acknowledged in his letter to the council that his original hope of finding a docile Anna and persuading her to return home and honor the agreement with her siblings had been thoroughly dashed. He now recommended that the council make no further efforts to reason with her.

 The Kindness of Kin

THE OLD SECRETARY'S LETTER DISTILLS THE CITY'S VIEW OF Anna's tossing of the agreement and the official response to her equally bumptious allegation of foul play on the part of the council itself. Later legal documents submitted by the council and Anna's siblings to the imperial commission inquiring into her case provide additional information on the circumstances of the agreement and the council's role in its creation. Particularly revealing are the allegations by her brother and sister, which, far from showing a spirit of compromise, were intended to deny her any inheritance whatsoever.

Philip and Agatha claimed to have helped their father draft his testament and to know its circumstances well. At the time of Hermann Büschler's death, both were convinced that Anna had no legal claim to a maternal inheritance and only a scant one to a paternal or family inheritance. The maternal inheritance had already been settled by the agreement signed with her father in 1528 and by the council's ruling in 1534, directing her eventual compensation for Lindenhof. As for a paternal or family inheritance, their father's testament left no doubt about his wishes for the disposition of his estate. Philip and Agatha believed that those wishes overrode any "natural or prior right" to such an inheritance Anna might invoke as an immediate blood relative. Indeed, the preamble of the testament unequivocally renounced all prior testamentary statements made by their father, including the marriage contract of 1495.[37]

All this notwithstanding, their father did believe that Anna should get something. So "out of fatherly kindness," as Philip and Agatha put it, and in consultation with them, he had bequeathed Anna what, in light of her scandalous behavior, the three in concert deemed to be a proper portion within the law.[38] What is left unsaid, however, but was well understood by all three at the time, is that the testament awarded Anna as little of the family estate as her father thought the law required.

Why, if her siblings believed that their sister had been treated properly and fairly in their father's testament, did they subsequently agree to increase her portion after his death? In explaining their turnabout, they protested that they too had "cause and legal right" to enforce their father's stringent testament against her. It was not because law or justice required it of them[39] that they subsequently attempted to rescue her from the legal limbo into which she had plunged herself by signing the restrictive agreement with her siblings. Their action now, like their father's earlier, was said to be an expression of "kindness" to their sister, one they calculated would have enabled her, solely on condition of her friendly cooperation, to increase her legal portion to more than three times what her father had decreed, thus gaining more than half of the legal "third."[40]

As her siblings recalled the discussions leading to the agreement, Anna had participated fully, and with the counsel of three legally astute relatives: her uncle and former bürgermeister Conrad Büschler, Sr., and her first cousins Conrad Büschler, Jr., and Hans Hornberger, both experienced politicians in Hall and Rothenburg respectively. Also, during the proceedings and at her own request, she had sworn an oath of citizenship and paid the required fee for its rights and privileges, thereby formally placing herself under the authority and protection of the city council.[41] And throughout it all, she had remained friendly with her siblings. After signing the agreement, she personally thanked those who had drawn it up. And in the weeks following, she was back and forth to her brother Philip's house. She even invited his children to dine with her at her house on Gelbinger Street outside the city wall. That date, however, was not kept, because before it could arrive, Anna had hastily departed Hall for Hohenlohe and Speyer, where she set in motion the litigation that now engulfed them all.[42]

It was no mystery to her siblings why Anna suddenly concluded that the agreement was a fraud and fled. Philip's refusal to pay the new debts that she continued to accumulate had precipitated the new crisis. In the weeks after signing the agreement, she had given Philip a list of the debts he was then obligated to pay, which by all accounts he dutifully set about paying. When new bills for purchases of silver and fabric arrived at his door, however, he refused to honor them. The agreement explicitly excluded the payment of such debts, and Philip was quick to complain to the council that his sister was ignoring its terms. In response, the council summoned Anna and rebuked her, reiterating to her that her siblings were obligated to pay up to twelve hundred gulden of the debt existing at the time of the agreement, not new debts incurred thereafter as well. Philip claimed to have relented for the sake of peace at this early stage of the agreement, paying the first wave of new debts anyway, while at the same time indicating to Anna that he would not do so again.[43] It was only at this point, her siblings claimed, that Anna discovered the agreement to be a "swindle" and returned to the courts.

Recalling these same events, Anna told a completely different story, one of conspiracy and coercion reaching to the highest levels of city government. In her version, her siblings had grabbed all the family property and possessions for themselves upon the death of their father, justifying their actions by his testament, which Anna claimed never to have seen or read, despite repeated requests for a copy.[44] But being impoverished and recently widowed, she was in no position to fight back. So she let herself be saddled with an agreement that gave her little and forbade her from asking for more.

Had she resisted her siblings at this time, she was convinced, they would have enforced, as they repeatedly threatened to do, the stringent terms of their father's testament. That would have given her only a fraction of what she believed to be rightfully hers, the despicable "third of a third,"[45] or approximately one-ninth of the true estate, as she calculated it. So as in 1528, when her father forced her to settle for less than what she deemed to be a fair maternal inheritance, she now seized the partial loaf her siblings offered, lest she be left with her father's paltry slice. Yet all the while, she believed she was entitled to a great deal more and remained determined to get it.

Anna's version of events further maintains that she initiated private discussions with her siblings and made informal appeals to the city council before giving up on the agreement and departing Hall. In the recollections of her siblings and councilmen, however, the contacts and conversations Anna initiated at this time were superficial and not in good faith. Anna, on the other hand, distinctly remembered making the case to her siblings that her father's disinheritance of her was illegal on the grounds that it contradicted the parental marriage contract, which Anna now insisted held legal priority over her father's testament. Had that primal document, which placed strict limits on each parent's freedom to dispose of family property, been enforced, as both parents had originally intended it to be, Anna believed she would have received a full and equal share of family land and movables.[46]

Even apart from the marriage contract, Anna argued that the law did not permit a father to ignore the needs of a natural child, nor to apportion testamentary property (*legata*) selectively from his estate, wrongdoing she believed her father knowingly committed. Hence her reference to his testament as an "alleged testament." Had her father not given favored son Philip many thousand gulden beyond what she and Agatha received? Was not testamentary property illegally awarded to Philip without any consultation with or compensation of the other heirs?[47] "According to law, a testator . . . is obliged to leave his *entire* livelihood to the children as their legal and proper portion," Anna lectured her siblings at the last hearing before her death.[48]

Another possible legal argument Anna might well have invoked to good effect was a qualifying clause in the law permitting a father to disinherit a daughter who opposed his will in marriage. By that law, if a father with a daughter under twenty-five years of age, acting in accordance with his position and wealth, made a good-faith effort to arrange a proper marriage for her, only then to have her reject his efforts and refuse his choice, defiantly electing instead to lead an unchaste life, then he could disinherit her. However, if it could be shown that a father had been negligent and had not arranged a proper marriage for a daughter within the time determined by law, that is, before she turned twenty-five, then the daughter could not be disinherited because of any subsequent unchaste behavior on her part, which by then would have to be attributed as much to paternal neglect as to natural desire. As the *Schwabenspiegel*, a law code dating from the thirteenth century, put it, she might lose her "honor" after twenty-five, but she could not lose her inheritance.[49]

Whether Hermann Büschler had done all he could and should to find Anna a suitable mate became a major issue in the two parties' assessment of blame for her scandalous behavior. Even though the above law precisely summarized Hermann Büschler's view of the matter and its qualifying clause nicely stated Anna's, neither side ever invoked it. That this legal course was not pursued is perhaps best explained by its double-edged nature, both sides perceiving it to be mutually negating. So while Anna blamed her behavior on her father's refusal to recognize any of her suitors as worthy of her, she defended her right to a full inheritance by appealing to her parents' marriage contract and to natural law. Likewise, her father insisted that she had rejected all the possible husbands he could find, yet he based his legal case on her willful disobedience of his parental authority and her public shaming of the family and the community.

In the end, none of Anna's arguments against her father's disinheritance prevailed. Convinced that her siblings were determined to leave her with the crumbs of her father's testament should she resist them, she silently did as she was told in 1543. Publicly at the time, she persisted in portraying herself as a poor, abandoned widow, besieged by creditors and with no one to turn to, forced in the end by her "poverty, fear, and inexperience" to take what seemed at the moment to be as good as she was ever going to get.[50] Only later, in the clear light of day, when the provisions of the agreement began to be implemented contrary to her expectations, did she discover how completely fooled she had been.[51]

Whereas her siblings portrayed their sister's glass as more than half full, Anna described it as more than half empty. Exactly reversing their alleged proportions, she decried the agreement for denying her "not only more than half of what was just, but three times as much and more."[52] On the single occasion when she mentions a specific figure, she accuses her siblings of cheating her out of more than two thousand gulden of her father's estate.[53]

As far as Anna was now concerned, the agreement of 1543 had been a charade from the start, shrewdly orchestrated by three of the most powerful men in Hall: her brother; city secretary Wurzelmann, the document's chief draftsman; and Leonhard Feuchter, soon to become the new bürgermeister and, with Wurzelmann, the city official appointed by the council to advise her during the negotiations.[54] Anna portrays her brother, who was soon to become bürgermeister, as Hall's "leading councilman and a man everyone [then] feared,"[55] hence one in a position to work his will on the council, given the support of Wurzelmann, who also had very good reason to dislike Anna. Clearly, Philip had the most to gain from an agreement that masked his father's bias toward him in apportioning the family inheritance. At the same time, the agreement promised to silence the only person (Anna) who had a reason to challenge Hermann Büschler's disposition of his estate. In Anna's opinion, Philip and his allies had played with a deck that could not have been more prejudicially stacked.

Anna might well have said of her father in the mid-1520s what she now said of her brother in the early 1540s, for her father had then been a heroic and unblemished man whom everyone respected and feared. And he too had successfully worked his will on her through the courts, thanks to strategically placed allies. The parallel between the two episodes may have crossed Anna's mind in a disturbing moment of hindsight.

Anna also claimed to have had no say whatsoever in the selection of the men who drafted the agreement with her siblings, nor of the city officials and relatives who advised her during the proceedings. In the end, she was presented with a finished document and instructed to sign it, unread.[56] As was also the case with her father's testament, she alleged that she had neither seen nor read the agreement, her requests for a copy again going unanswered by the council.[57] She remembered on the day of the signing being in the council room with her brother and sister, her court-appointed advisers, and the men who drafted the agreement. When instructed to sign the finished document, she had hesitated as if to protest, whereupon, at her brother's signal, a guard had entered the room and was ordered to take her away to the tower. It was at that moment, Anna claimed, that Wurzelmann had pressed the quill into her hand and stood over her as she signed the agreement at the place indicated to her.[58]

 Persona Non Grata

IT WAS CLEAR TO ANNA, AND SHE THOUGHT ALSO TO EVERYONE else present on that day in 1543, that she had signed the agreement with her siblings under duress. From this, she had derived her only comfort at the time, for she knew that an agreement made under such conditions would be ruled null and void at a fair hearing and the question of her inheritance reopened. No sooner had she departed the council room than she began to think how she might escape Hall and seek help against the city and her siblings.[59]

By January 1544 at the latest, she had in all likelihood taken refuge in Neuenstein, whence she now prepared her counterattack. Her first new legal action of record was a letter to the city council of Hall, written on January 23, 1544, in which she formally protested the agreement with her siblings and begged the council to intervene on her behalf. She accused her siblings of having taken away her natural inheritance, "contrary to law and fairness,"[60] and bound her to a punishing agreement based on their father's "fickle testament." Since signing that agreement, she had discovered the exact clause in her parents' marriage contract that forbade either parent from disposing of marital property beyond their immediate personal belongings. She now asked the council to sequester and inventory her father's estate and to block any further division of it, or transference of the case to another jurisdiction, without her foreknowledge and consent.

Already earlier, within weeks of the signing of the agreement, both sides had made informal appeals to the council to enforce its terms on all parties. At the time, Anna accused Philip of not paying her creditors and of even privately threatening to have her jailed if her carping and criticism continued. He in fact haled her before the city council in an effort to "silence eternally" her alleged slandering of his intentions.[61] It was after several months of such bickering that he and Agatha filed a defamation suit against their sister.[62]

Meanwhile, her vociferous criticism of Hall justice in Speyer and the insults and threats she had leveled at the Hall delegation during the famous meeting in Wurzelmann's house there had made her *persona non grata* with the city council as well, which looked on such indiscretion and disrespect by a citizen as virtual treason. Once again, powerful storm clouds had gathered around Anna.

On April 18, 1544, the council sent her the first of three summonses to appear at city hall to answer the charges of her siblings. As with two subsequent summonses (on May 17 and July 4), Anna did not comply. By midsummer, her presumed defiance of the council had thoroughly alienated Hall's magistrates.[63] Convinced that any further overtures on their part would only be met with "wanton rejection of authority,"[64] the council ordered her arrest for disobedience and insubordination, describing its action as singularly necessary "for the sake of public order and security."[65] Pursuant to that order, the city militia caught up with Anna and her lawyer in late August in the town of Münkheim, within Hall's jurisdiction. There they arrested her and brought her back to Hall, where she was confined in what the council described as "a completely tolerable woman's prison."[66]

The unfolding of these events would soon rival in personal terror Anna's earlier capture and shackling by her father. Again, her retelling of them completely contradicts the council's version. According to her account, she and her lawyer entered Hall territory freely and in good faith, en route to the city to meet her court date with the council, apparently in late August or early September. True, she was tardy in doing so, but not because of any disrespect for the council. She had hesitated only because the council had refused to send her a letter of safe-conduct before she departed Speyer for Hall. In the place of such a letter, it assured her that her citizenship would suffice to protect her once she was in Hall land.[67] With that assurance, she had, in the end, reluctantly set out for Hall. As in a similar situation eighteen years earlier, when the city's safe-conduct had failed to protect her from her father, her citizenship now proved, despite the official assurance, to be no guarantee of safety from her enemies in the council. Once again, the past seemed to be repeating itself for Anna Büschler.

Behind her arrest in Münkheim she saw the hand of her brother. She reasoned that her siblings now feared that the wrong they had done her by their clever agreement might come to light during their defamation suit.[68] To interrupt that process, they had instigated her arrest on other charges, namely, her alleged defiance of the city's summonses—again, much as her father had earlier interrupted a pending litigation in Hall by taking her captive in Esslingen on the authority of an imperial mandate. By now Anna was so cynical about Hall justice that she must have suspected that a hearing there under any conditions would produce the same result, regardless of the charges brought against her.

Soon after her arrival and imprisonment, tower officials took a deposition. In it, they describe her as a broken woman—angry, debilitated, despairing, refusing to talk to anyone or to receive any assistance. "She appeared to be completely wretched and ill," the deposition reported, "and cried out to God that she should come to such great ruin and suffering in body and soul because of the damned estate of her father," a condition in which she expected to die.[69] While she also had a jaundiced view of her lawyer, she blamed her present misfortune completely on her brother and sister, who had stopped her quarterly annuity payment. She saw no chance of reconciliation with them, nor any possibility of gaining any further assistance from them. The deposition quotes her as begging the council "to be her father and mother and to think kindly of her," as she now had no one else to turn to.[70]

What the council had described as a "tolerable woman's prison" Anna found to be "a wretched tower." There she was confined for a total of six weeks, during the last of which she fell ill and had to be transferred to the hospice, where her husband had died the previous year. There she was chained to her bed so that she could not escape, not an unusual practice for the insane. She claims that a special cell was then being built for her on the premises, within which the council intended to confine her for the remainder of her life.[71]

Despite misgivings about her lawyer, who had returned alone to Speyer after her arrest in Münkheim, the man proved in the end to be of some assistance to her, albeit belatedly and in predictably lawyerly fashion. Learning of her imprisonment in Hall, he had petitioned the Rottweil court for a penal mandate ordering her swift release. He wrote to Anna on October 8 to inform her of his success and the mailing of the mandate to the city council, in return for which services he requested three and a quarter gulden by return mail.[72]

The mandate proved, however, to be unnecessary, as Anna, ever resourceful, managed to escape to the safety of Neuenstein by her own devices. Nonetheless, in subsequent briefs against the city, she would cite the council's defiance of that very mandate as one of three ways it had broken imperial law when it took and held her captive. In addition to (1) leaving her in chains against the order of a higher court, the council had (2) illegally imprisoned a woman for a civil offense and (3) used that imprisonment as grounds for suspending a pending lawsuit with her siblings.[73] In a word, all of her many enemies in Hall had conspired quietly to put her away for life.

The Rottweil court subsequently fined Hall twenty marks of highest-quality gold for defying its order to release her—ten for the court and ten for Anna. The council appealed that fine on the grounds that Anna had already escaped by the effective date of the mandate, so that no punishable act of disobedience on its part had actually occurred.[74] Six years later that fine remained unpaid and was still being debated by the two courts (Hall and Rottweil). Anna, however, never stopped believing that the magistrates of Hall had knowingly deceived and bullied her throughout the entire episode.[75]

CONSVL·IS·EXPRESSOS·IN·IMAGINE
CERNERE · VVLTVS ·
CONRADI · BVSCHLER
PICTA·TABELLA·DEDIT ·

SEINES · ALTERS · 67 ·
· 1 · 5 · 7 · 9 ·

*C*onrad Büschler, Jr. (1512–79), Anna's council-appointed curator in
1543–44, was in his early thirties during the negotiations with her
siblings. His father, Conrad, Sr. (d. 1550), also played a prominent
official role during the negotiations. It was to his house that Anna first fled
in 1525, after her forced removal from her father's house.

CHAPTER
SIX

IN THE AFTERMATH OF HER ARREST UNTIL THE DAY SHE DIED, from the summer of 1544 to January 1552, Anna attempted to reopen the matter of her inheritance and to punish the city of Hall for maliciously arresting and jailing her. In this undertaking, she was assisted by a new husband, whom she married in 1546. His name was Johann von Sporland, a Neuenstein native and, judging by his activities on Anna's behalf, a man both knowledgeable in the ways of the law and certainly dogged. Unfortunately, the sources do not permit a judgment on whether he was the most unprincipled and cunning man available to her at the time, although the chances of finding such a man in the princely stronghold of Neuenstein were surely favorable. Sporland's persistence in the courts on Anna's behalf, both during her lifetime and after her death, suggests that she had had some success in fulfilling her infamous Speyer prophecy.

Between 1546 and 1550, the Sporlands petitioned the imperial court in Esslingen to invalidate Anna's 1543 agreement with her siblings and clear the way for Anna to receive a full inheritance. Of the few documents that appear to have survived from these years, one is a copy of the court's response to the Sporlands' indictment of Philip and Wolf Schanz, Agatha's husband, dated March 1548. It provides a glimpse at least of the ongoing conflict between the three siblings and the court's cool reaction to it. In it, the court instructs both parties, on pain of fine, to abide by the law in the resolution of their differences, thereby preserving the status quo, which did not favor Anna, while at the same time leaving the door of the court open to further litigation.[1] The Sporlands, however, wanted a grand review, and in the end that was exactly what they got.

Having watched the Büschler family feud fester for six more years, the imperial court intervened in what promised to be a decisive resolution between the spring of 1550 and January 1552. Intermittently during those twenty-odd months, four separate commissions, staffed by imperial court judges, visited Hall and conducted as many hearings, taking testimony from dozens of witnesses in an effort to end the dispute once and for all.

A combination of factors lay behind the decision to act at this time. First and foremost was the Sporlands' relentless pursuit of their claims, which never allowed the dispute to die. There was also the clear failure of the city council of Hall to bring the dispute to a final closure. In addition, the testimony taken during the hearings at mid-century make it clear that both conscientious members of Hall's city council and imperial officials familiar with the case at the courts of higher jurisdiction (variously, Rottweil, Esslingen, Speyer, and Augsburg) suspected that a great, unrequited wrong had been done Anna Büschler by her father. Imperial authorities also worried that the city council of Hall had broken imperial law and its covenant with one of its citizens when it arrested and imprisoned Anna in 1544. Not a few Hall citizens still remembered those six months in 1525 when the city council stood by and watched as Hermann Büschler made his daughter a prisoner in her own house. Finally, after almost three decades of feuding, everyone connected with this on-again-off-again drama, whether as participant, witness, or mere observer—both the Büschlers and the Leuzenbrunns/Sporlands, imperial judges and Hall councilmen, and a sizable segment of Hall's citizenry—was ready to see it end. Only the lawyers could have found a silver lining in its continuation.

In the presence of one or more of the four commissions, Anna, her siblings, and the city council each gave their version of events, both those surrounding the agreement of 1544 and its subsequent failure, and those leading to Anna's arrest by the city in the same year and its terrible aftermath. What Anna had to say about these matters so contradicted the account given by her siblings and the city council that the commissioners could only conclude that lies were being told on all sides.

Anna made two large accusations that bring to focus the key legal issues the commissioners now relied on witnesses to resolve. The first was that her siblings had coerced her into signing an agreement that was far more in their interest than in hers, and having done so, then refused to honor its key provision, the payment of her debts. Secondly, she accused the city council of deceitfully and illegally arresting her after the agreement's collapse, and, but for her lucky escape, intending to let her rot to death in a specially made prison cell. On both charges,

Anna sought compensation for her losses and injuries and appropriate punishment of her tormentors.

 Remembering Anna

WHILE ANNA PORTRAYED HER SIBLINGS AND LEADING CITY OFFI-cials as disingenuous and cruel, they portrayed her to the imperial commissioners as a near sociopath. The commissioners sought to de-termine the truth by taking testimony from approximately three dozen witnesses, who arguably either had been or were in a position to know the relevant facts. These were people who either had been present at crucial junctures in Anna's life, particularly in the 1520s, when the dispute began, or had had a close relationship over the years with one or more of the parties involved. Hence the colorful parade of citizens and subjects, relatives and friends, from Hall, surrounding villages and neighboring towns, and places as far away as Rothenburg.

There were thirty-nine witnesses in all, both male and female, rang-ing in age from twenty-three to eighty. They were both the powerful and the barely visible, landed noblemen as well as day laborers, with annual incomes as high as five thousand gulden per annum and lower than twenty—a "jury" not only of peers, but one that also represented a very large part of the social spectrum of sixteenth-century society, an indication of that society's integration and fluidity.

The commissioners left few stones unturned in assembling relevant witnesses. Well represented were local councilmen, territorial officials, and lawyers directly connected with the case over the years. There were also three domestic servants, two mercenaries, a housewife, a baker, a messenger, a law student, a salt-maker, a shoemaker, a tailor, and a plasterer filling out the ranks. The oddest witness may have been Margretha Keidmenin, a forty-year-old bath attendant, who thirty years earlier, at ten years of age, had worked for Anna's mother as a maid.[2] She was summoned to the Windberg hearings in the apparent hope that she might recall how Anna, who would then have been in her early twenties, had behaved upon returning to her father's house after her mother's death, information pertinent to an assessment of Anna's character. Having left the Büschler household before the death of Anna's mother, Margretha could not, unfortunately, comment directly on Anna's conduct, nor was she able to provide the commission with any other relevant information.

By a preponderance of the testimony before the four commissions, which was taken at different times and often from the same witnesses, the commissioners expected to expose the lies, resolve the contradictions, and determine the truth of Anna's accusations. Only two witnesses testified at all four hearings: Leonhard Feuchter, Hall's reigning bürgermeister; and physician Anthony Brellochs, who had known Anna's mother and father before their marriage and had continued to have a close personal relationship with the family thereafter. Two other witnesses testified at three of the hearings: the octogenarian nobleman and several-times councilman Volk von Rossdorf (d. 1554), the oldest witness, and one who had some sympathy for Anna; and councilman Hans Eisenmenger, a loyalist, who adhered strictly to the city's version of events. Seventeen other witnesses testified at two of the four hearings.

A case could be made that third-party testimony was weighted against Anna. The largest single group of witnesses, all basically unsympathetic, was Hall councilmen, of whom there were ten. A number of other witnesses had had confrontations with her, which might cast suspicion on their testimony. This is certainly true of her father's servants, Lienhard Vahmann and Barbara Dollen. It was Vahmann who had recovered the two barrels of his master's goods that Anna had stolen and shipped to Kirchberg with the intention of selling there, and in one of which her scandalous love letters had been discovered. This and other of her misdeeds, which he had observed, had left Vahmann with mixed feelings about her at best. Barbara Dollen had endured both disrespect and alleged death threats from Anna, and she manifestly disliked her. At least one witness, salt-maker Gilg Menger, had lent Anna money, which she only slowly repaid, yet he spoke up in her favor. On the other hand, cousin and curator Conrad Büschler, Jr., whose unqualified support she might have expected to receive, contradicted her testimony on key points. A few councilmen, however, broke ranks and spoke good words as well as bad on her behalf. In a complex story such as Anna's, where the protagonist is both a fearless sinner and boldly sinned against, a seeming friend might prove an enemy, a presumed enemy a friend, and not a few could play it both ways. For Anna tempted her contemporaries to take a second, critical look at their public lives and heroes, and to compare their own private desires with what society required of them—a prospect both frightening and exhilarating.

On one issue a solid majority of witnesses agreed: Anna had been a well-informed and willing participant in the deliberations leading to the disposition of the family estate. Councilman Hans Eisenmenger and Wimpfen's city secretary, Lienhart Bleimeier, a man in Maternus Wurzelmann's employ, testified that Anna had had too many distinguished advisers at her side credibly to claim that she had not fully understand what was happening around her.[3] Wurzelmann's central role in the drafting and implementation of the agreement, which Anna viewed as sinister, was also praised by Eisenmenger and Bleimeier. They portrayed the old *Stadtschreiber* as an honest broker with nothing to gain from the agreement, which he had crafted only with Anna's well-being in mind.[4] At least one councilman, however, could not honestly say whether Wurzelmann had favored one side or the other.[5]

Those present throughout the negotiations describe Anna as having been a cheerful and enthusiastic participant from start to finish. Bleimeier remembered thinking at the time how absorbed and pleased she was by what she heard, although he acknowledged that he could not say "from what impulse" she had in the end embraced the agreement.[6] According to councilman Melchior Wetzel, no one at the signing threatened her in any way. Only once did she interrupt the proceedings, and then only to confer briefly in private with her curator. Returning to the council room, the two posed a question or two, which having been satisfactorily answered, her curator announced that she would abide by the agreement.[7] Eisenmenger remembered watching as she then held her right hand over her left breast and swore allegiance to the agreement in the council room, thereafter exclaiming to the assembly: "Praise God that I am thus provided for and now have my livelihood!"[8] Another prominent person present throughout the negotiations, bürgermeister Leonhard Feuchter, recalled that in the days after the signing of the agreement, she had been completely at peace with her brother and was frequently at his house, which she dearly loved.[9]

On the other hand, Johann Hornberger had heard others say that Anna was not at all happy with the agreement and had departed Hall at her earliest opportunity, fully intending to challenge it.[10] Volk von

Rossdorf had even heard rumors that she had been drunk at the time it was drawn up, and for that reason was refusing to abide by it.[11]

It was uncharacteristic of Anna to play a waiting game; her instinct was always to act up, to take immediate and decisive action. While it can hardly be said that she was ever in the dark during the negotiations with her siblings (she rather understood all too well what was occurring), she did find herself at the time in what was for her the most stressful of situations, namely, one she could not control. Hence, the contradictory assessments of her behavior.

 ### *A Conspirator in Curator's Clothing?*

IF ANYONE WAS IN A POSITION IN 1551 TO PROVIDE A CREDIBLE account of Anna's behavior seven years earlier and confirm one or the other narrative of events, it was surely cousin Conrad Büschler, Jr., her council-appointed curator. He made two statements under oath about these crucial matters, the first in response to her siblings' testimony that she had freely joined in the agreement, the second in response to Anna's testimony that she had signed the agreement against her will and under the threat of jail. He agreed that she had "freely and willingly" sworn to abide by the terms of the agreement, something he knew for a fact because he had stood by her side in the council room when she did so.[12] On the other hand, he gave her some slight benefit of doubt when she protested that she had signed the agreement out of fear. Because he had not been present during the deliberations that created the final document and had no prior knowledge of any coercion, he could not say for sure whether in the end she had signed the agreement under duress,[13] although to all appearances he believed she had not.

At another hearing, testifying on the very same matter for a second time, Conrad Büschler stated emphatically that she had freely and willingly signed the agreement. Never did he hear a word from her about being threatened with jail if she did not. Indeed, "she asked to sign [the agreement] herself ... there was not the slightest coercion ... [and] she freely accepted, praised, and swore allegiance to it." He assumed that such had truly been the case because he never heard her protest the agreement, nor did she ever instruct him in any way to contest it on her behalf.[14]

So according to the person arguably in the best position to know, Anna had entered the agreement knowingly, willingly, even pleasantly. If any coercion had been involved, only she and her intimidators knew about it at the time. It was not until she had fled Hall and begun denouncing her brother and the city council on the streets of Speyer that her curator, and presumably everyone else involved in the case, realized that appearances had belied reality.

For any judges who may have doubted it, Conrad Büschler's testimony added new weight to her siblings' allegation that Anna had become disenchanted with the agreement only after the fact and had not opposed it from the start. If that was the case, as the vast majority of witnesses testified, her only compelling legal argument for overturning it—that she had acted under duress—was groundless.

On still other, less subtly argued issues, her curator also contradicted Anna's testimony, again giving credence to her siblings' and the city council's version of events. Some of these issues were minor. He did not, for example, believe that her father's wealth was as great as the twenty thousand gulden she claimed,[15] or that her brother Philip was the fearsome councilman she portrayed him as being. "He was . . . a member of the council, but not the entire council," as Conrad Büschler put it.[16] He also disputed Anna's statement that her siblings had stopped paying her annuity. It was rather she who had refused to accept payment, after deciding to challenge the legality of the agreement. And even after that decision, her siblings continued to deposit[17] her eighty gulden with the city council, where it was held more or less in escrow until she decided to resume receipt of it.

If such testimony seemed to aid and abet the enemy, more disturbing still to Anna must have been her curator's revelation that he, like her, had never actually read Hermann Büschler's testament, nor so much as seen the parental marriage contract. And being thus unfamiliar with the key documents on which her case was being disputed, he declined to offer an opinion on the crucial question of whether the testament contradicted the marriage contract.[18] Inasmuch as the claimed higher legal authority of the latter, wherein Anna's right to a full and equal inheritance was secure, had been Anna's main argument in challenging her father's discriminatory testament, she might have expected greater care and effort on the part of the man appointed to protect her interests. On the other hand, another relative and key adviser, her Rothenburg cousin Johann Hornberger, also deferred to the lawyers on the question of whether a father's testament might override a parental marriage contract.[19]

Despite his claim never to have read Hermann Büschler's testament, cousin Conrad could still cite its provisions freely and in detail. He knew, for example, that it gave Philip a twelve-hundred-gulden bond, along with the family house and the Lindenau manor, and that sister Agatha, but not Anna, had been appropriately compensated for the latter properties, which made up a sizable part of the joint family property.[20] These were new grounds for Anna to suspect, as she would soon allege, that her curator had all along been conspiring with her enemies.

Conrad Büschler's ability to cite the provisions of her father's testament sight unseen was not, however, a *prima facie* case for a conspiracy. The details of the testament were readily available to him, as they were to any other interested party, through Anna's siblings, who were eager to have them known, since the testament so strongly favored them. The testament had also been publicly read to the entire family at an official ceremony, which Anna and her curator attended. So cousin Conrad could have known its key provisions without actually having held it in hand. Even so, one in his position should not have relied so trustingly on such biased communication for his knowledge of data so vital to his client, especially if there were the slightest grounds for suspecting that her siblings were conspiring with the council against her. And it could hardly have been proper conduct for her curator not to have demanded copies of all the pertinent documents and to have studied them with great care.

Whether they were justified or not, Anna had her doubts about her curator's loyalty, which she obliquely expressed when she protested that he had not been properly sworn to his office. By that she meant that he had not, as was ordinarily required of one in his position, taken a personal oath of loyalty to her, a fact he and other witnesses frankly acknowledged during the hearings. His was rather an ad hoc appointment by the city council, which empowered him to act in an official capacity on her behalf only and until she and her siblings could reach agreement on her share of the family inheritance.[21] In other words, his was not a normal curatorship, but a special assignment occasioned by a specific conflict, the resolution of which also terminated his responsibility.

By making her curator's failure to take the customary oath of his office grounds for nullifying the agreement with her siblings, Anna and her lawyer were citing what they believed to be both a technical violation of the curatorial position and an improper representation of her case by one who might be deemed to have been all too compliant with city hall.

 Surviving the Fittest

IF ANNA HAD BEEN MANIPULATED BY HER SIBLINGS AS BLATANTLY as she claimed, surely someone else would have recognized it as well at the time. It is not credible that those who allegedly conspired against her also succeeded in co-opting absolutely everyone involved in the case. A more likely scenario is that Anna had been motivated by something other than fear of her siblings and the city council when she acquiesced so politely in the agreement of 1543. She could reasonably have favored the agreement at the time simply for its immediate benefits, only later to be repulsed by its terms, when they proved to be less generous over the long run than she believed they would and should be. In other words, it is possible that both sides were telling the truth about what had happened on October 16, 1543.

A telling clue to Anna's state of mind in the months surrounding the agreement with her siblings appears in the testimony of cousin Johann Hornberger during the Machtolff hearings. He had watched her on that day in 1543 when her father's testament was read aloud to the assembled family, and her reaction had stuck in his mind. "She began to weep," he testified, "because she knew the trouble it would bring her."[22] Her disinheritance had been her father's *coup de grâce*, and he had delivered it at precisely the right time. By her own description, Anna was then more vulnerable than ever before or after in her life. The sudden death of her husband, a scant month after her father's, had left her a widow with a mountain of debt, and her health had been failing at the time as well, in addition to all of which she was now to be disinherited.

Just how dire her situation had become would be confirmed nine months later, in July 1544, when the Hall militia arrested her in Münkheim as she attempted to travel from Speyer to Hall for her famous nonhearing before the city council on charges of defaming her siblings. In the intervening months, she had effectively scuttled the agreement with her siblings and fled to Neuenstein and then on to Speyer, where she intended to challenge it in the imperial court.

In choosing this course of action, she had given up her new furnished house in Hall and her tidy eighty-gulden annuity. At the time of her capture in Münkheim, the only possession on her person was a traveling case, or "bundle," as bürgermeister Feuchter described it. When opened and searched, it was found to contain the residue of a harsh life: a few letters, pieces of leftover food, some strands of dirty red yarn, and two "Heilbronn roots," or "herbs of grace,"[23] a popular medicinal plant of Eurasian origin used as a cure-all.

None who knew Anna's condition in those days doubted that the agreement, in giving her anything at all, was to her advantage.[24] There is also no reason to doubt that that had been Anna's point of view as well when she signed it. She had good, pragmatic reasons for reaching a prompt agreement with her siblings on her father's legacy, even if it meant the immediate forfeiture of any further claim to what she believed to be a full and fair share of that legacy.

That does not mean, however, that her siblings and some city officials did not knowingly and in concert take advantage of her condition and profit from the agreement. For Anna, it was another situation in which agreeing to take half a loaf made more sense than being handed much less. Everyone had something to gain by the agreement. For Anna, it meant immediate debt relief and a basic livelihood. For her siblings, it was a modest act of generosity that promised to pay big dividends. By it they expected to silence their sister's criticism, sanction their greater inheritance, and perhaps even soothe their own consciences, to the extent that the latter were pained. For the city council, the accord promised to veil the misdeeds of a former bürgermeister and to end a family feud that had gone on much too long and was threatening once again to bring the unwanted intrusion of a higher court into local affairs.

Their Sister's Keeper

WHY HAD AN AGREEMENT THAT SEEMED TO SERVE THE INTERESTS of so many collapsed so quickly? There is evidence that it was not Anna but Philip and Agatha who actually sowed the seeds of its destruction. They did so by making the negotiations difficult from the start, and then, after the agreement was signed, by fulfilling their obligations in as slow and tedious a fashion as possible. According to one witness, Philip and Agatha had at first not wanted to increase Anna's portion of the inheritance at all, and even when they recognized that peace with her was in their own best interest, they resented the concessions they felt forced to make.[25] And when in fulfillment of the agreement they had to pay off her creditors, they proceeded cautiously and reluctantly, so much so that councilman Georg Bernbeck had to spur them to action.[26] By all reports, Philip was a creditor's nightmare, poring over each claim and requiring documentation for every pfennig. And at every opportunity, he and Agatha piously reminded Anna of their magnanimity and her unworthiness.

Such presumption on the part of her siblings was particularly galling to Anna, who cited it among her grievances. If anything, she believed herself to be the more righteous party and the one whose cause was just. In so believing, she was not without her supporters. Volk von Rossdorf declared her to be "no bastard" and thought her father had been wrong to treat her as such.[27] He also stated that the main gossip he had heard about her was that she had been treated unfairly[28]—an indication that at least in the matter of her inheritance, popular opinion was by no means completely against Anna. Heidelberg law student David Schmidlin, who may have gotten to know Anna only after the events of 1544 (he was seventeen when they occurred), shared the view that her father had no right to recant the terms of the marriage contract with her mother,[29] and he believed that she had been "defrauded" by her siblings.[30] Plasterer Philip Strobel from Oehringen (near Neuenstein in the county of Hohenlohe) concurred in this judgment, for he had seen with his own eyes the worn pewter Anna had been given as her share of chattel.[31]

The majority of witnesses still thought the agreement with her siblings, despite its inequities, benefited Anna, and most were at a loss to explain why she rejected assistance she so urgently needed. Several cited Philip's refusal to pay new debts along with the old as triggering her action, which was also her siblings' explanation.[32] A more cynical explanation, and one her siblings may also have entertained, is that she had knowingly entered the agreement with mischievous intentions, believing that once it was firmly in place and her creditors had been turned her brother's way, he would be persuaded, or even forced, to pay her new debts as well as old. It was then only when Philip emphatically turned away new creditors that Anna opportunistically threatened a new round of litigation.

Despite Anna's complaints about the agreement, her siblings did pay a sizable number of debts. The Heilbronn lawyer, Jacob Ehinger, claimed that most of her creditors, both Jewish and Christian, had been paid.[33] Councilman Georg Bernbach personally acted as a middleman for Philip and Agatha with Jewish creditors in Frankfurt, delivering 325 gulden to them in payment of Anna's debts.[34] And Gilg Menger, Anna's friend in Hall, got back from her brother the forty gulden he had lent her.[35]

If there is an initial act that may be said to have begun the unraveling of the agreement, it was most likely Philip's exceedingly meticulous negotiations with his sister's creditors. In fairness to Philip, curators and guardians at this time were expected to be tough. According to witnesses, he summoned each creditor to his house and required that he explain why, by how much, and since when his sister had been indebted to him, and to document his claim fully with bills and receipts. Philip intended thereby to learn the exact nature of each loan and put himself in a position to distinguish between fair and exorbitant interest. In that undertaking, every record was suspect, no question out of bounds, and rudeness a proper tool.

Needless to say, Philip bruised many egos in the process. When he found everything to be in order and aboveboard, he promptly paid the debt in full. When he believed that the conditions of a loan had been unfair or in error, he either bargained the creditor down or sent him away unpaid. Moses of Beihingen, the only creditor Anna mentions by name, was alleged by Philip to have demanded more than double what Philip thought to be fair and, in the end, agreed to pay.[36] Moses was only the most persistent of Anna's creditors, and by no means the only one angered by her brother's intense scrutiny. Several others also complained to the city council that Anna's legitimate debts were not being paid, despite the agreement with her siblings.[37] And Anna, to her great dismay, found her creditors, with Moses of Beihingen in the lead, back on her doorstep.

According to David Schmidlin, it was this series of events, triggered by her brother's scrupulosity, that ended the initial post-agreement amity among the three and drove Anna back into the courts. When her creditors started hounding her again, she concluded that her brother did not intend to keep his part of the deal, refusing not only to pay debts incurred after the agreement, but a number incurred before.[38] That conclusion, perhaps a bit hasty on her part, was further bolstered by her siblings' refusal to allow her to take from her father's house pieces of furniture to which she was particularly attached and which she greatly desired to have as her own.[39]

The majority of witnesses, however, rejected Anna's charge that her siblings had refused to pay her annuity, and that this refusal had justified her return to the courts. While it is true that she did not receive the annuity for several years, unwillingness on the part of her siblings to pay it was not the actual cause. According to Conrad Büschler, direct payments to Anna had stopped after the first quarterly payment,[40] and thereafter her siblings, per order of the city council, faithfully deposited the amount specified by the agreement with the city. Exactly what the city did with the accumulating money during the interim is unclear, but in March 1548, by order of the imperial court in Augsburg, the council paid Anna and her new husband the accumulated sum. Thereafter, regular quarterly payments to the Sporlands resumed, receipts for which exist until July 1551.[41]

There is plenty of testimony to her siblings' fidelity to the agreement. Nobleman Georg Senft boasted to the commissioners of his brother-in-law Philip's goodwill in meeting his obligations: not only did he pay many of Anna's debts in 1544, but he had also continued to pay her annuity to the present day (1551)—something Senft could personally attest, as he had a few weeks earlier placed another thirty-gulden installment in Johann von Sporland's hands.[42] So the dispute over Anna's annuity was a settled matter after 1548. That part of the 1543 agreement, at least, had survived the agreement's collapse, albeit in a somewhat tortured fashion.

✵ In 1541, Emperor Charles V visited the city and dined in Hermann Büschler's house, today part of the Hotel Adelshof. A figure of the emperor, commemorating this and a second visit in 1546, stands over the entryway on Market Square (see pp. 145-146).

(Credit: Steven Ozment)

The Ruins of Castle Limpurg. In 1575, the Haller demolished Castle Limpurg, although not yet to the point depicted here, which portrays the ruins in 1910, much as they are today. When visiting, Anna came through the entry gate (above the end of the front wall) and gained access to the castle via the inner bridge (between the entry gate and the tower remains), under which one passed into the castle's lush, protected gardens. *(Credit: G. Schmidt, Stadtarchiv Hall (HV BIII/1503)*

⬛ The entryway to Castle Limpurg, through
which Anna passed many times.
(Credit: Steven Ozment)

⬚ Daniel Treutwein's family coat of arms (see p. 75) as displayed on the gravestone of Conrad Treutwein (d. 1438).
(Credit: Stadtarchiv Schwäbisch Hall)

⬚ Erasmus, his wife Anna of Lodron, and their three children (see p.100). In the Schenks' room, Comburg cloister.
(Credit: Stadtarchiv Hall)

¶ Bey Hans Glaſer brieffmaler zu Nurnberg hinter S. Lorengen auff dem plag.

A Cavalryman and His Girlfriend. *I am a Born Cavalryman Elected and Destined to War.* Cavalryman: "Come with me my little maid/ And we'll be off to Italy.../I'll provide you with a horse or wagon/ And dress you up in silk or satin/With me, you'll never know hunger/You'll have chicken boiled and fried/I have many taler and ducats/Which shall all become yours/If only you'll stick by me." *(Credit: Niklas Stoer,* Max Geisberg, The German Single-Leaf Woodcut: 1500-1550, *IV, rev. and ed. by Walter L. Strauss (Hacker Art Books Inc.: New York, 1974), p.1355.)*

The Hohenlohe castle in Neuenstein was one of several Hohenlohe castles in the region. There, Anna, apparently with the assistance of Erasmus, found a refuge from her father (see p. 98). Here, the castle's inner courtyard is portrayed.

(Credit: Steven Ozment)

The gravestone of Anna's sister Agatha Schanz (d. 1559). The banner around her head reads: "O, Lord Jesus, have mercy on me." The Büschler (top left) and Hornberger (top right) coats of arms are clearly visible. In St. Michael's Church.

(Credit: Steven Ozment)

ridicule of her brother at the imperial diet.[45] The seventy-year-old Limpurger and sometime city servant and messenger Hans Stahel also had a log for the fire. He had known Anna for forty years, going all the way back to the time when she worked for the Schenkin in castle Limpurg. After the collapse of her agreement with her siblings in 1544, he frequently heard her complain about her brother's success in driving her out of Hall. It enraged her no end that Philip remained in their parents' house and enjoyed their property while she was once again living a near vagabond's life. Stahel heard her vow to get even with her brother through the courts.[46]

Several witnesses testified that Anna had carried incriminating letters on her person when Hall militiamen arrested her in Münkheim. Some of these letters she apparently managed to destroy before they could be taken from her and read. According to reports, she shredded several with her teeth while in transit to Hall, and threw them away with her excrement to ensure their loss. The confiscated surviving letters were sent to the imperial court, evidently to document the city's charges of her vicious slandering.[47] Although the witnesses offer no summary of their contents, an Oehringen shoemaker testified that one of the letters was from a physician in Speyer (perhaps a medical prescription), while another was a copy of the defamation charges lodged against her by her brother.[48]

As for Anna's treatment during her imprisonment in Hall, witnesses for the city insisted that she had been given "food, drink, and every care,"[49] and they scoffed at her charges of mistreatment. Hans Stahel, who had orders to feed her "according to need" during her weeks in the tower, could recall no complaints from her about the treatment she received.[50]

As for Anna's charges that the city had plans to confine her for life, councilman Melchior Wetzel acknowledged that a special room had been under construction for her, but had not been completed because of her escape.[51] And Lienhard Bleimeier confirmed that the council had indeed ordered a special cell to be built, although he could not recall the council's exact intentions at the time.[52]

Witnesses from outside the council had also heard talk about an "eternal prison" for Anna. Barbara Dollen knew about it, but she could not say whether Anna was to be put there for life.[53] Nicholas Schmidlin, a tailor who worked for Count Georg of Hohenlohe, tes-

Gelbinger street, where Anna moved after the settlement with her siblings (see pp. 149-150), was a "suburb" outside Hall's walls. Today, the only surviving structure Anna would immediately recognize is the ancient tower known as the Josenturn.

(Credit: Steven Ozment)

 Collections of official documents (like the Büschler family trial records) were stored in great oaken cabinets, which were in turn placed in locked vaults. The one shown here contains the papers and deeds of the Sybilla Egen Foundation. Sybilla Egen (ca. 1470-1538) lived three doors down from the Büschlers and established foundations for needy students and artisans, poor girls, pregnant women, and widows. In Hällisch-Frankisches Museum.
(Credit: Steven Ozment)

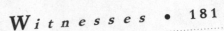 *The Weight of the Evidence*

WHAT HAD BEEN AT STAKE FOR PHILIP AND AGATHA IN THESE long-drawn-out proceedings was their right to keep a grossly disproportionate share of the family inheritance. Although a case was made on Anna's behalf, in the end she got no more of it than what the agreement with her siblings had originally provided, and not even all of that. Still, given the circumstances of her case, the settlement seemed a fair one to the majority of witnesses and some righting of the injustice done her by her father's testament.

More was at stake for the city council. Anna had accused the city not only of illegally arresting her, but also of brutalizing her while she was held prisoner in the tower and, after falling ill, chained to a bed in the hospice. If those allegations were true, the city was guilty of denying due process to a citizen and thereby threatening public order. The willingness of the imperial court in Rottweil to fine Hall for breach of safe-conduct clearly indicates that the imperial government was no more of a mind to tolerate such anarchy in its cities than it was among factious noblemen in the countryside. Because of Anna's challenge, Hall faced still another confrontation with a higher court and possible new punitive fines, a most burdensome prospect for an imperial city jealous of its sovereignty and weary of conflict with Anna Büschler.

Although Anna's failure to answer three summonses became the immediate legal ground for her arrest and incarceration in 1544, witnesses make it clear that her public attacks on the city council in Speyer played the larger role. According to councilman Conrad Seither, her "contemptuous letters" to the council and her siblings and her "disdaining of the council hither and yon" were "not the least reason" the militia seized her in Münkheim.[43] She was arrested, another testified, "for the sake of good order, after having been heard to say inappropriate things about the council in Speyer and elsewhere, and even to threaten the city with harm"—behavior deemed completely unbefitting a citizen sworn to uphold her government.[44]

Council witnesses also recalled her intemperate remarks in Wurzelmann's house, when she subjected Hall's delegation to "many threatening and sarcastic words," as well as her equally embarrassing public tified that Anna had first been confined in the tower, but had fallen ill there and had had to be placed in the hospice, where her attendants had chained her to a bed in a small room. It was at that time that he had heard rumors about the construction of a special room for her with iron grates that opened and closed,[54] although he acknowledged that he never actually saw such a cell himself.

On the other hand, bürgermeister Lienhard Feuchter emphatically denied that the city council ever contemplated imprisoning Anna for life: "No, by no means did anyone want to arrest or imprison her eternally; [our intention was] only to place her in a safe, womanly custody for a while."[55] Despite the bürgermeister's protestations, at least one councilman remembered the episode with embarrassment and regret, indicating that there had indeed been division within the council over the action. According to Michael Seiboth, Anna's imprisonment was "undeserved"[56] and should never have happened, "because more things may be overlooked in a woman than in a man."

That sentiment was typical of the age and shared by a number of witnesses, who, on the one hand, disapproved of Anna's behavior, yet, on the other, thought her father and the city council also held some responsibility for it. Women at this time were believed to be physically, intellectually, and morally weaker than men, and hence more vulnerable to harm, deceit, and temptation, and thus in greater need of protection and supervision by the men in their lives. That, however, did not, as logic would seem to dictate, increase male tolerance and sympathy for the weaker sex when, as biology allegedly inclined it to do, it succumbed to its weaker nature. A woman caught in adultery might legally be executed on the spot by her husband, but not the presumably stronger husband caught in adultery by his wife. And only men living in the Middle Ages could deem it a kinder execution for a capital crime to drown, bury alive, or burn a woman at the stake rather than decapitate, hang, or tear her apart on the wheel, as was done with men.[57] If, however, unlike Michael Seiboth, the other councilmen of Hall had no apologies for treating Anna like a man, neither did any of them step forward to proclaim her arrest and imprisonment, evidently for eternity, to be the city council's finest hour.

The Grieving Mary, from an entombment scene sculpted from Linden wood in Kunzelsau around 1470. On display in Hall's Hällisch-Frankisches Museum.

CHAPTER

SEVEN

The Moral

TO THE CITY'S GREAT RELIEF, THE IMPERIAL COURT ACCEPTED ITS argument that Anna had escaped her cell before the council could act on the penal mandate ordering her release,[1] thereby voiding her charge that the city had willfully disobeyed the higher court's order to release her. To all intents and purposes, Anna's two other charges—that her siblings had forced a devious and unkept agreement on her and that the council had unlawfully arrested and imprisoned her—were rendered moot as well by her sudden death in January 1552. Her widowed husband kept the litigation going until 1554, seeking in vain to win an all too belated justice for Anna as well as a share of the Büschler family inheritance for himself as her surviving spouse. The majority of witnesses did not, however, support Anna's charges, and had she lived to hear a final ruling from the imperial commissioners, the judgment would most likely have been a great disappointment to her.

Although lacking a happy ending, our story is not, however, without salutary lessons. For in that distant age, as in our own, rationality and madness accompanied one another, the one as prominent and real as the other.

The most immediate lesson of the Büschler family history is that protracted, self-destructive litigation is no novelty of the twentieth century. Particularly during the second half of the sixteenth century, when the witch craze peaked in Germany, ordinary people proved all too willing to resolve their petty grievances with their neighbors by accusing them of harmful magic, and the clergy and the politicians learned to enlarge their powers by trying old women and men in the witch court, all to the delight and profit of the rapidly growing legal profession.[2] In this regard, the Büschler family litigation was another sign of the times.

The three courts in which Anna directly pled her case, however, were no witch courts, and she did not end up on a pyre, or chained forever to a table in her father's house, or left to rot in the eternal prison contemplated for her by the city council. Year after year, one court or another heard and acted on her complaints, and some of what she demanded she eventually got. Indeed, many of her contemporaries believed she was treated better than she deserved, given her defiant trampling of the values and expectations of her age.

Another obvious lesson of our story is that the conflation of legislative, executive, and judicial powers in a single body can indeed be as perilous to the rights and well-being of individuals as the American founding fathers warned in the eighteenth century.[3] The political theorists of the sixteenth century knew that too, however, and they warned their fellow citizens no less urgently and eloquently of the danger of concentrating political power in the hands of a few. Our modern concepts of representative government and the right of lower officials to depose tyrants for the good of the body politic also have their origins in these early centuries. Specifically, these now self-evident truths grew out of the experience of late medieval churchmen, who battled a self-aggrandizing and schismatic papacy in both books and councils, and the suffering of German Lutherans and French and Netherlands Calvinists, who endured defeat and tyrannous rule at the hands of imperial Spain.[4]

If, despite the successful constitutional struggle of 1510–1512, the city council of Hall still appears to have remained a petty aristocracy of wealth and privilege throughout the sixteenth century, that same council also prized, celebrated, fought to retain, and foresaw the enlargement of the political representation the city had by that time attained. And the council was as ready to retire, or punish, a bürgermeister for moral and ethical failings, which it did in the case of Hermann Büschler, as to depose, or ostracize, councilmen for resisting self-interested, real-political change, as those who opposed the Reformation after 1523 discovered. Anna Büschler may not have received justice and fairness in her home court sufficient to assuage the modern conscience, but she was heard there. And because the city council was not a legal island but subject to a network of imperial courts willing to prod and override it, she did not end up empty-handed. But that also happened in part because the city council itself, for all its many failings, remained a principled body, some of whose members sympathized with her plight.

Still a third clear lesson of Anna's story is that women at this time were not powerless victims of male rule. They had both the ability and the opportunity, in the absence of modern equality, to define themselves and their self-worth in fully satisfying ways through the spheres of life and work then available to them both within and outside the home.[5] Despite the limited nature of women's educational and vocational opportunities in comparison with men's, and the fact that women could participate in the most important civic and political activities only vicariously, they still had inalienable rights and significant access to the courts, by which they could climb onto the stage of history and leave their mark, as Anna did.[6] Although women everywhere faced an ancient gender-based discrimination that men did not, its effect on them was not altogether unlike the discrimination most contemporary males experienced because of their inferior social standing. Gender alone did not entitle any man to the rights and protections of citizenship (*Bürgerrecht*), which the widowed Anna could purchase on October 17, 1543,[7] thanks to the new property and wealth she (momentarily) received after the settlement of the family estate with her siblings. Nor could gender alone qualify males to hold public office. Only wealth, property, and social standing gained such rights, protections, and privileges for both males and females. Nor could the vast majority of men, any more than women, expect to receive a university education and pursue a lucrative career in theology, law, or medicine. Most urban males succeeded to the handicraft trades and businesses of their fathers and grandfathers as predictably and docilely as women followed their mothers into the textile and food-processing industries.[8] A substantial number of males were also accused of witchcraft; approximately one out of every five of the perhaps 80,000 to 100,000 people suspected, tried, and/or executed for witchcraft between 1400 and 1700 was a male.[9] As in modern times, one's material position in the world was as much one's destiny as biology.

Anna's story suggests that the "sexism" that seems so pervasive in the literature and laws of late medieval and Renaissance Europe[10] was not as prominent or severe in actual family life and social practice. The dark portrayals of women that appear in rare, fringe tracts like the infamous *Malleus Maleficarum* (1487), the Church's great manual for the detection and punishment of witches, certainly merit the label "misogynous": hating and dismissive of women. Written by two German Dominican inquisitors, who were obsessed with the alleged seductive and violent nature of womankind (they believed, for example, that witches had sex with the devil and could make men's penises magically disappear), this pornographic classic provoked lurid interest in perverse women among the new reading public, and for a century and a half it placed in the hands of both Church and state an insidious tool for self-aggrandizement.[11]

The imaginations of two fifteenth-century clerics cannot, however, be read as serious commentary on the real-life relationships between men and women in late medieval Germany. For all their crudity, ridicule, and worry over womankind's weaknesses, the mainstream didactic literature and popular entertainments of these centuries were far more inclined to encourage a woman's moral striving and inner talents than to dismiss or to demonize them.[12]

In both everyday life and times of crisis, women in the sixteenth century had access to effective personal and legal resources. As Anna demonstrated for almost a quarter of a century, even "bad girls" could challenge manifest abuse and lawbreaking at the highest levels of their societies, commanding public attention, and do so with a degree of success. Society's general attitude toward women at this time is more accurately described as condescending and protective than as hateful and dismissive. To his fellow citizens, Hermann Büschler's treatment of his daughter was both unusual and unacceptable and was neither condoned nor left unpunished. And although the consequences were not of a magnitude capable of satisfying a modern sense of justice any more than they could Anna's at the time, the bürgermeister did lose his position in the city council, which, after much outside prodding, also forced him to give his daughter some of what was legally hers.

There is a final lesson to be learned from Anna's story that is not as obvious as the aforementioned. It is one about human nature and character that transcends gender and politics and may be more important than both. Anna's story is both stranger than fiction and truer than history, and neither the novelist nor the historian has yet done it any justice. Despite her prominence in the historical record, she has been given scant attention from modern scholars, and even that little bit has been obscured by the larger figures and events in her life. On the few occasions when she has popped up in a literary or historical work, it has been in the most opprobrious of roles: a disobedient daughter, a promiscuous woman, a disloyal citizen, an ungrateful sibling, a hateful widow.

In 1922, German novelist Leonhard Frank published a popular bi-

ography of Hermann Büschler, into which he inserted, under a pseu-
donym, a fictitious recreation of Anna's life.[13] The novel's focus was
on the constitutional crisis of 1510–1512 and the heroic role Hermann
Büschler played in it.[14] From the perspective of the 1920s novelist, the
bürgermeister's feat was a memorable victory for the political freedom
of the German people. Hermann Büschler appears in the novel as an
ordinary man who is said to have become the "darling of the common
man" and "the hero of Hall" because he "listened to the voices of his
forefathers [and heeded] the call of history."[15]

The high point of the story is the dramatic meeting with the emperor, set in Frankfurt, when Hermann Büschler, clad in his "marvel-
ous attire," literally put his life on the line for Hall's nonnoble burghers
and artisans. In the novelist's account, Emperor Maximilian reminisces
for a few moments with his bold supplicant after the encounter, recalling a visit he had made to Hall a decade earlier, at which time he
lodged in the home of Hermann Büschler's father, a man he claimed
still to remember well.[16]

Anna appears in the story as the bürgermeister's beautiful but way-
ward daughter, Suzanne, a girl who loves to dance and defy her parents, and whose behavior poses for her famous father a test of paternal
devotion and courage almost as great as the testing of his political will
by the city's constitutional crisis. Suzanne's story is told to extol Hermann Büschler's heroic qualities as a father, complementing his heroic
qualities as a politician. If the novelist's account of her life is not totally
the product of his own imagination, some of it may derive from local
legends about fathers with difficult daughters, for the "Anna" found
here is not the woman of historical record.[17]

In the story, Suzanne is "caught in the mysticism of love" with a
worthless ensign named Hans (Daniel Treutwein?), a convicted felon
who once spent three months in jail. Defying her parents, she persists
in seeing him. She also has a respectable suitor from a good Hall family,
Georg Seiferheld (Erasmus of Limpurg?),[18] a man with solid connections and a certain future, who once brought her a personal greeting
from Albrecht Dürer. To her parents' dismay, however, Georg has not
been able to win her heart.

When Suzanne runs away with the unworthy Hans, Georg to his
credit and ultimate peril, tracks them down, eventually finding Suzanne in Frankfurt, "deceived, dishonored, and abandoned," and living

By all odds, Anna should have been crushed by the forces arrayed against her and never have appeared prominently in the historical record. Yet she survived far beyond what either contemporaries or a modern reader might reasonably have expected. There were even some modest spoils of victory along the way, and there might have been more, had she been more inclined to accept one-sided compromises. The astonishing thing is that she held out for so long and managed so well against such formidable opposition.

How she did it is no mystery. She had her supporters on her mother's side of the family and other friends as well, and thanks initially to Erasmus and her Rothenburg connections and later to her two husbands, she cultivated her own noble counselors and friends in high places, who helped her make the most of her rights and opportunities. The imperial courts to which she turned never took her charges lightly, and even the city council of Hall could not look the other way when it found itself confronted by clear evidence of her father's transgression of the law. And among the townspeople who followed her trials and tribulations, there were some who believed she deserved better than she got. In the end, however, it was up to Anna herself to make these various connections and resources work to her advantage. To the extent that it can be so described, Anna Büschler was her own success story.

The defining moment was surely her father's stunning cruelty in 1525. That terrible event created in Anna a lifelong rage, which complemented her youthful defiance. Righteous anger inspired her through all the subsequent decades of deprivation and litigation. The opportunism of her siblings and the manipulation of the city council further fed that anger. Hers was the same emotional stuff out of which contemporary religious reforms and peasant revolts were born: the transforming experience of having been bullied and defrauded by people and institutions she had believed she could trust and rely on, and from which she might reasonably have expected some forgiveness for her youthful failings and a more certain justice for the crimes she believed had been committed against her.

Anna always understood what neither the novelist nor the historian could see: a father who knew better had injured his child, and finding himself unobstructed by a city government aware of his actions and in a position to stop them, he compounded the injury for decades all the way to his grave and hers. Her siblings and the city council understood the situation well enough, but neither were deeply moved by it. After her father's death, her brother and sister tried in their own way to make amends by providing her with a more generous, if still grossly disproportionate, share of the family inheritance. Although the gain seemed small to Anna by comparison with what she believed she had lost, she would have been well advised to accept it gratefully and stifle her anger. The indignity she suffered in her mid-twenties had been too great to allow her to do that, however, and by 1543, she had simply lived with its memory for too long. Partial compensation only poured salt in wounds that would not mend; accepting half a loaf now could only be a way to temporize.

There are injuries to the human spirit which can never be healed, and in the presence of which modern ideals of justice and fairness seem only to pale and even to punish. They are situations in which there is nothing one can say or do to make the injured whole again or to compensate the loss; such emotional recrudescences are constant and inevitable. For those who behold such injury, the episode is simply over and done, and it makes little difference whether one curses the darkness or lights a candle, for what has been broken cannot and will not be fixed this side of eternity.

History is littered with such indelible injuries. The only saving grace in these situations is the injured party's own refusal to go quietly. There is a shriek of recognition, a redeeming sarcasm, a slap of defiance, which ennobles a person's destruction and distinguishes it from abject defeat. By such resolve Anna redressed her own injury and departed the world with a sense of her own worth, knowing her life had been neither a pity nor in vain.

From this perspective, Anna Büschler's petty thievery and heavy petting, rejection of paternal and conciliar authority, and embarrassment of her family and hometown, were not the only scandal in sixteenth century Hall. There were also the cruelty of a father, the miserly kindness of a brother and a sister, and the indifference of a city council, each of whom might, even by sixteenth century standards, have accommodated this unfortunate woman at modest expense to themselves. Although little note has been taken of Anna Büschler in history books and novels, and even that little bit has been unkind, in the inner battle for human dignity, which goes on in every individual life beneath the great wars and reforms of an age, Anna may have been more heroic than the bürgermeister of Hall and the Schenk of Limpurg.

NOTES

CHAPTER ONE: THE STORY

1. There were two periods of negotiation and/or litigation between Anna and her father (1525–1528, 1534) and two with her siblings (1543–44, 1550–52). From these confrontations resulted a significant number of pertinent documents and over a thousand manuscript pages of witness testimony. The greater part of both was gathered during hearings held by imperial commissioners between late 1550 and early 1552. Thanks to the survival of these sources, Anna's story can today be told. The entire collection of sources presently catalogued in the HSA Stuttgart is described in *Akten des Reichskammergerichts im Hauptstaatsarchiv Stuttgart A-D, Inventar des Bestands C3*, ed. Alexander Brunotte and Raimund J. Weber (Stuttgart, 1993), pp. 387–89.

2. "Hall" here means Schwäbisch Hall and is not to be confused with Halle on the Saale. It was apparently designated "Swabian" in 1191, when the Hohenstaufens included the city with Rothenberg and Wimpfen in the duchy of Swabia—thus, a larger political, not a regional ethnic, designation. Eduard Krüger, *Schwäbisch Hall. Mit Grosskomburg, Kleinkomburg, Steinbach und Limpurg. Ein Gang Durch Geschichte und Kunst* (Schwäbisch Hall, 1953), p. 27. According to Wilhelm German, the addition of "Schwäbisch" to Hall is a possible dark reminiscence of the mother church of Hall-Steinbach, which belonged to the Swabian bishopric of Augsburg ("Komburg-Steinbach" was originally "Schwäbisch-Augsburgisch"). *Chronik von Schwäbisch Hall und Umgebung. Von den ältesten Zeiten bis zur Gegenwart* (Schwäbisch Hall, 1989; reprint of original edition of 1900), p. 39.

3. *Specificationes eins erbern Rath der statt Hall gegen Anna Büschler*, or *Der Herrnn Beclagten Defensional Articull* [henceforth, *Defensional Articull*], in *Beweisrodel des ksl. Komissars lic. Johann Machtolff* [henceforth, *Machtolff*] (1552), HSA Stuttgart, C3 Bü 529 (7, Q32).

4. Robert S. Gottfried, *The Black Death: Natural and Human Disaster in Medieval Europe* (New York, 1983); Rudolf Hirsch, *Printing, Selling and Reading, 1450–1550* (Wiesbaden, 1974), pp. 10–23; Lucien Febvre, "The Origins of the French Reformation: A Badly-Put Question?" in *A New Kind of History and Other Essays: Lucien Febvre*, ed. Peter Burke, trans. K. Folca (New York, 1973), pp. 60–65.

5. Helmut B. Koenigsberger and George L. Mosse, *Europe in the Sixteenth Century* (New York, 1968), p. 230.

6. For a summary of this scholarship, see Steven Ozment, *Protestants: The Birth of a Revolution* (New York, 1992).

7. Anke Wolf-Graaf, *Die verborgene Geschichte der Frauenarbeit. Eine Bildchronik* (Weinheim, 1983), chs. 2–6; Lyndal Roper, *The Holy Household: Women and Morals in Reformation Augsburg* (Oxford, 1989); cf. Sherrin Marshall's perceptive critique of the latter: *Journal of Modern History* 65 (1993): 887–89.

8. Krüger, *Schwäbisch Hall*, p. 12.

9. *Ibid.*, pp. 9–13, 19; German, *Chronik von Schwäbisch Hall*, pp. 9–11.

10. Gerd Wunder, "Rudolf Nagel von Eltershofen (d. 1525) und Hermann Büschler. Stättmeister der Reichsstadt Hall," in *Lebensbilder aus Schwaben und Franken*, ed. Max Miller and Robert Uhland (Stuttgart, 1960), pp. 35–38; Gerhard Wunder and Georg Lenckner, *Die Bürgerschaft der Reichstadt Hall von 1395–1600* (Stuttgart, 1956), no. 1149, p. 161.

11. Heide Wunder, *"Er ist die sonn', sie ist der Mond." Frauen in der Frühen Neuzeit* (Munich, 1992), pp. 94–99.

12. Gerd Wunder, *Die Bürger von Hall. Sozialgeschichte einer Reichsstadt 1216–1802* (Sigmaringen, 1980), p. 173; Anette Völker-Rasor, *Bilderpaare—Paarbilder: Die Ehe in Autobiographien des 16. Jahrhunderts* (Freiburg, 1993), p. 120.

13. Shulamith Shahar, *Childhood in the Middle Ages*, translated by Chaya Galai (London, 1992), p. 229.

14. Gerd Wunder, *Die Bürger von Hall*, p. 177.

15. "Ein seltsams leben hetten sie mit einander gefurt." Councilman Bernhard Werner, response to *Uff dise nachgeende Fragstuck . . .*, in *Beweisrodel der ksl. Kommissare Johann Ludwig Windberg* [henceforth, Windberg] (1551), HSA Stuttgart, C3 Bü 530 (7, Q30/31).

16. Wunder, *Die Bürger von Hall*, p. 76. See below. The embarrassment the two caused the town may explain why, despite the survival of memorials to her siblings, no representations of Anna or her father to the best of my knowledge exist.

17. "Die erbarn alten geschlechten." Johann Herolt, *Chronica, zeit- unnd jarbuch vonn der statt Hall ursprung unnd was sich darinnen vrloffen unnd wasz fur schlösser umb Hall gestanden [1540–45]*, ed. Christian Kolb (Stuttgart, 1894), pp. 170–175.

18. Gerd Wunder, *Die Bürger von Hall*, pp. 163, 186.

19. German, *Chronik von Schwäbisch Hall*, pp. 34, 38–40; Krüger, *Schwäbisch Hall*, p. 24.

20. German, *Chronik von Schwäbisch Hall*, p. 42.

21. Herolt, *Chronica*, pp. 98–99, n. 3; Gerd Wunder, "Die Haller Ratsverstörung von 1509 bis 1512," *Jahrbuch des historischen Vereins für Württembergisch Franken*, N.F. 30 (1955): 57–68; 62; Gerd Wunder, *Die Bürger von Hall*, p. 73; and especially Gerhard Wunder and Georg Lenckner, *Bürgerschaft der Reichsstadt Hall*, pp. 43–49; German, *Chronik von Schwäbisch Hall*, pp. 70, 73.

22. Gerd Wunder, *Die Bürger von Hall*, p. 179.

23. Herolt, *Chronica*, p. 170.

24. The richest was worth 19,000 gulden. Gerd Wunder, "Die Haller Ratsverstörung": 62–63.

25. "Er möcht . . . auff die stuben zum wein gehen aber zu gleichen stubherrn nemen sie in nit." Herolt, *Chronica*, p. 170.

26. *Ibid.*

27. "Die gemainen rathsherrn und ehrlich burger." Herolt, *Chronica*, p. 171; Gerd Wunder, *Die Bürger von Hall*, p. 74.

28. Herolt, *Chronica*, p. 171.

29. Gerd Wunder, "Die Haller Ratsverstörung": 61.

30. *Ibid.*: 61–62; Herolt, *Chronica*, p. 172. These alterations of the original constitution "bedeutete praktisch eine Zementierung der Vormacht des Adels." Gerd Wunder, *Die Bürger von Hall*, p. 75.

31. "Das wohlhabende Bürgertum strömt in Rat und Gericht ein." Gerd Wunder, "Die Haller Ratsverstörung": 67; Herolt, *Chronica*, pp. 173–174; Hildegard Nordhoff-Behne, *Gerichtsbarkeit und Strafrechtsfplege in der Reichsstadt Schwäbisch Hall seit dem 15. Jahrhundert* (Schwäbisch Hall, 1971), pp. 22–23. Two patricians who remained in the council at this time, Gilg Senft and Volk von Rossdorf, would be witnesses forty years later at the Büschler family hearings. Gerd Wunder, *Die Bürger von Hall*, p. 76; see below.

32. Gerd Wunder, "Rudolf Nagel . . . und Hermann Büschler," p. 38.

33. Gerd Wunder, "Die Haller Ratsverstörung": 67.

34. "Hab ein unzuchtigs leben gnug getriben/aber der vatter habs darzu gezogen." Salt-maker Gilg Menger, to *Fragstuckh/Philipsen Buschlers unnd Schentzin contra Anna Buschlerin* [henceforth, *Fragstuckh Philipsen Buschlers*], no. 1, in

Beweisrodel der ksl. Lic. Daniel Hornung [henceforth, Hornung II] (1551), HSA Stuttgart, C3 Bü 530 (7, Q30/31).

35. *Exceptiones Articulate ... Anna Buschlerin gegen Stetmeister und Rath zu Schwebischen Hall*, HSA Stuttgart, C3 Bü 1546.

36. "Sich brechtig mit klaidung und geschmuck/mehr dann ir geburt gehalten." Councilman Adam Gutmann, to *Defensional Articull*, no. 1 (Machtolff); Volk von Rossdorf, to *ibid.*

37. Barbara Lienhard Dollen, to *Superelisif Articul Philipsen Buschlers et Consorten contra Anna Buschlerin* [henceforth, *Superelisif Articul Philipsen Buschlers*], no. 2 (Windberg); councilman Hans Eisenmanger, to *ibid.* Gerd Wunder misreads "feinberlein" (fine pearls) as "Weinbeerlein," a beret of grapes, which the finished product may have appeared to be. Gerd Wunder, "Liebesbriefe aus dem 16. Jahrhundert," *Württembergisch Franken*, N.F. 30 (1955): 69–89, 85.

38. *Fragstuckh/Philipsen Buschlers*, no. 4, to *Articuli Elisivi Anna Buschlerin gegen Philipsen Buschler und Agatha Schäntzin*, no. 3 (Hornung II).

39. It is unclear whether he had been present at the time or had received a first-hand account from the visiting friar himself.

40. "Herman Buschler sie umb ihr ungeburlich kleydung gestrafft/nemlich das sie die kleyder nit so weyt solte lasen ausschneiden/das man ihr den blossen leib sehe." Arnold Engel, to *Fragstuckh/Philipsen Buschlers*, nos. 4 and 5, to *Articuli Elisivi Anna Buschlerin*, no. 3 (Hornung II).

41. "Wan der Clegerin vatter selig/kein gefallen darab gehabt/so hette er sie nit also cleydet." Philip Strobel, to *Fragstuckh/Philipsen Buschlers*, no. 1, to *Articuli Elisivi Anna Buschlerin*, no. 3 (Hornung II)

42. German, *Chronik von Schwäbisch Hall*, pp. 179–180. Jakob and Wilhelm Grimm, *Deutsches Wörterbuch* (Leipzig 1899; Munich, 1984), vol. 15, pp. 1678, 1685–6; 2267.

43. "Ehr habs ein zeitlang gelitten/aber ihr nachmals abgestellt/ob es aber ime gefallen oder nit/hab er zeug kein wissen." Nobleman Gabriel Senff, Philip Büschler's brother-in-law, to *Fragstuckh/Philipsen Buschlers*, no. 1, to *Articuli Elisivi Anna Buschlerin*, no. 3 (Hornung II).

44. "Dem vatter uber seine zinsbrieff unnd gelt khamen/und sich darvon klaidt/klaineten und weibs gezierdt gemacht unnd ettwa vil davon verschmuckhet." Councilman Michael Seiboth, councilman, to *Defensional Articull*, no. 1 (Machtolff).

45. Her brother describes the letter as a "hauptbrieff auff 1200 gulden haubtgutt." *Superelisif Articul Philipsen Buschler contra Anna Buschlerin*, no. 2 (Windberg). The city officials of Hall also allege that she stole "all kinds of things from her father and especially several [such interest-bearing] letters." *Fragstuck eins Erbern Raths der statt Schwebischen Halle contra Anna Buschlerin* [henceforth, *Fragstuck eins Erbern Raths*], no. 2, to *Positiones et Articuli [Anna Buschlerin]*, nos. 5–13, in *Verhör von Zeugen aus Schwäbisch Hall und Oehringen durch ksl. Kommissar Lic. Daniel Hornung* [henceforth, Hornung I) (1551) HSA Stuttgart, C3 Bü 529 (7, Q29); Lienhard Vahmann, to *Superelisif Articul Philipsen Buschler contra Anna Buschlerin*, no. 2 (Windberg).

46. "Ein poden mit treidt in der Gelbingen gassenn zum theil gelert/unnd one sein wissen/verkaufft ... uber zehen scheffel nit mer doben gewesen." Barbara Dollen, to *Superelisif Articul Philipsen Buschler contra Anna Buschlerin*, no. 2 (Windberg). "Sie hinder jrem vatter/nach dem miller geschickt/unnd frucht austragen lassen." Volk von Rossdorf, to *Defensional Articull*, no. 1 (Machtolff).

47. To *Superelisif Articul Philipsen Buschler contra Anna Buschlerin*, no. 2 (Windberg).

48. *Fragstuckh/Philipsen Buschlers*, nos. 8–9, to *Articuli Elisivi Anna Buschlerin*, nos. 4–6 (Hornung II).

49. "Ubel hauset." Hans Hornberger, to *Superelisif Articul Philipsen*, no. 2, and *Uff dise nachgeende Fragstuckh*, no. 5 (Windberg).

50. "Das Daniel Treutwein seliger nach jr der clegerin oder sie nach ime gestelt hab." Anthon Brellochs, M. D., to *Der clegerin übergebene Fragstuck*, no. 4 (Machtolff). The other suitor named is Caspar Schenk from Oehringen. Lienhard Feuchter, to *Fragstuckh/Philipsen Buschlers*, no. 4, to *Articuli Elisivi Anna Buschlerin*, no. 1 (Hornung II). The priest Arnold Engel claimed to know several men in Dinkelsbühl and Hall who had courted Anna, but could not remember their names. To *Fragstuckh/Philipsen Buschlers*, no. 4, to *Articuli Elisivi Anna Buschlerin*, nos. 1–2 (Hornung II).

51. "Bey nechtlicher weyl haimlich hindern zum haus herauss gelassen." Vahmann, to *Der Clegerin übergebene Fragstuckh*, no. 2 (Machtolff).

52. To *Superelisif Articul Philipsen*, no. 2 (Windberg). Dollen: "Offtmals/wan der altt geschlaffen/unnd Daniel Treutwein vorhalben gewesen/gemissigt jr wein zu hollen jns vatters keller/unnd do sie zeugin das nit thun wöllen hett sie clegerin jr ein plos messer ans hertz gesetz dergestalt/sie zum drittenmal ir entlauffen miessen." To *ibid.*

53. To *ibid.*

54. To *ibid.*, no. 4 (Windberg).

55. To *Uff dise nachgeende Fragstuckh*, nos. 3–4 (Windberg). "Als sie mannbar gewesen/sich wider irem vatter widersetzig erzaigt." Michael Seiboth, to *Defensional Articull*, no. 1 (Machtolff).

56. *Der Clegerin übergebene Fragstruck*, no. 4 (Machtolff).

57. "Item sagt wahr/das viel eherlicher gesellen/umb sie Clegerin werben lassen/ aber gantz one/das dem vatter eynicher gefallen wöllen/das gelt lieber dann die dochter gehabt." *Articuli Elisivi Anna Buschlerin*, no. 2 (Hornung II).

58. "Er hab etwa hören sagen/das die Clegerin vill werber gehapt/jr vatter hab nie khain willen darzu geben wellen." Michael Seiboth, to *Der Clegerin übergebene Fragstuckh*, nos. 4–5 (Machtolff): "Allein am vatter erwunden/das die heurath nit fortgang." Arnold Engel, to *Fragstuckh/Philipsen Buschlers*, no. 4, to *Articuli Elisivi Anna Buschlerin*, nos. 1–2 (Hornung II).

59. *Fragstuckh/Philipsen Buschlers*, to *Articuli Elisivi Anna Buschlerin*, nos. 1–2 (Hornung II).

60. "Er hett von Herman Büschler wol gehört/das seiner dochter Annen/etlich gutt heuratt fur gestannden/sie hett aber ime nit volgen wöllen." Councilman Bernhard Werner, to *Uff dise nachgeende Fragstuckh*, no. 3 (Windberg).

61. "Er hab von alten wol gehört/das er der Annan halben, sie angesprochen werden, er wiss aber kein zu nemen . . . Ware sie der und der gern gehapt aber der vatter nit willigenn wöllen." To *Uff dise nachgeende Fragstuckh*, nos. 2–3.

62. Gerd Wunder et al., *Die Schenken von Limpurg und ihr Land* (Sigmaringen, 1982), p. 9.

63. Also "Erbschenken" or "Reichsschenken." Herolt's contemporary description is "erbschenken des heilligen Römischen reichs und semperfrey." *Chronica*, p. 70.

64. Gerd Wunder et al., *Die Schenken von Limpurg*, pp. 13–14, 18.

65. *Ibid.*, pp. 24–26.

66. German, *Chronik von Schwäbisch Hall*, p. 111.

67. *Ibid.*, pp. 107–10.

68. Herolt, *Chronica*, p. 121; *Das Land Baden-Württemberg*, vol. IV, ed. Der Landesarchiv-direktion Baden-Württemberg (Stuttgart, 1980), pp. 391–94.

69. German, *Chronik von Schwäbisch Hall*, p. 136.
70. It was normal practice to keep the original draft of a letter and to mail a finished copy. That Anna had some of her letters to Erasmus in her possession as well as his to her resulted from the fact that she sometimes kept the drafts of her letters. See Georg Steinhausen, ed., *Deutsche Privatbriefe des Mittelalters*, I: *Fürsten und Magnaten, Edle und Ritter* (Berlin, 1899), II: *Geistliche und Bürger* (Berlin, 1907); Steven Ozment, *Three Behaim Boys: Growing Up in Early Modern Germany* (New Haven, 1990).
71. "Das sy unzuchtige brief so kheiner eerlichen dochter unnd junckhfrauen zugestannden hin und wider geschriben habe." *Superelisif Articul Philipsen*, no. 1 (Windberg).
72. The letter is among the Windberg documents.
73. "Es ist ein Mann haist Herman Büschler/wan der selb nit wer wolt ich mir vill ding ein ennd schaffen."
74. "Wann derselbig nit werhe/wolt sie wol gutter ding gegen jr schenkin komen." Vahmann, to *Uff dise nachgeende Fragstuckh*, no. 5 (Windberg).
75. "Sein dochter Anna/durfft irem sun nit hembder machen/sie wolt jren sun noch selber wol bekleiden. Durch ein sollichs dann der vatter/sie auss den hauss zu jagen verursacht." *Ibid.*
76. When Erasmus's father died impoverished in 1530, he divided his modest realm between Erasmus and his older brother Karl (1498–1558). Erasmus received Limpurg (the original holding) and Obersontheim, where he later built a new, more modest castle, while Karl got the wealthier holding of Speckfeld, a new possession Gottfried had inherited only in 1521. Gerd Wunder et al., *Die Schenken von Limpurg*, pp. 36–37; Karl O. Müller, "Das Geschlecht der Reichserbschenken zu Limpurg bis zum Aussterben des Mannesstammes (1713)," *Zeitschrift für Württembergische Landesgeschichte* 5 (1941): 215–43.
77. *Der Clegerin übergebene Fragstuck*, nos. 2–3 (Machtolff).
78. "Offtmals sie ein bose schlangen gehaissen." Anthon Brellochs, to *Defensional Articull*, no. 1 (Machtolff).
79. Heide Wunder, *"Er ist die Sonn', sie ist der Mond,"* p. 59.
80. Richard von Dülmen, *Kultur und Alltag in der Frühen Neuzeit*, I: *Das Haus und seine Menschen 16.–18. Jahrhundert* (Munich, 1990), pp. 185–89; Völker-Rasor, *Bilderpaare—Paarbilder*, pp. 121, 267; Steven Ozment, *When Fathers Ruled: Family Life in Reformation Europe*, (Cambridge, MA, 1983), ch. 1.
81. Rudolf Weigand, "Ehe- und Familienrecht in der mittelalterlichen Stadt," in *Haus und Familie in der spätmittelalterlichen Stadt*, ed. Alfred Haverkamp (Cologne, 1984), p. 166.
82. Von Dülmen, *Kultur und Alltag in der Frühen Neuzeit*, p. 188; Völker-Rasor would make the Reformation responsible for this. *Bilderpaare—Paarbilder*, pp. 150–52.
83. In St. Gall, a first offense of adultery brought the offender three months on bread and water, a second, six months plus a year's exile, the third, whipping and banishment. Zeeden, *Deutsche Geschichte in der frühen Neuzeit*, pp. 202–6. On sodomy, see Von Dülmen, *Kultur und Alltag in der Frühen Neuzeit*, pp. 195–96.
84. According to Edward Shorter, "Before 1750, the lives of most young people were resolutely unerotic. . . . traditional society succeeded quite effectively in suppressing (sublimating if you prefer) the sex drives of the unmarried." *The Making of the Modern Family* (New York, 1975), p. 99. For evidence of the contrary, see Von Dülmen, *Kultur und Alltag in der Frühen Neuzeit*, pp. 185.
85. Barbara Beuys, *Familienleben in Deutschland* (Reinbeck bei Hamburg, 1980), p. 170.

86. On the sixteenth-century experience in German and Swiss towns, see Thomas Max Safley, *Let No Man Put Asunder: The Control of Marriage in the German Southwest: A Comparative Study, 1550–1600* (Kirksville, MO, 1984).

87. Beatrice Gottlieb, "The Meaning of Clandestine Marriage," in *Family and Sexuality in French History*, ed. Robert Wheaton and Tamara K. Hareven (Philadelphia, 1980), p. 73. See also Weigand, "Ehe- und Familienrecht," pp. 173–77.

88. Elisabeth Koch, *Maior dignitas est in sexu virili. Das weibliche Geschlecht im Normensystem des 16. Jahrhunderts* (Frankfurt am Main, 1991), pp. 92–93.

89. *Ibid.*, pp. 95–96.

90. Ozment, *When Fathers Ruled*, pp. 25–44; Safley, *Let No Man Put Asunder*.

91. Beuys, *Familienleben in Deutschland*, p. 227; Völker-Rasor, *Bilderpaare—Paarbilder*, pp. 267–69; Ozment, *When Fathers Ruled*, pp. 84, 93.

92. Ozment, *When Fathers Ruled*, p. 150.

93. Friedrich Beyschlag, ed., "Ein Vater an seinen Sohn (1539)," *Archiv für Kirchengeschichte*, 4 (1906) : 296–302; Ozment, *Protestants*, p. 109.

94. Cornelia N. Moore, *The Maiden's Mirror: Reading Material for German Girls in the Sixteenth and Seventeenth Centuries* (1987), pp. 17, 30, 34.

95. Edward Bodemann, "Höhere Töchtererziehung im 17. Jahrhundert: Ein Testament oder Verordnung der Frau von Quitzau ihren beiden Töchtern hinterlassen," *Zeitschrift des historischen Vereins für Niedersachsen* (1890): 309–13, cited by Moore, *The Maiden's Mirror*, pp. 105–6.

96. See below.

CHAPTER TWO: THE AFFAIRS

1. Gerd Wunder, "Liebesbriefe": 83–84.

2. Krüger, *Schwäbisch Hall*, p. 46. Cf. Bernd Moeller, "Piety in Germany Around 1500," in Steven Ozment, ed., *The Reformation in Medieval Perspective* (Chicago, 1971), pp. 50–75.

3. As recounted by Johann Herolt; Gerd Wunder, *Die Bürger von Hall*, p. 103.

4. The original statue of the Madonna was made around 1320, and before 1440, the church had been known as the Church of the Holy Cross. After the miracle of the hare and the church's transformation into a popular pilgrim shrine, the name was changed to the Church of Mary and became very well endowed, thanks to the generosity of the pilgrims. The Madonna was only slightly damaged by the Allied bombs. It was in the years following the war that vandals and relic collectors dismembered her. Today, the only remains of the "Madonna of the Hare" appear to be her upper torso, discovered in the summer of 1994 by the author and Mathias Beer in the attic of the new church that now stands on the site.

5. Gmelin, *Hallische Geschichte* (Hall, 1896–99), pp. 657–58; Gerd Wunder, *Die Bürger von Hall*, pp. 34–36. Cf. Richard Auernheimer and Frank Baron, eds., *Das Faustbuch von 1587: Provokation und Wirkung* (Munich, 1991).

6. Krüger, *Schwäbisch Hall*, pp. 44, 53; Gerd Wunder, *Die Bürger von Hall*, p. 129; German, *Chronik von Schwäbisch Hall*, pp. 183–84.

7. The following summary of the highlights of the Reformation in Hall are taken from Krüger, *Schwäbisch Hall*, p. 47; Herolt, *Chronica*, pp. 112, n. 1, 189; Gerd Wunder, *Die Bürger von Hall*, pp. 103–4; and German, *Chronik von Schwäbisch Hall*, pp. 149–52.

8. Cited by James M. Estes, *Christian Magistrate and State Church: The Reforming Career of Johannes Brenz* (Toronto, 1982), pp. 81–88.

9. German, *Chronik von Schwäbisch Hall*, p. 151.

10. Herolt, *Chronica*, pp. 189–90.

11. A. Rentschler, "Einführung der Reformation in der Herrschaft Limpurg," *Blätter für Württembergische Kirchengeschichte* N.F. 20 (1916): 97–134; 107.

12. *Ibid.:* 110.

13. *Ibid.:* 113–14, 121.

14. "Ohn all Umbständ." *Ibid.:* 129. Rentschler opposed the then (1916) reigning view that Erasmus had remained comfortably Catholic until 1544, challenging two poorly documented actions on Erasmus's part that had theretofore been cited in evidence: (1) his insistence, in 1541, as a condition of the sale of castle Limpurg to Hall, that a Catholic priest be appointed to the parish church of lower Limpurg, and (2) his refusal, in 1544, to join other area Schenks in signing the Lutheran Augsburg Confession. See *Heinrich Preschers Limpurgischen Pfarrers zu Gschwend Geschichte und Beschreibung der zum Fränkischen Kreise gehöriger Reichsgrafschaft Limpurg*, I (Stuttgart, 1789), pp. 301–5. Rentschler demonstrated that in both instances, Prescher had misread the evidence in Herolt's *Chronica* and other sources. Rentschler, "Einführung der Reformation": 102–7. While basically correct in his revision, Rentschler may have exaggerated the importance of the 1537 oath as proof of Erasmus's Protestantism. Reform-minded Catholic princes and prelates elsewhere, including the Holy Roman Emperor, also admonished biblical preaching and might in good conscience have administered the very same oath to their clergy.

15. Rentschler, "Einführung der Reformation": 122–23.

16. *Ibid.:* 101–2.

17. Krüger, *Schwäbisch Hall*, p. 50; Rentschler, "Einführung der Reformation": 123–24; Gerd Wunder, *Personendenkmale der Michaelskirche in Schwäbisch Hall* (Hall, 1987), no. 8, p. 12; German, *Chronik von Schwäbisch Hall*, p. 155. The event is memorialized on the wall of St. Michael's Church in a scene which appears to confuse a Hall merchant named Philip Büschler (d. 1570) with Philip Büschler the bürgermeister (d. 1568).

18. Gerd Wunder, *Die Bürger von Hall*, pp. 37–38.

19. Gerd Wunder, "Liebesbriefe": 88, n. 4.

20. "Es ist aber denen von Hall der gelt zweyen wert/dan sich all tag zanckh des zols und gefreisch zutrungenn." Herolt, *Chronica*, p. 260.

21. Gerd Wunder et al., *Die Schenken von Limpurg*, p. 38.

22. "So gesegen mir Gott das bad"; literally, "as God blesses my bath."

23. I.e. from other sources, while she can know about him only as he writes to her.

24. "Schnur." Originally the term indicated a close relationship (a daughter-in-law, for example, was said to be the *schnur* of her mother-in-law), but here it designates a woven bracelet worn about the wrist as a bond of friendship or love.

25. "Wann ich wol weiss, dass ich euer gnad nit gemiess bin, wann ich euer gnad nit zulaid wolt than. Darumb geriethe man vil wesen wol." Gerd Wunder, "Liebesbriefe": 69.

26. The penultimate sentence is poetic: "lang mich und mach mir die weil nit lang." *Ibid.:* 70. The letters exist only in copies made by sixteenth century notaries, which are now preserved in the Hauptstaatsarchiv Stuttgart, C3 Bü 529 (7, Q32). All of my references are to Wunder's transcriptions ("Liebesbriefe," 69–83) and follow his numbering either directly or in brackets. His transcriptions have been read against the originals, and I have added one letter he chose to delete from his edition, while paraphrasing and discussing several other omitted letters. Some of the letters are signed, while others are not.

27. On Erasmus's various posts, see Karl O. Müller, "Das Geschlecht der Reichserbschenken zu Limpurg bis zum Aussterben des Mannesstammes (1713)," *Zeitschrift für Württembergische Landesgeschichte* 5 (1941): 215–43; 233–34.

28. Gerd Wunder, "Liebesbriefe," April 8, 1521: 70.

29. *Ibid.*, May 9, 1521: 71–72.

30. There had been a previous marriage alliance between Hohenlohe and Speck-feld in the late fourteenth century, when Elisabeth of Hohenlohe married Schenk Friedrich III of Speckfeld (1394). The House of Hohenlohe was again entertaining such an alliance. After the death of Schenk Friedrich of Speckfeld in 1521, Eras-mus's father, Gottfried, Friedrich's younger brother, inherited Speckfeld. If there was to be another alliance between the House of Hohenlohe and the Schenks of Limpurg, it would have to be negotiated with Erasmus and his father. Elisabeth of Hohenlohe might more logically and profitably have inquired whether Eras-mus's elder brother Carl had any interest in her; Carl inherited Speckfeld upon his father's death in 1530. It is unlikely that Elisabeth had contemplated a marriage with Friedrich before his death; there was a twenty-seven year difference in their ages, and he had remained single lifelong. Wunder, *Die Schenken von Limpurg,* pp. 30–31, 36.

31. Ludwig II (1498–1538). One of his sons married Erasmus's sister Anna, who was Anna Büschler's age and likely also a friendly advocate for her among the princes of Hohenlohe. As for Elisabeth, she ended up marrying Baron Georg of Hohen-Höwen. Gerd Wunder, "Liebesbriefe": 88, ns. 14, 17.

32. Bishop Georg, Erasmus's uncle.

33. "Zerreyss den brief, es mechts sonst frau mutter inne werden." Gerd Wunder, "Liebesbriefe": 73.

34. Doubtless Erasmus is meant.

35. "Schlechte rechnung."

36. On gender roles in this period: Beuys, *Familienleben in Deutschland,* pp. 223–98; Merry Wiesner, *Working Women in Renaissance Germany* (New Bruns-wick, NJ, 1986); Moore, *The Maiden's Mirror.*

37. "Was . . . euern gnaden geschriben hat, das willen ich sitzen heilen bis zu mein letzen end." Gerd Wunder, "Liebesbriefe," n.d. (no. 12): 74.

38. "Spitzige red."

39. "Gemachten kragen."

40. "Dieweil der ein Thrum ist." Gerd Wunder, "Liebesbriefe": 74–75.

41. "Ein luederlin geben."

42. "Ir habt villeicht sorg es mecht leben und mecht euch einmal zuteil werden, so werdt ir mir gantz zu hüpsch dartzu."

43. If not mere excuses, meaning apparently that the presence of his or her father in Hall would have provided a legitimate reason for Erasmus to be there, and then to have had the opportunity to meet secretly with her.

44. German, *Chronik von Schwäbisch Hall,* pp. 87, 147.

45. Renate Dürr, "Ursula Gräfin—der Lebensweg einer Haller Magd und ledigen Mutter im 17. Jahrhundert," *Württembergisch Franken* 76 (1992): 169–70.

46. The two had apparently made private "future vows" of marriage, or what we today would call an engagement, not private "present vows" of marriage, which would have made them man and wife on the spot in the eyes of God. Both future and present vows were legally binding.

47. Within weeks of the case's dismissal, he married a burgher's daughter, who was also pregnant by him at the time. Dürr, "Ursula Gräfin": 172.

48. *Ibid.:* 171–76.

49. "Ich erpiet jr . . . gutt lassen sein."

50. HSA Stuttgart C3 Bü 529 (L32), p. 115. This letter is among those deleted from Wunder's transcription.

51. Thus, Trotula (eleventh century) and Lanfranc (late thirteenth century). In Edward Grant, ed., *A Source Book in Medieval Science* (Cambridge, MA, 1974), pp. 764, 800. While medical authorities recommended regular bleeding, normally twice a year, as an aid to good health for both men and women, bleeding was

deemed to be harmful to a woman once she became pregnant. Bleeding a pregnant woman from the median vein would have been considered life-threatening at least to the fetus.

52. Lanfranc in *ibid.*, p. 801.

53. On the recent history of this misguided belief, see Mathias Beer, "Kinder in den Familien deutscher Städte des späten Mittelalters und der frühen Neuzeit," *Zeitschrift für Kulturwissenschaften* 6 (1994): 25–48; Klaus Arnold, *Kind und Gesellschaft im Mittelalter und Renaissance* (Paderborn, 1980), pp. 11–15.

54. "Und als ich vor 2 jarnzu Forcheym gewesn, ward ich an ein frauen gewisen, die auch vil fruezeitige Kinder gehabt het, die saget mir schrepfen het ir geholfen, doran kont ich mein weib koum bringen, bis das sie es auch tet, wiwol ich acht, das gross gepet zu unserm heiland hab uns unsern Samuel vom got Israhel erworben, der frist im in seinen wegen sein leben." In Heinrich Herrwagen, "Bilder aus dem Kinderleben in den 30-er Jahren des 16. Jahrhunderts," *Mitteilungen aus dem Germanischen National Museum* (Nuremberg, 1906), p. 96; Matthias Beer, "Kinder in den Familien deutscher Städte": 32–33. On the Scheurl children, J. G. Biedermann, *Geschlechtsregister des Hochadelichen Patriciats zu Nürnberg* (Bayreuth, 1748), Tabula CCCCXLIV. I devote a chapter to the Scheurls in a forthcoming study of the traditional family.

55. Gerd Wunder, erroneously, I believe, ascribes letter 13 [16] to Anna rather than Erasmus. He cites records indicating Hermann Büschler's attendance at the imperial diet in Nürnberg and at a meeting of cities in Esslingen in the fall of 1522, and suspects this to be the "absence" referred to in both letters 13 [16] and 14 [18]. "Liebesbriefe": 88, n. 24. However, the second letter dates the departure from Hall on August 14, while the first letter has the traveler away for "two weeks or longer," suggesting a return home well before late September. Two distinct absences appear to be described by the two letters: Erasmus's father in the first letter and Anna's in the second. This interpretation is also supported by the different style of the two letters and subsequent letters in the correspondence.

56. Apparently the best option envisioned by Erasmus is that she come on Sunday, using church as a pretext for a visit to castle Limpurg.

57. Gerd Wunder, "Liebesbriefe," n.d. (no. 19): 76.

58. Margrethe, daughter of bürgermeister Konrad Büschler. *Ibid.*, June 13, 1523 (no. 25): 79–80.

59. It is unclear what misfortune Erasmus has in mind, but he may mean the suspicion and scrutiny of his parents, who would not have been pleased to learn the full extent of his involvement with Anna and who would certainly have been embarrassed by its public disclosure. Other women, however, brought Erasmus greater misfortune. See below.

60. "Des leibgedings halben."

61. "Frümer"; that is, more high-minded than to think that he would put money above his feelings for her.

62. Might Anna have been seeking Erasmus's assistance in having her father's keys reproduced after he took hers away? See above.

63. At this time, lovers frequently asked one another to wear their favorite color, and ashen appears to have been Erasmus's. Or might he have suggested ashen because of its penitential connotations in light of her romance with Daniel Treutwein?

64. On their financial dealings, see below.

65. Herolt, *Chronica*, p. 58; Georg Widmann (1486–1570) (not to be confused with Georg Rudolf Widmann, author of the *Faustbuch* [1599]), in Gerhard Wunder and Georg Lenckner, *Die Bürgerschaft der Reichsstadt Hall*, p. 182.

66. Gerd Wunder, *Die Bürger von Hall*, p. 153; Karl Steiff and Gebhard Mehring,

Geschichtliche Lieder und Sprüche Württembergs (Stuttgart, 1912), pp. 193, l. 237f, 186, l. 421f.

67. "Ein weis judenhaubt sampt der brust on arm, mit einem braidten judenhuet unnd schnur under dem kyn herumb gezogen, in einem rotten feldt." The coat of arms is preserved on a gravestone of Conrad Treutwein (d. 1438) on the north wall of St. Michael's Church in Hall. Herolt, *Chronica*, p. 58.

68. Friedrich Pietsch, *Die Urkunden des Archivs der Reichsstadt Schwäbisch Hall*, vol. 1 (1156–1399), vol. 2 (1400–1479), (Hall, 1967, 1972), 2: 546–47; Gerhard Wunder and Georg Lenckner, *Die Bürgerschaft der Reichsstadt Hall*, p. 182; Gerd Wunder, *Die Bürger von Hall*, p. 94.

69. See the complaints about Jewish gouging by Paul II Behaim during his student years in Padua. *Deutsches Studentenleben in Padua 1575–1578*, in Wilhelm Loose, *Beilage zur Schul- und Universitätsgeschichte* (Meissen 1879), pp. 11–38, no. 3, p. 14.

70. John Edwards, *The Jews in Christian Europe 1400–1700* (London, 1988), pp. 12, 16.

71. *Ibid.*, pp. 25–26, 29–34, 58–60.

72. On the fantasy of ritual murder, see Ronnie Po-Chia Hsia, *The Myth of Ritual Murder: Jews and Magic in Reformation Germany* (New Haven, 1988).

73. Herolt, *Chronica*, p. 150, n. 2; Gerd Wunder, *Die Bürger von Hall*, pp. 94–95. The emperor's generosity to the Haller in this episode may have riled the local clergy. Although criminal fines at this time rarely had any restitutionary purpose (they simply went into the state treasury), it was customary for humane civil authorities when fining participants in pogroms to give some, even all, of the collected fine to the local clergy to assuage the Church, whose own law, unlike the emperor's, was not as kindly toward Jews. On the different treatment of Jews in imperial and canon law, see Solomon Grayzel, "Popes, Jews, and Inquisition: From 'Sicut' to 'Turbato,'" in Solomon Grayzel, *The Church and the Jews in the XIIIth Century . . . 1198–1254* (Philadelphia, 1933), pp. 49–59; *The Church and the Jews in the XIIIth Century*, II: *1254–1314*, ed. Kenneth R. Stow (New York, 1989), pp. 1–47

74. Gerd Wunder, *Die Bürger von Hall*, pp. 94–95.

75. Herolt, *Chronica*, p. 58.

76. Cf. Heiko A. Oberman, ed., *Deutscher Bauernkrieg 1525. Zeitschrift für Kirchengeschichte* 85 (1974): 157–72.

77. H. C. Erik Midelfort, "The Revolution of 1525: Recent Studies of the Peasants' War," *Central European History*, 1978, pp. 189–206. Midelfort discusses the old, but hardly dated, views of Günther Franz, *Der deutsche Bauernkrieg*, 10th ed. (Darmstadt, 1975), and the new, and now highly questionable, views of Peter Blickle, for whom the peasants' revolt was the crescendo of the Reformation's social promise, not its opportunistic exploitation. Peter Blickle, *The Revolution of 1525: The German Peasants' War from a New Perspective* (Baltimore, 1981; originally published 1975). See my discussion of Blickle's work and other speculative present-day efforts to interpret the Reformation definitively through the Peasants' War. *Protestants*, pp. 118–34.

78. Gerd Wunder, *Die Bürger von Hall*, p. 31.

79. Herolt, *Chronica*, p. 19.

80. Herolt describes his forced service in detail. *Chronica*, pp. 199–20; also Prescher, *Geschichte der Reichsgrafschaft Limpurg*, pp. 215, 223.

81. German, *Chronik von Schwäbisch Hall*, pp. 195–97.

82. Herolt, *Chronica*, p. 205; Prescher, *Geschichte der Reichsgrafschaft Limpurg*, pp. 244–47; German, *Chronik von Schwäbisch Hall*, p. 220.

83. Herolt, *Chronica*, pp. 242–44; Prescher, *Geschichte der Reichsgrafschaft Limpurg*, p. 166; German, *Chronik von Schwäbisch Hall*, p. 220.

84. Herolt, *Chronica*, pp. 270, 296–97; Prescher, *Geschichte der Reichsgrafschaft Limpurg*, pp. 268–71; German, *Chronik von Schwäbisch Hall*, p. 221. Both massacres are celebrated in contemporary poetry. Steiff and Mehring, *Geschichtliche Lieder*, pp. 210–52.

85. "Ein Sündenregister Herzog Ulrichs, zur Warnung vor ihm aufgestellt" (1520). Steiff and Mehring, *Geschichtliche Lieder*, pp. 189–208.

86. "Wyrtenbergscher Spruch wider die stet des bunds." *Ibid.*, pp. 151–57, 164. There are two versions of the poem, the original in 1519 and a new, Protestantized version in 1524.

87. Herolt, *Chronica*, pp. 58–9, 92–93, n. 3; Joseph Baader, ed., *Verhandlungen über Thomas von Absberg und seine Fehden gegen den Schwäbischen Bund*, 1519–1530 (Tübingen, 1873), p. 222.

88. Baader, *Verhandlungen über Thomas Absberg* (Stuttgart, 1873), p. 228; *Fehde Hanns Thomas von Absberg wider den Schwäbischen Bund* (Munich, 1880).

89. See letter 19. On Daniel's age, see appendix.

90. Herolt, *Chrourica*, pp. 182–83, 189.

91. HSA Stuttgart, C3 Bü 529 L32, pp. 137–45. The numbering follows the archive's arrangement. None of the letters are dated and only two are signed.

92. Ostensibly Daniel's immediate commander, but possibly someone Anna's father asked to keep an eye on Daniel, when he and Anna were traveling in the same region.

93. It is unclear who this is, but apparently a trusted messenger.

94. Erasmus's namesake was the patron saint of people suffering intestinal disorders, especially colicky children. In the late Middle Ages, he became one of the fourteen "Holy Helpers," chosen for this distinction from among hundreds of other patron saints.

95. This letter could be read as Anna's if the last sentence is read as her play on Daniel's stock closing.

96. Sulz is a castle near Kirchberg an der Jagst on the margravine of Hohenlohe, see below pp. 98–99.

97. A Hall councilman.

98. The letter is apparently written on or shortly after New Year's Day.

99. "St. Gilgien." Erasmus is meant. St. Giles was the patron saint of cripples, hermits, horses, lepers, and mothers, and like St. Erasmus was popular in late medieval Germany as one of the fourteen "Holy Helpers." Daniel may associate him with Erasmus because he knew Erasmus suffered from a crippling illness. See below.

100. Money is apparently meant.

101. "I b o. zweiffeln"; elsewhere, "I B O Z."

102. Apparently their frequently mentioned priestly intermediary, to whom the letter is being sent for safe delivery to Anna.

103. Daniel may be referring to an intemperate outburst on his part over Anna's continuing relationship with Erasmus, which has temporarily alienated her, but which he believes she will later appreciate as a good deed on her behalf.

104. Johann Mangolt, Doctor of Jurisprudence and city secretary in Hall (1509–1520), later lower judge (*Assessor*) in the imperial supreme court in Speyer; Herolt, *Chronica*, p. 146. Anna may at this time have been seeking legal counsel because of the deteriorating relationship with her father.

105. The reference is to the food and wine the two shared, or, according to Hermann Büschler, "stole," from his house.

106. It is unclear what these letters are; possibly legal papers aborning.

107. It is unclear whether the bailiff or Hermann Büschler is meant.
108. Probably another loan.
109. It is unlikely that this is Hans Kitzinger, Erasmus's faithful servant.
110. In the district of Scheinfeld in middle Franconia.
111. Apparently from her father in the wake of his discovery of the full extent of her "stealing" and cavorting with Daniel, which was now town gossip.
112. "Ein Vater an seinen Sohn (1539)," *Archiv für Kirchengeschichte* 4 (1906): 296–302, no. 13.
113. "Einlegen in das holtz."
114. *Guajakbaum* or *Pockholz*.
115. Apparently elder brother Karl was Erasmus's conduit for family funds.
116. See above.
117. Rainer Jooss, *Kloster Komburg in Mittelalter: Studien zur Verfassungs-, Besitz- und Sozialgeschichte einer fränkischen Benediktinerabtei* (Sigmaringen, 1987), p. 141.
118. See below.

CHAPTER THREE: ON THE RUN

1. *Verneute Ordnung und Verbott der Hoffart, eines... weisen Raths der Statt Nürmberg was unter ihrer Burgerschafft... jedem in seinem Stand... in Beklaidungen zugelassen und verbotten wird* (1618). British Museum 5511.aaa.18.
2. "William Smith, A Description of the Cittie of Noremberg... 1594, übersetzt," trans. William Roach, *Mitteilungen des Vereins für Geschichte der Stadt Nürnberg* 48 (1958): 233.
3. *Ibid.*: 213–14, 216–17, 222.
4. Ozment, *Protestants*, ch. 5.
5. "Das vetterlich hertz von ime [Hermann Büschler] gethon." *Exceptiones Articulate... Anna Buschlerin gegen Stetmeister und Rath zu Schwebischen Hall*, no. 5.
6. "Sie auss seinem hauss unverschulter sachen gantz ungestimmiglich gejagt." *Articuli Elisivi Anna Buschlerin*, no. 4 (Hornung II).
7. *Exceptiones Articulate*, no. 4.
8. "Domit sie nicht in weltlich schanden fallen durfft." *Exceptiones Articulate*, no. 6. The following account of Anna's activity after her expulsion is drawn from her own reconstruction of events in three major legal documents: *Exceptiones Articulate*; *Der Clegerin übergebene Fragstuck* (Machtolff); and *Articuli Elisivi Anna Buschlerin* (Hornung II).
9. Hornberger, to *Der Clegerin übergebene Fragstuck*, no. 8 (Windberg).
10. Dollen, to *ibid.*, no. 35 (Windberg).
11. *Exceptiones Articulate*, no. 6.
12. "Ja, hett die dochter Annen gern wider im hauss gehabt." To *Uff dise nachgeende Fragstuckh*, no. 7 (Windberg).
13. According to her brother and sister, "Sy sich allenthalben im landt so ergerlich gehalten/unnd allerley ungerathen verdechtlich gesinndt an sich gehenckt." *Superelisif Articul Philipsen Buschlers et Consorten contra Anna Buschlerin*, no. 4 (Windberg).
14. A forty kilometer ride northeast of Hall, and just south of Rothenburg.
15. "Sie sag sie well ewer vest inn grossen schaden fieren im Cammergericht." Dated the Sunday after Easter, 1525 (Machtolff).
16. Leinlin von Blaufelden's undated letter to Anna discussing the legal efforts on her behalf and Apollonia Prenner's letter to Anna's father demanding her re-

moval are among the documents submitted to the Machtolff hearing. Cf. also Gerd Wunder, "Liebesbriefe": 86–87.

17. *Anna Buschlerin schrifftlich Bitt um tagsatzung und glait gegen irem vatter* (August 19, 1525), HSA Stuttgart, C3 Bü 1546.

18. Karl-Ernst Küpper, "Das Reichskammergericht," in *Deutsche Rechtsgeschichte 1500–1800 im Spiegel der Bestände der Historischen Bibliothek der Stadt Rastatt,* ed. Historische Bibliothek der Stadt Rastatt (Rastatt, 1991), pp. 321–24; Hajo Holborn, *A History of Modern Germany: The Reformation* (New York, 1961), pp. 43–44.

19. Karl-Ernst Küpper, "Das Rottweiler Hofgericht," in *Deutsche Rechtsgeschichte,* pp. 321–24.

20. *Anna Buschlerin schrifftlich Bitt um tagsatzung und glait gegen irem vatter/ und daruff ervolgtte antwort und glayt* (August 19, 1525), HSA Stuttgart, C3 Bü 1546.

21. Nordhoff-Behne, *Gerichtsbarkeit und Strafrechtspflege,* pp. 23–24, 57–61.

22. Ozment, *Three Behaim Boys,* p. 12. That widows nonetheless played a major role in the rearing and education of their children can be seen in the example of Friederich Behaim's (1563–1613) mother. *Ibid.,* pp. 94–96.

23. Rudolf Huebner, *A History of Germanic Private Law,* trans. Francis S. Philbrick (Boston, 1918), pp. 61–68; Gerhard Köbler, "Das Familienrecht in der spätmittelalterlichen Stadt," in *Haus und Familie in der spätmittelalterlichen Stadt,* ed. Alfred Haverkamp (Köln, 1984), pp. 136–60; Merry E. Wiesner, "Women's Defense of Their Public Role," in *Women in the Middle Ages and the Renaissance,* ed. Mary Beth Rose (Syracuse, 1968), pp. 1–28; Gabriele Becker et al., *"Aus der Zeit der Verzweiflung." Zur Genese und Aktualität des Hexenbildes* (Frankfurt am main, 1977), pp. 49–50.

24. Heide Wunder, *"Er ist die Sonn', sie ist der Mond,"* pp. 107–11.

25. See below.

26. Köbler, "Das Familienrecht," pp. 155–56. On the law's regulation of the rights and testimony of women under different circumstances in a court of law, see Koch, *Maior dignitas est in sexu virili,* pp. 75–90.

27. "Ain sicher frey stadtsgeleyt fur meniglich unnd sunderlich fur die jhennen so sie mechtig sein zu rechten zugegen unnd zugestelt haben." *Exceptiones Articulate,* no. 13.

28. *Ibid.,* nos. 16–18.

29. Holborn, *A History of Modern Germany,* pp. 44–46, 48.

30. John Witte, Jr., kindly pointed out this possible explanation of Esslingen's seeming self-contradiction and negligence.

31. "Mandat per surrepnans et abrepnans." *Exceptiones Articulate,* no. 22. "Die gefenncklich anzenomen unnd innzusetzen." *Der Clegerin übergebene Fragstuck,* no. 19 (Machtolff). "Fenckliche einziehung und verwarung." *Defensional Articull,* no. 2 (Machtolff)

32. *Vom Reichsregiment in Esslingen ausgest. ksl. Geleitsbrief betr. ungehinderte Verbringung der Anna Buschlerin in väterlichen Gewahrsam,* HSA Stuttgart, C3 Bü 528, (7, Q10).

33. Gerd Wunder, *Die Bürger von Hall,* p. 180.

34. See the example of Benoite Ameaux, in Robert M. Kingdon, *Adultery and Divorce in Calvin's Geneva* (Cambridge, Mass., 1995), pp. 60–61.

35. To *Uff dise nachgeende Fragstuckh,* no. 24 (Windberg).

36. *Exceptiones Articulate,* no. 31.

37. To *Uff dise nachgeende Fragstuckh,* no. 24 (Windberg).

38. To *Der Clegerin übergebene Fragstuck,* no. 33 (Machtolff); Hermann Büschler's "nahe freunnd und schweger," according to Conrad Büschler, *ibid.*

39. *Copey Margrave Casimir Befelchs Anna Buschlerin halben aussgangen* (1526), HSA Stuttgart, C3 Bü 529 (7, Q7/8); Herolt, *Chronica*, p. 182.

40. *Exceptiones Articulate*, no. 35; *Defensional Articull*, no. 4 (Machtolff).

41. Nordhoff-Behne, *Gerichtsbarkeit und Strafrechtspflege*, pp. 26–28.

42. "Grusamlich gepeiniget."

43. "Wider junnckfrolich zucht verjagt."

44. *Urteilsbrief des Hofgerichts Rottweil* (1526), HSA Stuttgart, C3 Bü 1546.

45. *Der Clegerin ubergebene Fragstuckh*, nos. 24–30 (Machtolff).

46. ". . . *Sich beclagt* die Ersame Junckgfrau Anna Buschlerin von Hall . . . wiewol die anntwurter [= Angeklagten] jr Clegerin ain frey sicher schrifftlich besigelt glait unnd trostung in die stat Hall zukhumen gegeben unnd zugeschickt haben/So sey doch solch glait an jr Clegerin (uber unnd wider das sy sich glaitlich gehalten) gebrochen worden und nit gehalten. Indem das sy Clegerin auf jr anntwurter vergunnden/in der stat Hall durch jre Statknecht fanngklich angenomen/und jren vatter uberlifert/unnd also ob ainen halben jar fanngklich gehalten unnd grusamlich gepeiniget worden/unnd so jr der allmechtig nit gehollffen/also das sy hohenndt zu einem laden aussfallendt/entloffen were/hette sy als wol zuvermueten/one betracht des gegeben glaits/jren anntwurter halben in fanngkhnus muessen erfulen unnd sterben/dardurch sy Clegerin in grosse schwer verliembdung jrer eeren halber/schmach/schannd/spott krannckheit jrs leibs/unnd entgweltigung jrer klainater unnd klaider khumen/unnd also wider junnckhfrolich zucht veriagt im jamerlichen ellenndt umbtziehen muessen/damit sy anntwurter jr zuvil unnd zum hochsten gewallt unnd unrecht gethon/unnd sy Clegerin vil lieber funnfft tusennt gulden/wo sol[c]hs in jrern vermogen/verlieren oder nit haben wellt/dann sol[c]h gefanngkhnus/schannd/schmachheit/verlust/wie oblaut/nochmals gedulden/In hoffnung das sy die anntwurter schuldig jr Clegerin hierumb mit funf tusent gulden abtrag zuthun/doch in dem allem Ewer gnaden richterlichen taren [= wagen = es darauf ankommen lassen] unnd messigung vorbehallten mit bekherung aller kosten unnd schaden/oder das darumb zu inen allen mit aucht [= Aechtung] und anlaiten [= Einsetzung eines um Schadenersatz Klagenden in des beklagten Güter]/wie recht gericht werde." *Hofgericht Rottweil: Anna gegen Schwäbisch Hall*, HSA Stuttgart, C3 Bü 1546.

47. *Vidimus der stat Schwabischen Hall* (Tuesday after St. Matthew's, 1526; recorded in Speyer May 6, 1527), HSA Stuttgart, C3 Bü 1546.

48. "Dieweil die sach ain Glaitsbruch unnd also ain Eehafftin disen loblichen hovegerichts betreffen ist/So weist man den handels nit." *Hofgericht Rottweil.*

49. *Petitio stettmaister unnd statt zu Schwabischen Hall contra Anna Buschlerin*, HSA Stuttgart, C3 Bü 1546.

50. "Ein Predigt, dass man Kinder zur Schulen halten solle" (1530), *D. Martin Luthers Werke: Kritische Gesamtausgabe* (Weimar, 1883), 30/II, p. 532; Ozment, *When Fathers Ruled*, p. 153. "All authority has its root and warrant in parental authority. . . . All who are called masters stand in the place of parents and from them must obtain authority and power to command. In the Bible they are called fathers, because in their government they perform the functions of a father and should possess a fatherly heart toward their people. . . . The Romans and others of ancient times. . . . called their princes and magistrates *patres patriae*, fathers of the country; and it is a shame that we who wish to be Christians do not so call our rulers or, at least, treat and honor them as such." *Dr. Martin Luther's Large Catechism* (Minneapolis, 1935), p. 72.

51. *Petitio stettmaister unnd statt zu Schwabischen Hall contra Anna Buschlerin*; see also *Exceptiones et in eventum conclusiones Stetmaister unnd Rath zu Schwabischen Hall gegen Anna Buschlerin*, HSA Stuttgart, C3 Bü 1546.

52. "Ist mein underthenig bitt E. Mt. wellen mich zu dem aid der armut gnediglich zulossen damit ich zum rechten kumen moge." *Supplicatio Anna Buschlerin gegen Schwebischen Hall*, HSA Stuttgart, C3 Bü 1546.

53. "Die Citation hab ich uff der Mauern jn ein schiss loch gelegt/und davon gangen/hat sich die gnanten Anna Busslerin umbgewendt und die Citation auss dem loch genomen/ Das ist gescheen am funffundzwenzigisten tage des monets Februarii, Anno 1527" (Machtolff).

54. *Exceptiones Articulate*, nos. 37–40.

55. *Ibid.*, no. 37.

56. Gerd Wunder, "Rudolf Nagel . . . und Hermann Büschler," p. 38.

57. "Before 1531." Gerhard Wunder and Georg Lenckner, *Die Bürgerschaft der Reichsstadt Hall*, no. 1149, p. 161. Most likely by the summer of 1529.

58. *Urkundenbuch der Stadt Heilbronn*, III (1501–1524), ed. Moriz von Rauch (Stuttgart, 1916), nr. 2620, pp. 583–84; Wunder, "Rudolf Nagel . . . und Hermann Büschler," p. 39.

59. "Herman Buschlers dritte hausfraw Barbara Eytelwein von hailpronn," *Ratsprotokollen*, 1502–69, p. clxxix, Stadts- und Hospital Archiv Schwäbisch Hall.

CHAPTER FOUR: HALF A LOAF

1. Bonney, *The European Dynastic States*, pp. 103–4; J. J. Scarisbrick, *Henry VIII* (Berkeley, 1968), pp. 137–38.

2. Bonney, *The European Dynastic States*, pp. 104–5.

3. On these events, G. R. Potter, *Zwingli* (Cambridge, England, 1976).

4. On Anabaptism, Claus-Peter Clasen, *Anabaptism: A Social History, 1526–1618* (Ithaca, N.Y., 1972).

5. Potter, *Zwingli*, p. 338.

6. *Uff dise nachgeende Fragstuckh*, no. 32 (Windberg).

7. It was a brief marriage, because Hermann Büschler married Barbara Eitelwein, from Heilbronn, sometime before 1531. Gerhard Wunder and Georg Lenckner, *Die Bürgerschaft der Reichsstadt Hall*, no. 1149, p. 161.

8. Gerhard Köbler, "Das Familienrecht in der spätmittelalterlichen Stadt," in *Haus und Familien der spätmittelalterlichen Stadt*, ed. Alfred Haverkamp (Köln, 1984), p. 157.

9. *Ibid.*, p. 158.

10. *Ibid.*

11. Huebner, *A History of Germanic Private Law*, pp. 629, 645, 662–63, 666.

12. Her brother Sebald, who was a student at Heidelberg in 1529, died in 1532, and Anna also received a share of his maternal inheritance, for which she paid taxes on April 24, 1532, according to the *Bürgerbuch*. Gerd Wunder and Georg Lenckner, *Die Bürgerschaft der Reichsstadt Hall*, nr. 1168, p. 162. I have been unable to confirm the death dates of Anna's three deceased siblings (Hermann, Jr., Sebald, and Bonaventure). See notes 19 and 20 below.

13. Anna claimed that her debts at the time of her brother's death had been more than double the 397 gulden the pair ended up getting in settlement of the maternal inheritance. To *Uff dise nachgeended Fragstuckh*, no. 46 (Windberg).

14. Huebner, *A History of Germanic Private Law*, pp. 633–34.

15. "Alle und jegliche jr hab unnd guter ligende unnd varende/nichts davon ausgenomen." *Heiratsbrief zwischen Hermann Büschler zu Schwäbisch Hall und Anna, Tochter des Sebold Hornberger* (1495), in *Acta Hermann Buschlers gegen Hansen von Leutzenbrun und sein hausfrau: Verfahrensfehler in Streitsache betr. Entfremdung vergangenen elterlichen Erbes durch Verkauf bzw. im Fall des Lindenhofes, dessen Uebermachung an Sohn des Kl. Philipp Büschler, ohne Konsens*

der Miterben (also, *Akten von Stättmeister und Rat der Stadt* [1534], HSA Stuttgart, C3 Bü 528 [7]). On laws regulating *Heyratsgut,* see Koch, *Maior dignitas est in sexu virili,* pp. 41–55.

16. "So mag er auch als ain rechtunnde person bey den kinden in witwenstuhl pleiben sitzen und solle der kinde auch des guts getreulich walten/unnd so die kindt zu iren vogtbarn jaren komen nach baiden taile freunde rathe auch aussteuren und beratten." *Heyratsbrief* (1495).

17. "Und die ersten unnd nachgenden kindt furter Hermann Büschlers ir vatterlichs erbe unnd gut gleich mit ainander erben und tailen. Also das der ersten kind ainem als vil als der nachgenden kindt ainem davon volg und werde alles ungeverlich [= *unbefangen,* impartial]." *Ibid.*

18. "Und zubeschluss dis heyrats/so ist mit nemblicher worten beredt das der obgenant Hermann Büschler der vorgenanten sein eeliche hausfrau der obgenanten irer heymsteuer/widerlegung und morgengabe/in erbarn zivilichen form versichern und beweyssen soll/damit sie und ire erbern/der habent und versorgt sein/mög." *Ibid.*

19. When Anna's mother died in 1520, there were six surviving children: four sons, Hermann, Jr., Philip, Sebald, and Bonaventure (a cloth-maker), and two daughters, Anna and Agatha. *Positiones et Articuli,* nos. 1–3 (Hornung II); Leonhard Feuchtner, to *Positional Artikel,* no. 3 (Hornung II). Both Hermann and Sebald were dead by 1528; Bonaventure is mentioned in Hermann Büschler's testament (1543) as missing and presumed dead. See below.

20. *Urkundenbuch der Stadt Heilbronn,* IV, ed. Moriz von Rauch (Stuttgart, 1922), nr. 3081, p. 349. Referring to the settlement with the Leuzenbrunns, Hermann Büschler's testament (1543) later mentions Anna's receipt of eighty gulden as her share of deceased brother *Sebald's* portion of the maternal inheritance, which she received in 1532 (see note 12 above). *Testament Hermann Büschlers,* HSA Stuttgart, C3 Bü 530 (7, Q28). According to witness testimony, the death in 1528 that triggered the discussions of Anna's maternal inheritance was that of Hermann, Jr., for which the city council awarded Anna a fifth of his maternal inheritance, which would logically also have been eighty gulden. Perhaps her father here confuses the two sons in his testament, written many years after the fact, or is citing Anna's second receipt of a share of fraternal maternal inheritance and forgetting the first. Leonhard Feuchter, to *Peremptorial Articul Philipsen Buschlers unnd Agatha Schantzin,* no. 3 (Windberg).

21. *Ibid.,* no. 43 (Windberg); Feuchter, to *Preemptorial Articul,* no. 3 (Windberg).

22. "Das der . . . HB/mir AB/fur mein muterlich erbe und fell/clainat geschmuckt und gebende . . . bis uff dato dis brieffs geschehen raichen und geben solle drey hundert sibenundneutzig gulden an muntz gemeiner Landswerung. Dagegen sol ich . . . den HB mein vatter dweil er lebt ainichs zugelts oder aussteur claider/oder clainat halben mit oder aus recht nit belestigen oder anziehen. Dartzu soll auch . . . mein vatter/und sein erben/mit meinen schulden gerichts scheden und zerungen wie die durch mich gemacht und herkomen nichts ausgenomen/weder zuschicken noch zuschaffen haben/sonder der gar und gentzlich frey/und zubezalen nit schuldig." *Erbvertrag zwischen Hans von Leuzenbronn bzw. dessen Ehefrau Anna geb. Büschler und Hermann Büschler* (1528), in *Acta Herman Büschler,* HSA Stuttgart, C3 Bü 528 (7).

23. *Fragstuckh/Philipsen Buschlers,* to *Articuli Elisivi Anna Buschlerin,* no. 8 (Hornung II).

24. *Uff dise nachgeende Fragstuckh,* no. 45 (Windberg).

25. "An statt der ausssteur." *Articuli Elisivi Anna Buschlerin,* no. 9 (Hornung II).

26. Children under twenty-five could be disinherited if they married without parental consent. See below.

27. "Zum drittentheil all meiner verlassen hab unnd guter [als] ir legitima unnd angepurenden theil." *Testament Hermann Büschlers.*

28. *Ibid.*

29. *Ibid.*

30. "Impartible things, and also lands, were frequently not alienated, but instead abandoned to one of the heirs, who was then bound to compensate the others either by payment of a certain sum of money or by a rent charged upon the land (so-called 'Erbegelder,' heir money)." Huebner, *A History of Germanic Private Law*, p. 709. On the different inheritance practices in German Protestant and Catholic lands, see Paula S. Fichtner, *Protestantism and Primogeniture in Early Modern Germany* (New Haven, 1989). Also on these subjects: Peter Ketsch, *Frauen im Mittelalter*, II (Düsseldorf, 1984), p. 181; Köbler, "Das Familienrecht," pp. 157–58.

31. "Doch so sollen/in allen vorgeschriben puncten/artickeln/und sachen die ee-genanten zwey eeleut alwegen an leben oder am tode gwalt und macht haben/nemlich er solt sein pfert/claider/harnisch/und sie ire claider/kleinott/geschmuck und gepende zu ir jedes leibs gehorung hinzugeben zuverschaffen oder zu ver-machen/durch got/oder eere/wem und wohin jr jedes wil." *Heiratsbrief*, in *Acta Hermann Büschlers.*

32. "Auch hab ich als ich der bosen huren die vier hundert gulden must geben zu willen gehabt das ich sylbergeschirr wolt auch angreiffen und verkauffen." Letter to Philip (1530), in *Acta Hermann Büschlers.*

33. In Leuzenbrunn's summary before the council: "Nun aber wurde ich bericht unnd in meines schwehers aigen hanndtgeschrifften/inhalt der hiebey eingelegten copein finde/das genanter mein schweher sich unnderstanden die ligende guetter zum tayll/auch das sylbergeschirr nit alain zuverkauffen/sonnder auch dieselbigen verschafft/Und ain gut umb Tausent gulden angeschlagen/das do zway taussent gulden woll wert ist/welcher doch nit alain wider den heyratbrieff/sonnder auch wider alle billichait." *Acta Hermann Büschlers* (prologue).

34. "Das . . . mein schweher sein heyratsbrieff hinder ain erbarn Rathe erlege/unnd jerlichs seins einnemens und aufgebens vor den verordneten unnd obersten vormunder rechnung tue/oder aber im curatores setzen unnd benennen lasse/die gutter zuverwalthen/wie der stat Hall brauch unnd gewonhait/und ander burgern auch geschehen ist/damit dieselbigen guter also verkaufft wider erstatten und her-bey zuthun/nit geschwecht. Und so es zum fall komen wurde/mein hausfrau als der rechten und naturlichen erben ainer/derselbigen nit spoliert und entsetzt werde." *Ibid.*

35. See Ozment, *Three Behaim Boys.*

36. Köbler, "Das Familienrecht," p. 159.

37. "Wo die kinder understeen ire eltern an Testamenten und verschaffungen/zu iren und zuhindern/so haben die eltern wol ain ursach sy zuenterben/Und die leibs narung zuwaigern/derowegen ich dan hie auch bezeugt und mir vorgestelt haben will/was mir die recht zulassen." *Exceptionsschrifft*, in *Acta Hermann Büschlers.*

38. "So die kinder verpieten iren eltern, gepürliche testament oder gescheft ze-tun." *Nürnberger Reformation*, in *Quellen zur neueren Privatrechtsgeschichte Deutschlands*, I, ed. Wolfgang Kunken (Weimar, 1936), Nnb 15.2, pp. 19–20.

39. "Hern Herman Büschler hat bis hieher das geschrey nit gehabt/das er vil golds umb ain ay geb/auch noch nit hat/das er das sein verspill oder verbüb." *Exceptionsschrifft*, in *Acta Hermann Büschlers.*

40. Response to *Exceptionsbrief*, in *ibid*.

41. It is unclear whether he means his second wife, Elisabeth Krauss, or his third, Barbara Eitelwein, the former deceased, the other divorced from him at this time (1534).

42. "Hab aber ich Anna Buschlerin und irem eevogt dem Leutzenpronner/fur muterlich auch bruderlich erb laut den quittantzen funfhundert gulden weniger dreyundzwanzigk gulden gereicht und geben . . . ich ir mer geben hab/dan ich jr vermogs heyratsbrieffe schuldig gewest bin/und ist mir durch bede freundtschafft also geratten worden . . . ich hab ir geben ir mutterlich gut/dabey ich mein lebenlanng der beysitz het mogen haben/und sovil gethon als were sy mir gehorsam gevolich kind gewesen. . . ." Response to Leuzenbronn, in *Acta Hermann Büschlers*.

43. "Erkhennt ain erbar rathe zurecht das Herman Buschler uber den mit weilund Anna Hornburgerin hailigen uffgerichten heyratsbrieve/seinem sone Philipsen/ ausserhalb beder thail freundschafft/unnd sonderlich L[euzenpronner] und seiner hausfrauen rathe den hove zu Lindenau seines gevallens zuzestellen unnd zuverendern nit geburt habe/unnd sich hinfuro/uff deren/so an sein Herman Buschlers inhendigen gutern/von den der heyratsbrieve meldung thut/interesse und kunfftigt erbforderung haben begern/mit jerlicher rechnung seines einnemens und ausgebens/neben getrewer verwalthung der selbigen guter/obangezaigtem heyratsbrieve gemess unnd gleichformig zuhalten/und auch ime Leuzenpronner seine in diser rechtvertigung uffgeloffen cost und scheden/yedoch nach rechtlicher erkantnus und messigung zubezalen schuldig sein solle." *Ibid*.

CHAPTER FIVE: SIBLINGS

1. Bonney, *The European Dynastic States*, p. 106.

2. Ozment, *Age of Reform*, pp. 402–6.

3. *Ibid*.; Williston Walker, *A History of the Christian Church* (New York, 1959), pp. 340–42.

4. German, *Chronik von Schwäbisch Hall*, pp. 164–65.

5. This is translated from the actual menu, which has been reconstructed from Hermann Büschler's surviving bill of fare and contemporary cookbooks, and served at the Hotel Adelshof in the summer of 1994. On the meal, see also German, *Chronik von Schwäbisch Hall*, p. 165.

6. *Ibid*., p. 166.

7. Michael Seiboth, to *Der Clegerin übergebene Fragstuck*, no. 3 (Machtolff).

8. Gerd Wunder, *Die Bürger von Hall*, pp. 166–68.

9. Huebner, *A History of Germanic Private Law*, pp. 695–97, 753.

10. To *Positiones et Articuli*, no. 2 (Hornung I).

11. "Prelegaten."

12. David Schmidlin, to *Articuli Elisivi Anna Buschlerin*, nos. 13–15 (Hornung II).

13. "Sagt zeug er wiss durch das Herr Philipp unnd die Agatha miteinannder abgetheilt . . . das der Hermann Buschler im lezten Testament gedachtem seinem sune 1200 gulden zu eim Legat/darzu auch das Haus fur 1000 unnd dann ein Hoff (so er ime zum heurat gutt gegeben) nur fur tausent gulden angeschlagen unnd verordent habe/doch gegenn der Agathen/die zwei stuck zuvergleichen." To *Uff dise nachgeende Fragstuckh*, no. 54. (Windberg).

14. David Schmidlin described Hermann Büschler's estate as being "under 15,000" gulden (to *Fragstuckh/Philipsen Buschlers*, no. 2 [Hornung II]), while Anna believed it to be 20,000. *Der Clegerin übergebene Fragstuck*, nos. 49–51 (Machtolff).

15. To *Fragstuckh Philipsen Buschlers*, nos. 20–21 (Hornung II).

16. "Die bemelt Anna Buschlerin/sich solliches testaments um vatterlichen ord-nung/als jrenthalben etwas zu hardt unnd unmildt/durch ehegemelten jren lieben vatter seligen gemeint beschwern/dan jre in crafft ermelten testaments von sollichen hab und gutern/nit sovil damit sie jre glaubigen zufriden sollen/Unnd von dem ubrigen jr gepurliche leibs narung die ubrigen tage jres lebens gehaben er-volgen und zustehen wirde." *Verträge der Büschler-Erben 1543*, HSA Stuttgart, C3 Bü 530 (7, Q28); a shortened version, also untitled, is in Machtolff. Later in the document, Anna's hardship is phrased in such a way as to suggest that she was not expected to live long: "nit sovil ervolgen unnd gedeihen hett mogen darmit sie jre merckliche gelt schulden bezalen/und die wenigern tag jres lebens jr not-turfftige underhaltung gehaben mogen." *Ibid.*

17. Wolf Sünwald, Schultheiss in Hall, to *Uff dise nachgeende Fragstuckh*, no. 75 (Windberg).

18. Agreement with Siblings (untitled) (Machtolff).

19. *Testament Hermann Büschlers.*

20. "Auch Hermann Buschlers uffgericht ehafft Testament/jhr Anna nit mher fur vetterlich erbschafft dann ein dritthail eines drithails fur ir legitima geburt/wie dann in angeregtem vertrag sie Anna mer dan dreymal/ultra dimidium/sollichs ires angeburender legitima/verfortheilt kan sein wordenn." *Fragstuckh/Philipsen Buschlers*, to *Articuli Elisivi Anna Buschlers*, no. 24 (Hornung II). See below.

21. Gerd Wunder, *Die Bürger von Hall*, p. 290; Gerhard Wunder and Georg Lenckner, *Die Bürgerschaft der Reichsschaft Hall*, no. 115r 9, p. 162.

22. Anna's "Renunciation" (untitled) (Machtolff).

23. Herolt, *Chronica*, pp. 129–35; Krüger, *Schwäbisch Hall*, pp. 49–50.

24. German, *Chronik von Schwäbisch Hall*, pp. 210–13. On the county of Ho-henlohe, Thomas Robisheaux, *Rural Society and the Search for Order in Early Modern Germany* (Cambridge, 1989).

25. "Bosen hönischen [worten] zu schuben." *Defensional Articull*, nos. 10–13 (Machtolff).

26. He served that post between 1532 and 1546.

27. *Uff dise nachgeende Fragstuckh*, nos. 79–80 (Windberg).

28. "Sie were in dem verthrag uberfiert." Letter of Maternus Wurzelmann (Mach-tolff).

29. "Hette als ein betrangte und eingesperte uff dem hause fertigen miessen/dann so sie das nit gethonn hette man sie inn das gewelb gelegt." *Ibid.*

30. "Wie dann zwen des Raths mit ein annder geredt/das sie darumben/sie usser Hall gewichen ain gutt schmerbain [*smerbaum* = acorn-bearing tree on which pigs feed; *smerbein* = a fat bone] gehapt. Darumben sie mit anwesen nimermehr geen Hall. Dieweil auch jr bruder sage sy seye unbesindt. So khanndte sie alss ein unbesindte khain glüpt/ayde/noch verthrag binden. So habe man jr auch jres junckenn Sigel zerschlagen wollen/welches jres Manns freundt nit zuguttem ver-schien werden." *Ibid.*

31. "So sie inn beschehenenn furhalten als bedacht gewesen/als jetze/wolte sie vor ewer fursichtig weisheit miten inn der Rathstuben mit züchten nider hauert unnd zum grobsten was gehandlet haben." *Ibid.*

32. "Das auch jres vatters heuser, ehe unnd dann der verthrag uffgericht in schlechten/aber jetz inn hohen werdt angeschlagen." *Ibid.*

33. "Wo sie jrer oberkhait sollliche schmach und schand beweysen das gethonn hette oder noch thete/dazu gehörte ein stain an hals unnd in ain wasser." *Ibid.*

34. "Sie wolt den ergsten buben den sie finden khönt, der miesste auch ain langen spizen im kopff haben." *Ibid.*

35. Christina Larner, *Enemies of God: the Witchhunt in Scotland* (Baltimore 1981), pp. 97, 125.

36. *Fragstuck eins Erbern Raths*, no. 4, to *Positiones et Articuli*, nos. 5–13; *Defensional Articull*, no. 14 (Machtolff); *Superelisif Articul Philipsen*, no. 7 (Windberg).
37. "So widerruff unnd widersprich ich hiemit/in besser form/all ander satzung/ordnung/testament/letsten willen/unnd heiraths beredung/so hievor uffgericht/und durch mich verordirt so ver und wo sie diessem meinem letsten willen abbruchlich oder widerwertig sein mochten/unnd will das dieselben crafftloss/ab und von unwirden seien." *Testament Hermann Büschlers.*
38. "Auss vatterlicher mildt und güttigkeitt sy in seinem testament/unnd letzten willen/mit der Legittima ganntz vetterlich bedacht." *Peremptorial Articul: Philipsen Buschlers unnd Agatha Schantzin*, no. 8 (Windberg).
39. "Keinen schuldigen gerechtigkeit." Leonhard Bleimeier, to *Uff dise nachgeende Fragstuckh*, no. 61 (Windberg).
40. See Chapter IV, note 5.
41. On women and citizenship, Wiesner, *Working Women in Renaissance Germany*, pp. 18–19.
42. *Fragstuckh/Philipsen Buschlers*, to *Articuli Elisivi Anna Buschlers*, nos. 16–26 (Hornung II).
43. *Ibid.*, no. 29 (Hornung II).
44. *Der Clegerin übergebene Fragstuck*, no. 70 (Machtolff).
45. "Ein drittingtheil der Legitima." *Ibid.*, no. 41 (Machtolff). See above, p. 160.
46. *Ibid.*, no. 42 (Machtolff); *Uff dise nachgeende Fragstuckh* ... nos. 47–51 (Windberg).
47. *Uff dise nachgeende Fragstuckh* ..., nos. 54–55. "[Hermann Büschler hat] seinem sun Philips ... legats weiss verschafft/unnd nach verschaffung der Legata allerst legitimam seinen dreyen kindern vermeynlich institutions weiss geordnet/dem rechten starks zu wider." *Articuli Elisivi Anna Buschlerin*, no. 14 (Hornung II).
48. "Muss ... testator von seiner ganzen narung den kindern legitimam lassen." *Positiones et Articuli*, no. 13 (Hornung II). "Wo ein vatter ein testament machen will/das er seinen kindern Legitimam nature/vonn alles dessen nahrung Iusticicionis weiss zuverschaffen schuldig." *Uff dise nachgeende Fragstuckh*, no. 53 (Windberg).
49. "So die töchter sich nit wolten bestatten lassen zu der ee, so der vater sie nach seinem vermögen, vor und eedann sie fünfundzweinzig iar alt worden weren, het geestatten wollen, sonder darüber ein unkeusch leben und wesen auserwelt hett; und so aber der vater an söllicher irer bestattung seumig were und sie in eegstympter zeit und maynung nit verheyrat hett, so sollte sie darumb nit enterbt sein." *Nürnberger Reformation*, Nnb 15.2, p. 20. On the *Schwabenspiegel*: Ketsch, *Frauen im Mittelalter*, II, no. 15, p. 192. See above, p. 139.
50. "Auss grosser armut/forcht/unnd unmundt verursacht/in ein billichen richtigen vertrag zu willigen." *Articuli Elisivi Anna Buschlerin*, no. 19 (Hornung II).
51. "Eyn uberbeschwerlichen/fortheylhafftigen/auch der Clegerin hoch nachtheyligen vortrag." *Ibid.*, no. 20 (Hornung II).
52. "In dem vermeyntenn vertheylhafftigen vertrag/nit allein ultra dimidium justi/sonder wol drey mal mehr und weythers vernachthailt worden." *Ibid.*, no. 21 (Hornung II).
53. "Gutt." *Der Clegerin übergebene Fragstuckh*, no. 53 (Machtolff).
54. *Fragstuckh/Philipsen Buschlers*, no. 5, to *Articuli Elisivi Anna Buschlerin*, nos. 16–24 (Hornung II).
55. *Der Clegerin übergebene Fragstuck*, nos. 58–63 (Machtolff).
56. *Ibid.*, nos. 45–47 (Machtolff).
57. "Das sie Anna coppey dess verthrags/unnd Testaments von irem geschwes-

terig/unnd von eim Rath/der Statt Halle/jr zuzustellen (dann sie weder das Testament noch verthrag nie gesehen noch gelesen) begert habe." *Ibid.*, nos. 70–71 (Machtolff); *Articuli Elisivi Anna Buschlerin*, nos. 27–28 (Hornung II).

58. *Der Clegerin ubergebene Fragstuck*, nos. 72–74, 80 (Machtolff); *Articuli Elisivi Anna Buschlerin*, nos. 29–30 (Hornung II).

59. *Der Clegerin ubergebene Fragstuck*, nos. 80–83 (Machtolff); *Articuli Elisivi Anna Buschlerin*, no. 31 (Hornung II).

60. "Wider Recht und billicheit." Letter to city council (Machtolff).

61. *Positiones et Articuli*, nos. 4–7 (Hornung I). "Eyn citation wider die Clegerin erhalten/die ihr auch verkundt worden/ire beschwerd des vertrags halben furzupringen/oder zusehen unnd hören jr ein ewig stillschweigen uffzulegen." *Articuli Elisivi Anna Buschlerin*, no. 32 (Hornung II)

62. *Positiones et Articuli*, no. 8 (Hornung I); *Defensional Articull*, no. 13 (Machtolff).

63. Council's account of summonses, in Machtolff.

64. "Sich anders nit versehen mögen/dann alles unraths böser muttwilligen zuschub/gewalts unnd bevehdung." *Defensional Articull*, nos. 15–17 (Machtolff).

65. "Nichts dann versicherung vor gwalt und bösen meytereyen gesucht." *Ibid.*, no. 20.

66. *Ibid.*, no. 19.

67. "Sie als ein Burgerin bedurffte sich keins aigens versehens." *Uff dise nachgeende Fragstuck* . . . , nos. 105–6 (Windberg).

68. "Die beclagten an ihrem rechten gezweiffelt/unnd gewusst/das sie der clegerin unrecht gethon/unnd mitt dem abgerungenen vertrag sie hoch vernachteylt/on das weren sey, bey ihrer aussbeachter Ladung unnd angefengtem Rechten verbliben/das gar keins wegs verhindert/sonnder desselben usstrags erwartett." *Articuli Elisivi Anna Buschlerin*, nos. 39–40 (Hornung II).

69. "Gehebt sich ganntz jemerlich unnd übel sprichenndt das es gott geklagt/das jr verdampt jrs vatters gutt/so zu grossem verderben unnd nachtail an seel unnd leib khomen soll." *Dergleichen Ir Frauw Anna Büschler beschehene Urgicht* (Machtolff)

70. *Ibid.*

71. "Ihr ein ewige gefangnus bawen lassen." *Positiones et Articuli*, nos. 9–11 (Hornung I). "Ein gemach . . . darin [der Rat] die beclagten/in zeit ires lebens gefenglich zuenthalten vorgehabt." *Uff dise nachgeende Fragstuckh*, no. 113 (Windberg). Also *Der Clegerin übergebene Fragstuck*, nos. 86–89 (Machtolff).

72. Letter, in Machtolff.

73. *Positiones et Articuli*, nos. 13–19 (Hornung I); *Uff dise nachgeende Fragstuckh*, nos. 109–10 (Windberg).

74. *Positiones et Articuli*, nos. 14–20 (Hornung I); *Defensional Articull*, nos. 21–23 (Machtolff).

75. "Fur und fur listiglich unnd gewaltiglich gehanndlet worden sey." *Der Clegerin übergebene Fragstuck*, nos. 96, 98 (Machtolff); *Uff dise nachgeende Fragstuckh*, nos. 114–15 (Windberg).

CHAPTER SIX: WITNESSES

1. Esslingen court's letter to Sporlands, in Machtolff.

2. She describes herself at the time as "ein jung medlein" and "kinds medlein." To *Superelisif Articul Philipsen*, no. 2 (Windberg).

3. Bleimeier, to *Defensional Articull*, no. 5 (Machtolff); Eisenmenger, to *Uff dise nachgeende Fragstuckh*, no. 66 (Windberg).

4. Bleimeier, to *Defensional Articull*, no. 5 (Machtolff): "Wiss . . . nit zu was vorteil [Wurzelmann] den auffgericht/kin gedenckhen sie der clegerin mer zu guttem

dann zu argem geschehen." Eisenmenger, to *Uff dise nachgeende Fragstuckh*, no. 80 (Windberg).

5. Bernhard Werner, to *Uff dise nachgeende Fragstuckh*, no. 79 (Windberg).

6. To *ibid.*, nos. 65, 67 (Windberg).

7. To *Der Clegerin übergebene Fragstuck*, nos. 74–80 (Machtolff).

8. To *Fragstuck eins Erbern Raths der Statt Schwäbisch Hall contra Anna Buschlerin*, nos. 4–5 (Hornung I); to *Articuli Elisivi Anna Buschlerin*, no. 30 (Hornung II).

9. "Alle puncten unnd articul des vertrags/fur die handt genommen/und denselbigen nach lengst inn des Herman Buschler hauss/im ecke vor der stuben/bewogen." To *Articuli Elisivi Anna Buschlerin*, no. 24 (Hornung II). "Er hab sie nach dem vertrag/aus und ein sehen ghon/in das Philipsen Buschlers haus/wann ihr geliebt." To *Fragstuckh Philipsen Buschler*, no. 1, to *Articuli Elisivi Anna Buschlerin*, no. 26 (Hornung II); confirmed also by Johann Hornberger, to *Der Clegerin übergebene Fragstuck*, nos. 35–37 (Machtolff).

10. To *Defensional Articull*, no. 9 (Machtolff).

11. "Zur zeit uffrichtung dess verthrags/die Clegerin voller weins gewest/und daruff nachvolgenns der verthrag der ursachen das sie mit wein beladen gewesen nit halten wollen." To *Der Clegerin übergebene Fragstuck*, no. 58 (Machtolff).

12. "Das sie sollichen verthrag vor sitzendem Rath/mit dem leiplichen ayd bestetigt habe dann er zeug jr clegerin als zu einem curator zugeordnet selbs dabey unnd mit gewesen da sie sollichen ayd erstattet/hab seins wissen sollichen ayd guttwillig gethon unnd sich dessen nit gewidert." To *Defensional Articull*, no. 6 (Machtolff).

13. "Als ein curator sey darbey und mit gewesen als die clegerin vor einem Ersamen Rathe/den aydt dess verthrags gethonn/das sie aber darzu genöt worden/ sey ime nit wissent/ob sie aber den verthrag willigklichen oder nit angenomen/ hab/dabey unnd mit sey er nit gewesen/unnd jm nit wissen." To *Der Clegerin übergebene Fragstuck*, no. 83 (Machtolff).

14. To *Uff dise nachgeende Fragstuckh*, nos. 93–99, 103 (Windberg).

15. To *ibid.*, no. 54 (Windberg).

16. "Einer des Raths gewessen/ . . . aber nit ein ganntzer Rathe/derhalben ime jeder förchten möchten." To *ibid.*, no. 84 (Windberg).

17. "Hinderlegt," not "hindergehalten." To *ibid.*, nos. 87–88 (Windberg).

18. To *ibid.*, no. 63 (Windberg).

19. To *ibid.*, nos. 48–51 (Windberg).

20. To *ibid.*, no. 54 (Windberg).

21. "Nit sunderlichen eidt thon." Hans Eisenmenger, to *ibid.*, no. 100 (Windberg). "Sagt zeug [Conrad Büschler]/er als ein curator gemelter Clegerin/habe wie er die curatorschafft annemen sollen/unnd derhalben durch die obrigkeit beschickt worden/ pflicht gethonn." To *ibid.*, no. 100 (Windberg).

22. "Feig sie an zu wainen/dann sie thet sich dess beschweren." To *Der Clegerin übergebene Fragstuck*, no. 39 (Machtolff).

23. "Heilbronner rürlin." To *Positiones et Articuli*, no. 11 (Hornung I).

24. "Der angenommen vertrag sey ihr nit nachtheylig/dann man hab viel schulden von ir wegen miessen bezalenn." Anthony Brellochs, to *ibid.*, nos. 2–3 (Hornung I); Hans Eisenmenger, to *Uff dise nachgeende Fragstuckh*, no. 69 (Windberg).

25. Priest Arnold Engel, to *Positiones et Articuli*, no. 2 (Hornung I).

26. Florian Bernbeck, to *ibid.*, no. 5 (Hornung I).

27. To *ibid.*, no. 6 (Hornung I).

28. "Man hab der Anna unrecht gethon." To *Articuli Elisivi Anna Buschlerin*, no. 41 (Hornung II).

29. To *ibid.*, nos. 9–12 (Hornung II); Gerhard Wunder and Georg Lenckner, *Die Bürgerschaft der Reichsstadt Hall*, nr. 7761, p. 573.

30. "Verfortheilt." To *Fragstuckh Philipsen Buschlers*, nos. 20–21 (Hornung II).

31. "Das sie sich des hausraths/so Ihr geben worden/beclagt/so acht er zeug fur sich selbs/sie sy damitt verfortheilt worden/dieweyl das zinwerck vast blech gewesst." To *Positiones et Articuli*, no. 4 (Hornung I).

32. Nobleman Gabriel Senft, to *ibid.*, no. 5 (Hornung I); Hans Eisenmenger, to *Uff dise nachgeende Fragstuckh*, no. 86 (Windberg).

33. To *Uff dise nachgeende Fragstuckh*, no. 75 (Windberg).

34. To *ibid.*, no. 76 (Windberg).

35. To *Fragstuck Philipsen Buschlers*, nos. 2 and following; to *Articuli Elisivi Anna Buschlerin*, no. 16 (Hornung II).

36. "Das Phillips Buschler die gleubiger annderer gestalt nit angefarn/dann das er sich bey jnen erkhundiget/wie/wann unnd warumb die clegerin inn schuldig/dann ettwan einer meher gefordert/dann man jme schuldig gewesen/alss mit dem juden Mosse zu Beyingen beschehen/welcher meher dann zwaymal sovil gevordert alss man ime geben hatt." Georg Bernbeck, to *Der Clegerin übergebene Fragstuck*, no. 65 (Machtolff). Bleimeier describes Philip's modus operandi more simply: "welcher seiner schulden rechtgeschaffen unnd bestenndig erfunden der sie mit lieb bezalt worden/da man aber unnder dem hiettlein spielenn wöllen/hetten sie/wie pillich/eingehalten." To *Uff dise nachgeende Fragstuckh*, no. 86 (Windberg).

37. "Ettliche gleubiger fur ain rath und die oberkhait jrer schulden halben khomen/gegen denen sich Phillips Büschler hart gnug gehalten." Councilman and wine steward Bernhard Werner, to *Der Clegerin übergebene Fragstuck*, no. 65 (Machtolff).

38. "Philip und Agatha haben alle die schulden/so Anna vor dem bewilligtenn vertrag gemacht/bezalen sollen/dess sie aber nit gethon." *Fragstuck Philipsen Buschlers*, no. 8, to *Articuli Elisivi Anna Buschlerin*, no. 25 (Hornung II). "Philips unnd Agatha Buschlerin/seyen schuldig daran/am vertrag/das derselb nit gehaltenn worden/dann sie die schuldner nit bezalen wöllen/sonder wider uff die Annan gewisenn." To *Fragstuck eines Erbern Raths*, no. 1, to *Positiones et Articuli*, no. 4 (Hornung I).

39. In David Schmidlin's summary: Philip and Agatha had broken the agreement "in den puncten/das sie die schuldnerrn nit bezalen/unnd ihre ettlich haussrath irem gefallen nach nit geben wellen." To *Fragstuck eines erbern Raths*, no. 2, to *Positiones et Articuli*, no. 4 (Hornung I).

40. Conrad Büschler to *Uff dise nachgeende Fragstuckh*, nos. 87–88 (Windberg).

41. Gerd Wunder, "Liebesbriefe": 87.

42. "Das Philips Buschler viel schulden/fur sie Clegerin bezalt/unnd hab selbst irem jetzigenn hausswirt Hans Sprolland vor etlichen wochen/ob 30 gulden von wegen des leibgedings entricht." To *Fragstuck Philipsen Buschlers*, nos. 14–16, to *Articuli Elisivi Anna Buschlerin*, no. 23 (Hornung II).

43. "Nit die wenigste ursach sein/das sie eim Erbarn Raths etliche schmehe schrifften zugesanndt/sunst auch hien unnd wider/ein Erbarn Rathe/schmehelich/widder jr burger pflicht gehalten unnd beschreitt." To *Fragstuckh Philipsen Buschlers*, no. 108 (Windberg).

44. Bernhard Werner, to *Uff dise nachgeende Fragstuckh*, no. 108 (Windberg); nearly identical testimony from councilman Georg Beinbach, to *ibid.* (Windberg).

45. Jacob Ehinger, Heilbronn attorney, to *ibid.*, no. 75 (Windberg). "Sie die frau Anna Büschlerin zu Matternn Wurzelman altem Stattschreiber inn sein herberg khamen/unnd von uffgerichtem verthrag meldung gethonn/hab sie vil boser spitziger wort triben/unnd unnder anndernn sich threulichen vernomen lassen/sie

wolt jren sachen rechtthonn/und sonsten anndere mehr sherpffere wort gerett."
Ehinger, to *Defensional Articull*, no. 13 (Machtolff).
46. To *Der Clegerin übergebene Fragstuck*, no. 1 (Machtolff): "Er zeug alss bot-
ten weiss ettwann zu jr khamen/hab sie jme vill klagt wie es jr ganng mit jrem
bruder/dann jr bruder Phillips hab es zu wegen bracht/das sie uss der statt
vertriben/unnd miess jezo jm lannd umbziehen/unnd sitz er Phillips Büschler uff
jres vatters unnd muetterlichen gutt/dess thue er niessen/unnd sey sie davon ver-
thriben/unnd sie well jme mit Recht woll begegnen." To *Defensional Articull*, nos.
10–11 (Machtolff).
47. "Die brieff unnd gerechtigkeit belangenndt/sagt zeug/es seyen ettlich brieve/
inn lumplin gebunden/inn Rath bracht wordenn/unnd darbey anzeygt das Anna
Buschlerin ettlich brieff mitt den zemen zerissen unnd uff den weg von Munck-
heim einher ires kodt geworffen/die ubrigen so noch da gewesen/hab ein Erbar
Rath/uff beschehen schreyben/dem Chamergericht/uberschickt." Hans Eisenmenger, to *Positiones et Articuli*, no. 11 (Hornung I). More briefly and less sensa-
tionally, Florian Bernbeck, to *ibid.* (Hornung I).
48. Peter Bart, to *ibid.* (Hornung I).
49. "Aller pfleg." Councilman Georg Bernbach, to *Defensional Articull*, no. 18
(Machtolff).
50. "Sie seines wissenns unklagbar gewest." To *ibid.* (Machtolff).
51. "Ime woll wisendt sein/das ein Ersamer Rath zu Hall im spital ain gemach
zurichten lassen wellen. Ehe aber dasselbig ussgemacht sey sie clegerin selbs uss-
khomen." To *Der Clegerin übergebene Fragstuck*, no. 94 (Machtolff).
52. To *Uff dise nachgeende Fragstuckh*, no. 113 (Windberg).
53. To *ibid.* (Windberg).
54. "So hab man in einem anndern gewelb oder stublin/eysen gütter fur die fens-
ter/unnd denn offenn machen lassen/Also sey die sag gewesenn/man habs ihr
Anna Buschlerin machen lassenn." To *Positiones et Articuli*, no. 11 (Hornung I).
55. "Nein mit nichten/hett man sie zu ewigen gefenncknus angenomen oder be-
halten wöllen/sunder sie in ein weibliche verwarhung ein zeitt lanng verordnet."
To *Uff dise nachgeende Fragstuckh*, no. 113 (Windberg).
56. "Nit billich." To *Der Clegerin übergebene Fragstuck*, no. 95 (Machtolff).
57. Peter Ketch, *Frauen im Mittelalter*, II: *Frauenbild und Frauenrechte in Kirche
und Gesellschaft. Quellen und Materialien*, ed. Annette Kuhn (Düsseldorf, 1984),
pp. 181, 190.

CHAPTER SEVEN: THE MORAL

1. "Sie haben in die peen/articulirten mandats nit fallen können/dieweyl sie Anna
seins wissens/zuvor aus der gefengknuss khomen/ehe das mandat eim Rath insi-
nuirt worden." Florian Bernbeck, *Positiones et Articuli*, no. 19 (Hornung I); Leonhard Feuchter, *ibid.*
2. H. C. Erik Midelfort, *Witchhunting in Southwestern Germany* (Stanford,
1972); Gerald Strauss, *Law, Resistance, and the State: The Opposition to Roman
Law in Reformation Germany* (Baltimore, 1986).
3. I thank John Witte, Jr., for alerting me to this.
4. Broadly on the subject: Quentin Skinner, *The Foundations of Modern Political
Thought*, II: *The Reformation* (Cambridge, 1978). On the conciliar theorists of
the fourteenth and fifteenth centuries, Francis Oakley, "Walter Ullmann's Vision
of Medieval Politics," *Past & Present* 60 (1973): 1–10. On Lutheran political theory
and resistance, Heinz Scheible, ed., *Das Widerstandsrecht als Problem der
deutschen Protestanten* (Gütersloh, 1969); O. K. Olson, "Theology of Revolution:
Magdeburg, 1550–1551," *Sixteenth Century Journal* 3 (1972): 56–79; and Eike
Wolgast, *Die Religionsfrage als Problem des Widerstandsrecht im 16. Jahrhundert*

(Heidelberg, 1980). On Calvinist political theory and resistance, J. H. Franklin, ed. and trans., *Constitutionalism and Resistance in the Sixteenth Century: Three Treatises by Hotman, Beza, and Mornay* (New York, 1969); Donald Kelley, *The Beginning of Ideology: Consciousness and Society in the French Reformation* (Cambridge, 1981); and R. M. Kingdon and R. D. Lindner, eds., *Calvin and Calvinism: Sources of Democracy?* (Lexington, MA, 1970).

5. See Heide Wunder's sage comments in *"Er ist die Sonn', sie ist der Mond,"* pp. 267–68. For a lucid survey of the literature, Merry Wiesner-Hanks, *Women and Gender in Early Modern Europe* (New York, 1993).

6. Heide Wunder particularly stresses women's equal contribution to family wealth and cultural life by way of their dowries and wealth-creating ability both in and outside marriage, and their talents as homemakers and family historians. " 'Er ist die Sonn'." On women's direct participation in politics and war, see Marion Kobelt-Groch, *Aufsässige Töchter Gottes. Frauen im Bauernkrief und in den Täuferbewegungen* (Frankfurt am Main, 1993).

7. Gerhard Wunder and Georg Lenckner, *Die Bürgerschaft der Reichsstadt Hall*, p. 167. In 1600, women obtained citizenship in Hall with eighty gulden in propertied wealth, men with one hundred. German, *Die Chronik von Schwäbisch Hall*, p. 144. Urban women also possessed a "passive" citizenship through their husbands.

8. On men and women in the trades, Shulamith Shahar, *The Fourth Estate: A History of Women in the Middle Ages* (New York, 1983); Gabriele Becker et al., *"Aus der Zeit der Verzweiflung." Zur Genese und Aktualität des Hexenbildes* (Frankfurt am Main, 1977), pp. 63–66, 107–14; Barbara Beuys, *Familienleben in Deutschland. Neue Bilder aus der deutschen Vergangenheit* (Reinbeck, 1980), pp. 267–75.

9. Christina Larner has summarized the work of Macfarlane on England (Essex), Midelfort on southwestern Germany, and Soman on Paris, as well as her own findings for Scotland, and concluded that "the substantial proportion of male witches in most parts of Europe means that a witch was not defined exclusively in female terms . . . yet at least four out of five persons to whom [the characteristics of witches] were ascribed are women. Witchcraft was not sex-specific, but it was sex-related." *Enemies of God*, pp. 91–92.

10. For literature, Ian Maclean, *The Renaissance Notion of Woman: A Study in the Fortunes of Scholasticism and Medical Science in European Intellectual Life* (Cambridge, England, 1980). For law codes, Ketch, *Frauen im Mittelalter*, and Gernot Kocher, "Die Frau in spätmittelalterlichen Rechtsleben," in *Frau und Spätmittelalterlicher Alltag* (Vienna, 1986), pp. 175–86. However, as Kocher points out, even the law codes present positive as well as negative views: "Ingesamt gesehen, bietet die Position der Frau im mittelalterlichen Rechtsleben kein einheitliches Bild. Die Spannweite reichte von der weitgehenden Unterordnung der Frau durch Geschlechtsvormundschaft oder Munt über Lockerungen dieser personenrechtlichen Herrschaftsform bis zur selbständig in das Erwerbs- und Rechtsleben integrierten Frau," (p. 485).

11. *Malleus Malificarium*, in Alan Kors and Edward Peters, eds., *Witchcraft in Europe, 1100–1700: A Documentary Survey* (Philadephia, 1972), pp. 124–27, 145. On the phenomenon of witchcraft in the context of the times: Brian Levack, *The Great Witch Hunt in Early Modern Europe* (New York, 1988); William Monter, ed., *European Witchcraft* (New York, 1969); Richard Kieckhefer, *European Witch Trials* (Berkeley, 1976).

12. Numerous examples in Ozment, *When Fathers Ruled*, and Moore, *The Maiden's Mirror*.

13. Leonhard Frank, *Hermann Büschler: The Burgomaster of Schwäbisch Hall* (Hall, 1922).
14. See above, chapter 1.
15. Frank, *Hermann Büschler*, pp. 128, 241.
16. *Ibid.*, pp. 128–30, 225–26, 241.
17. Hermann Büschler had no daughter named Suzanne by his first marriage to Anna Hornberger. I have been unable to document the offspring, if any, of his brief second and third marriages. Inasmuch as he died in 1543, it is unlikely that he could have had a daughter old enough to have done the things Suzanne is alleged to have done, even if there were children from these last two marriages.
18. The Seiferheld family was one of Hall's oldest and among the first to manu-facture salt and serve on the city council. There is a prominent Georg Seiferheld (1482–1539), who was a contemporary with Hermann Büschler and also served on the city council. In 1513, he married Walburg Wetzel, who outlived him. His politically prominent eldest son, Georg (d. 1578), who married Kaila Krauss in 1537, would have been a contemporary of Anna. Gerd Wunder, *Die Bürger von Hall*, p. 279; Gerd Wunder, *Personendenkmale der Michaelskirche in Schwäbisch Hall*, p. 44. It appears that he was Frank's model, or at least a prominent city name he plucked, for Suzanne's fictitious lover. If he courted Anna in the 1520s, there is no surviving record of it.
19. Frank, *Hermann Büschler*, pp. 128–30, 187–88, 206.
20. Gerd Wunder, *Die Bürger von Hall*, pp. 74–76.
21. "Dem Rat missfiel Büschlers Eingriff in ein schwebendes Verfahren, und der mächtige Mann verlor darüber seinen Sitz im Rat." *Ibid.*, p. 180. The scandal also occurred at a time when the old bürgermeister's opposition to the Protestant Ref-ormation was limiting his usefulness to the council and numbering his days in office.
22. Gerd Wunder, "Liebesbriefe": 187.

APPENDIX:

BIOGRAPHICAL/GENEALOGICAL ESSAY

With the exception of Schenk Erasmus of Limpurg, complete genealogical charts do not exist for the major figures of our story, and hard biographical information is scarce and scattered for them all. Relevant, reliable profiles can nonetheless be drawn from official records and other existing information.

HERMANN BÜSCHLER (d. August 1543) served as a Hall councilman from 1497 to 1510 and from 1513 to 1527, and he was five times the city's bürgermeister (1508, 1514, 1517, 1520, 1525). On August 25, 1495, he married Anna Hornberger (d. December 16, 1520), the daughter of a Rothenburg nobleman, with whom he had six children: two daughters, Anna (1496/1498–1552) and Agatha (d. February 1559), and four sons, Hermann, Jr. (d. 1528?), Philip (d. July 1569), Sebald (d. 1532), and Bonaventure, a cloth-maker, who disappeared in the early 1540s and was presumed dead in 1543.

ANNA, the eldest child, married twice: the first time in 1526, to Hans von Leuzenbrunn (d. August 1543), a poor nobleman, and the second in 1546, to Johann Sporland (d. not before 1554), a native of Neuenstein in the county of Hohenlohe. Existing records contain no indication of offspring from either marriage. AGATHA married Wolf Schanz, the bailiff (*Amtmann*) of Wertheim, with whom she had five children. In his mid-teens, PHILIP matriculated at the universities of Heidelberg (1520) and Tübingen (July 1522). In 1532, he married Afra Senft (d. April 15, 1585), the daughter of a prominent Hall nobleman, a marriage that later assisted his gaining recognition as a junker in 1551. Like his father, he served many years as a Hall councilman (1538–1557) and twice held the post of bürgermeister (1549, 1551).

Hermann Büschler had two brief, childless marriages after Anna's departure from home: in 1528 to Elisabeth Krauss, which ended with her death apparently in that same year, and before 1531 to Barbara Eitelwein, a Heilbronnerin, which ended in divorce.

ERASMUS OF LIMPURG (1502–1553), the fourth of seven children and the third of five survivors, was a thirteenth-generation Schenk in a dynasty that traced its ancestry back to Walter I (r. 1200–1218), Schenk of Schüpf. Upon the death of his father, Schenk Gottfried (1474–1530), Erasmus became lord of Limpurg and its environs, the original family holding. His elder brother Carl (1498–1558) earlier inherited the other native jewel in the Limpurg Schenks' crown, the town of Speckfeld, which became Carl's after the death of their uncle, Schenk Friedrich, in 1521. In 1533, Erasmus married Anna, countess of Lodron (d. 1556), a union that produced three children: the future Schenk Friedrich VII (1536–1596) and two daughters. After Erasmus sold the little kingdom of Limpurg to the city of Hall in 1541, Obersontheim became his new castle residence. Obersontheim and Speckfeld remained the two centers of local Schenkish power until the dynasty died out in the early eighteenth century.

DANIEL TREUTWEIN was the eldest son of city chronicler Daniel Treutwein, Sr., who may have served with other young noble soldiers as a mercenary for the city during the last quarter of the fifteenth century and was still alive in 1519. Daniel, Jr., survives in various records as a "courageous cavalryman" (Johann Herolt), assistant to Duke Ulrich of Württemberg, about whom he wrote a surviving poem, and the lifelong bailiff of Boxberg. His younger brother, Eitel (d. 1536), matriculated at the University of Heidelberg in October 1501 and became a doctor of both civil and canon law. He held several high judicial and ecclesiastical positions, among them the deanship of the locally famous Komburg convent (1535–1536). To have matriculated at Heidelberg, Eitel would have had to be at least fifteen years old, suggesting that his elder brother had likely been born in the early 1480s and thus was in his early forties when he began romancing Anna Büschler, then in her mid-twenties.

On Hermann, Anna, Agatha, and Philip Büschler, see Gerhard Wunder and Georg Lenckner, *Die Bürgerschaft der Reichsstadt Hall von 1395 bis 1600* (Stuttgart, 1956), nos. 1149, 1156, 1159, 1168 (1529), pp. 161–62; nos. 7339, 7341 (1559), p. 552; *Testament Hermann Büschlers*, HSA Stuttgart, C3 Bü 530; and *Positiones et Articuli*, nos. 1–3 (Hornung II), *ibid.* On Erasmus, Schenk of Limpurg, see Gerd Wunder et al., *Die Schenken von Limpurg und ihr Land* (Sigmaringen, 1982), p. 46; Heinrich Prescher, *Geschichte und Beschreibung der zum Fränkischer Kreise gehöriger Reichsgraffschaft Limpurg*, II (Stuttgart, 1789), appended genealogy; and Karl O. Müller, "Das Geschlecht der Reichserbschenken zu Limpurg bis zum Aussterben des Mannesstammes (1713)," *Zeitschrift für Württembergische Landesgeschichte* 5 (1941):

215–43; 233–34. On Daniel Treutwein, see Gerd Wunder, *Die Bürger von Hall* (Sigmaringen, 1980), pp. 47, 61, 153; Gerhard Wunder and Georg Lenckner, *Bürgerschaft der Reichsstadt Hall*, p. 182; and Johann Herolt, *Chronica Zeit- unnd Jarbuch vonn der statt Hall, Württembergische Geschichtsquellen*, I (Stuttgart, 1894), p. 58.

ACKNOWLEDGMENTS

Like a new cake made from scratch, a biography of a virtually unknown woman must rely on numerous suppliers and speciality shops. In gathering my ingredients, I have received many kindnesses and much good advice from archivists and librarians, historians and Germanists, and my agent and editor.

Mathias Beer, leading scholar of the late medieval German family, assisted both by mail and on foot, as we retraced together on a memorable day Anna Büschler's movements from her father's house in Hall to Hohenlohe castle in faraway Esslingen. John Witte, Jr., American authority on the law codes of late medieval and Reformation Germany, provided both a primer in legal history and counsel on the interaction of law, religion, and society. Matthias Senger checked my translations of Anna's correspondence with her lovers. Heide Wunder, author of perhaps the wisest history of German women, read an early version of the manuscript, and Caroline Ford and Larissa Taylor commented on parts of it. Govind Sreenivasan lent his mapmaking skills, and Judith Hurwich and Ruth Mellinkoff responded to questions. The archivists and librarians of the city archives of Hall (Herta Beutter) and Ludwigsburg (Trugenberger), together with those of the state archives of Stuttgart (Bührlen-Grabinger, Krimm, and Wagner), where most of the relevant documents are today stored, were generous sources of information. The study began in the German collections on the second floor of Widener Library, Harvard University's crown jewel, where I first discovered Anna Büschler.

In icing the cake, I had the editorial assistance of my agents Lynn Chu and Glen Hartley, St. Martin's editor Robert Weil, Andrew Graybill, Miranda Ford, Pei Loi Koay, and copy editor Ted Johnson, whose complementary skills helped transform research into prose and a manuscript into a book. As always, I remain indebted to my wife, Andrea, still the smartest one when it comes to writing a book.

Steven Ozment
Newbury, Massachusetts

Index

STEVEN OZMENT is McLean Professor of Ancient and Modern History at Harvard University. He has taught Western Civilization at Yale, Harvard, and Stanford. He is the author of nine books. *The Age of Reform, 1250–1550* (1980) won the Schaff History Prize and was a finalist for the 1981 National Book Award. *Magdalena and Balthasar: An Intimate Portrait of Life in Sixteenth Century Europe* (1986) and *Three Behaim Boys: Growing Up in Early Modern Germany* (1990) were selections of the History Book Club, as was his most recent book, *Protestants: The Birth of a Revolution* (1992). He lives in Newbury, Massachusetts with his wife, Andrea, and daughters, Amanda and Emma.